"Itchy Balls" growing on a Sycamore tree.

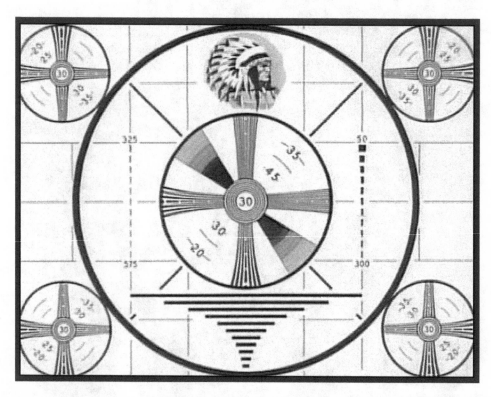

1950s television test pattern.

THE WAR OF THE
ITCHY BALLS

AND OTHER TALES FROM

Brooklyn

"If Brooklyn lore wasn't part of your life, it can be now." – Brian Williams, NBC News

A Half-Life Memoir by
WILLIAM A. GRALNICK

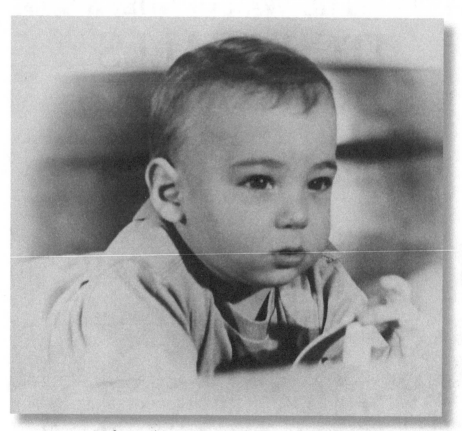

"A face only a mother could love," circa 1945.

Barringer Publishing, Naples, Florida
www.barringerpublishing.com
Cover, graphics, layout design by Linda S. Leppert

ISBN: 978-1-7339837-1-6

Library of Congress Cataloging-in-Publication Data
The War of the Itchy Balls and Other Tales from Brooklyn
Printed in U.S.A.

Dedication

To My Special Angel

Table of Contents

"We coulda been a city . . ."

PRELUDE

The Statler Brothers, the legendary Country and Western group known for its harmony and songs about nostalgia recorded, "Do You Remember These?" It is a sweet song that reminds the listeners of so many things that passed through one's life and on into memory. Styles of clothes liked pegged pants, hairdos like duck tails, girls or boys you've never forgotten and songs even if heard three times a week conger up the same memories of those girls and boys with the same wistful passion of the ended relationships.

If you'd like something a little more literary, let me offer the inscription from the keystone of the National Archives building, "Past is Prologue." It too fits. This book is about my past. Thought about while reading it, the reader will not only revisit his or her past, no matter where that past took place, but will wonder about at least two issues, both a bit darker than the book.

One could be called, "Bring in the Clowns" after the famous Judy Collins song from the then equally famous movie, *The Thousand Clowns*. Let me explore this with you in story form to warm you up for the book.

At age seventeen, I received an invitation to Mardi Gras from my older brother and his wife. My brother was just past the first stage of what would become a rocket-like career in television news. He had just been promoted and posted as the head of the CBS News Southern Bureau becoming the youngest at CBS ever to have such a title. He correctly thought that his kid brother still in Brooklyn would flip out to go to the Mardi Gras. Boy did he hit that nail on the head.

It was all arranged including tickets to one of the balls thrown by one of the crewes that allowed Jews to attend. Many didn't. You can read that again if you need to. True it was. Unfortunately, a few days before my departure there was a race riot I believe in Florida and in the '60s that's pretty much what the Southern Bureau's job was, covering folks who threw acid into swimming pools so they couldn't be integrated, or turned snarling dogs on men, women and children and such other things we as a nation are still trying to forget.

But for we three—the question was, "Is it appropriate in New Orleans for a teenager to stay with a young woman for a week without her husband being around?" We took our own counsel and voted unanimously that New Orleans could go to hell; I was comin' to town and staying with my sister-in-law. She even fixed me up with a date, a very pretty little thing with a drawl that caused me to remember my brother opining that he was in a state where "shit" was a three-syllable word. At dinner, this lovely drawl calmly produced these words in the matter-of-fact tone of "it's going to rain tomorrow." She said, "I wish someone would assassinate President Kennedy." Some months later someone did.

Welcome south, brother.

The week was mostly great fun and mostly uneventful or as near to uneventful as Mardi Gras could be. I thought I was doing as great a job entertaining my hostess as she was taking me to see the sights from street funerals to Voodoo rituals in the bayous. Then one night she said to me, "You know, you don't have to play the clown, constantly entertaining me. I will love you regardless." That was sort of a lightning bolt out of the hot, humid sky. It actually took me years to figure out what she was talking about.

The point? The typical thought when one thinks of clowns is the happy on the outside/sad on the inside character, or maybe the two masks that hang together one with a smile and one with a frown. So, my reader, assume that this book of mostly funny essays about mostly funny things has another side to it. Just because I've chosen to write a book without that side showing doesn't mean it isn't there. I'll bet as you remember your own childhood's pitfalls and pratfalls, you'll remember the sadness that they could bring while you were clowning it up with great bravado.

Then there is the iconic Charlie Brown. He illustrates point number two. Here is a character that embodied both *schlemiel* and *schlimazel.* For the uninitiated those are Yiddish words. The *schlemiel* is the one who drops the hot soup—all the time. The *schlimazel* is the one on whom it falls—all the time. Think of the world-trusting boy sure to a certainty that this time Lucy would not pull away the football, that the little red-haired girl didn't only want to be friends and that he as the hapless pitcher taking the mound would have better stuff for this game and wouldn't throw the pitch, hit so hard back at him, that it would knock his clothing off—in front of his team and the on-lookers. Charlie Brown was a sad little boy but soldiered on through life.

I chose to write this book this way—essays capturing episodes and snapshots of my youth—because I thought America at this juncture could use a book that wasn't deep, or dark, or even had a plot one had to worry over. One that had some clown to it. But just because it doesn't deal with the impact of being a *schlemiel* or *schlimazel* doesn't mean there isn't an impact, just because I didn't talk much about psychiatrists doesn't mean I didn't need one. I've just chosen to accept that the football will move and spare you the feelings from constantly ending up on my ass when it does, so you can enjoy yourself. Besides, with Ringling Brothers gone, someone has to bring in the clowns.

PREFACE

"You can take the boy out of Brooklyn ..."

"So, who am I to write a book's preface? No one you know, just a guy from Brooklyn."

The adage goes, "You can take the boy out of Brooklyn, but you cannot take Brooklyn out of the boy." It applies to many of us, including the author. In this heart-tapping book, Bill Gralnick epitomizes this saying. With a sensitivity and insight that so few writers have, Bill takes us all back into our childhood memories. The smells, the sights, the antics, and all the "foolish" things we did for fun come back to rekindle our senses. They are Brooklyn through and through, but also universal.

Bill is a Brooklynite to the core. Like a real Brooklynite, he doesn't come from New York, he comes from yes, Brooklyn. His stories are funny in a Brooklyn sort of way. They will all bring either a smile or a few drops of tears to your face. Maybe sometimes laughter hard enough to cause tears.

Brooklyn is a very unique place. It has its own aura, and if you lived there, it made you proud, even when it shouldn't have because it was a different kind of Our Town. From the Dodgers, Giants, Mets, Coney Island, Nathan's hot dogs, to Brighton Beach and the Mafia, they all made you feel like you belonged to a special place. That special place holds all of the memories stored in your heart, never to be taken away.

This book is a journey into our past. It does not matter if you grew up in Brooklyn. In it, you will find your childhood memories wherever they began.

Read the book . . . he's one hellofa story-teller.

> ~ Fred Goldstein, occasional poet,
> constant observer, and formerly of
> Sheepshead Bay, Brooklyn

ACKNOWLEDGEMENTS

To God, thanks for my still having a memory ...

To my parents: thanks for having me and playing a strong hand in making these memories possible—good and bad. Wish they could read them.

To my brother, of blessed memory, thanks for teaching me how to write, and being a player in a lot of these stories—good and bad—wish he could read them.

To Neil Simon, of blessed memory, thanks for telling me, "Writing (comedy) is not fun, it's work." And also, "If you take my advice and not be a writer, you shouldn't be a writer."

To my Andrea. Thanks writ large. "I'll go to my grave loving you" . . . glad she can read them.

To my friend, Dan, thanks for never being stingy with your critiques—or compliments.

To George Marks, a player in a lot of the stories—good and bad—but was also a neighbor with whom I've cross-continentally reconnected and is a current help with bits, pieces of memory, and some grand pictures. Thanks for your talent and willingness to share. Glad you've read some and helped some.

To Seth and sister, Jessica Chaves, thanks for having a younger memory than mine so that between you both, I was able to put names on a dog and a woman.

And oodles of thanks to the Barringer team without whom this work would be in a file cabinet not a book.

To all those other random souls, many gone, and some gone but still alive, as well as the many, probably about where I am now chronologically, who happened to trip across the stage on which my life was playing and exited at some point leaving an imprint strong enough to become a memory—good and bad—a plain, ole good-hearted thanks!

INTRODUCTION

*"In a moment that can only be described as Freudian,
I grabbed her ponytail—and it came off in my hand."*

How to start? A simple "hello?" Ruminating over this question brings to mind an old Jackie Gleason/Art Carney sketch from *The Honeymooners* about Carney's first foray onto the golf course. Gleason, of course, is giving the directions. He says, "First you have to introduce yourself to the ball. It is called addressing the ball." Carney gives him a quizzical look, shrugs his shoulders, leans over and says, "Helloooooooooooo ball!" Gleason smacks him.

The object of a book's introduction, however, is to acquaint the reader with what's to come, not about who wrote it. That in itself makes it an important piece of writing. Something terrible could happen after reading the introduction. You, the reader, could not read the book. Therefore, as much, if not more, thought went into this as went into what follows, so you'll continue on. It you want to know about me, well, there's some stuff on the cover and more stuff on my website: **www.williamgralnickauthor.com**.

The book is my perspective—my perspective on my life. Even after you read something about me you might well say, "Who the heck are you to be writing a memoir? Did you invent something? Did you build something? Did your philosophizing change anything?" No, no, and no. Yet, as I rummaged through the attic of my mind[1] to see what was up there, and if I thought it would have any interest, I discovered a lot that seemed pretty interesting, interesting just because I'm not famous. I think also that my encounters with life are universal, even though I'm from Brooklyn and you may not be, they'll resonate none-the-less.

In fact, I thought I would test that out. I picked a dozen friends. Each was different in one or many ways from the other—different birthplaces, economic status, religion, different cities where most of life was spent. I sent them the opening of the book and asked one question: "If this was the beginning of a book, would you read it?" Eleven said, "Absolutely!" The twelfth was a negative but he was a cousin, so it doesn't count.

To a person, the eleven commented that the content was universal and brought back memories, good and bad.

Unlike most memoirs, or autobiographies—I didn't learn the difference until I started this—this is a memoir told chronologically, but in story form. Each chapter is a story, a life event. The book will take you from about age three until the end of high school. There I pause. A sequel will follow to cover my college years.

What might you expect in these stories? Well, let's see . . . you'll meet my family and a bunch of characters from my neighborhood; you'll meet Salty, Wolf, Teri, and Shadow that are some of the dogs in my life; you'll meet an organ grinder and his monkey, and sense the wonder the trolley car gave little kids; you'll meet the "3 Rs" and several other girls over whom I tripped; you'll visit Coney Island in summer and winter; and you'll experience what could be called a gang fight, if anyone had fought, that is.

And there is so much more. The anxiety of starting elementary school, and the characters who taught it. Through my eyes, you'll experience the enormity of a big city high school, and the characters who taught in it. There is pathos—teachers with serious PTSD. There are tragedies—murder and suicide. Yes, you read that correctly—tragedy, murder, and suicide. There is humor, mostly the bungling of a pre-teen and teen as he sheds the skin of childhood. As he reaches for a semblance of adulthood, he invariably catches that skin on one thing or another.

One example: I went to pick up a date. She was someone I desperately wanted to go out with. Pretty and perky she was. I arrived. She perked down from the second floor of her house to say she'd be ready in a minute and whirled around in retreat. As she did, her ponytail flipped past my face and in a moment that can only be described as Freudian, I grabbed it. It came off in my hand. To say I was shocked into immobility doesn't come near what I felt thinking I'd just pulled her hair out. That's how I learned about a thing called "a fall," fake hair—but real news.

It's time to get started, so come along. I think you'll enjoy the read.

---

[1] Woody Allen

INTRODUCTION REDUX

"So, what is this? An Auto-oir? A Memography?"

Uh-oh. This isn't what I thought it was. I thought it was an autobiography. According to the experts, however, an autobiography focuses on the life story of a famous person written by that person. This is written by me. Not famous am I. And this tome is probably not going to change that. There is always hope though.

Then I read an article about writing a memoir. Hmmmm. "So, it's a memoir" methinks. Not! A memoir focuses on a piece of one's life. There isn't a piece of my life that would work as a book; actually there might be, but I'm not going to write it. Now isn't that intriguing? Sorry.

So, what the heck is this? An auto-oir? A memography? Seriously, my brother, a professional journalist and writer, once told me that I was a talented storyteller. What this book is then, is a series of stories that cover snippets, events, and moments of my life from elementary school through high school. The stories go from life with no hormones to one with almost all hormones. But doesn't most everyone's? And there you have it.

You are probably saying, "Have what?"

I don't blame you. One element that should be contained in both an autobiography and a memoir is a point. What point, or points, would be so important that the author is driven to write a book to drive them home?

Here it is. My point is this. Your life is more interesting than you probably think. True, some people manage to live deadly, boring lives. Some of them don't know any different, and that's fine with them. They sort of flatline through life—born, go to school, grow up, get married, have children, and die. Mind you, there is purpose to that, even a biblical purpose. But my bet, as with my life, is when you look at each set of words between the commas in the last sentence there are stories to be told. Some of those stories are pretty similar to everyone else's stories. They are the comfort food stories of life: first memories, the three-ring circus that is usually the story of the birth of one's first child, the loss of one's first pet and so on. Folks from other parts of this country, and hopefully others, are warmed and cheered by such stories because they bring back memories of their own life.

Then there's that other stuff. Weird teachers, scary neighbors, something that happened because you were somewhere you were told not to be at a time when something then happened that wouldn't have involved you "if you'd only listened to your mother." One's first encounter with a cop giving out a traffic ticket. One's first encounter with a ghost. These are the stories that elicit the "no way!" reaction; sometimes that reaction is from the writer as he or she scoops the stuff of these stories out of the goop that is one's memory.

So, my dear reader, my point is this: think about your life artfully, creatively, and you'll find that, first of all, it was more interesting than you thought. Secondly, maybe it was more interesting than mine, and you should be writing a book . . . be it an auto-oir or memography.

That said, I hope you enjoy the stories of my life as much as I did in remembering them, or should it be writing them?

Section One

"Hail, Hail the gang's all here . . ." kid with the glazed look is me at my bar mitzvah moving from table to table for the obligatory pictures.

The Family

. . . sort of **Meet the Fockers.**

"You can choose your friends but not your family." An ancient truism. Writers are told by editors that readers like to know a bit about them. Well, when you finish this, you'll know probably more than you need, if not more than you want.

But like you, I just didn't show up, like E.T. or Mork. I had as conventional a start as one can find in any biology textbook. No drama, just conception and birth. Yet, in child-rearing, there is an unfinished and probably unending argument about what molds an individual into what he/she becomes. The short form is, "nature or nurture." Do your genes make the most permanent impact on what you will become, or does your environment? I go for both.

Since I am not capable of, nor do I want to, write a histology textbook, you'll find here mostly nurture, mostly environment. Now that you've met me (and the golf ball), I thought it appropriate to introduce you to the family—like we finally came to the point in our relationship of having had a serious date, and you were invited over for dinner. This would be the primer you'd get, sort of *Meet the Fockers*.

I'll knock. Just follow me in when the door opens. Afterwards, you'll be armed with all the knowledge you need to proceed.

"Reading Bill Gralnick's book is a return for me to the streets, the families, the neighborhoods and wholesome culture of Brooklyn—my second hometown for ten exciting seasons with the Dodgers.

"I will never forget the great Ebbets fans cheering, 'We're which ya Oisk.'"

– Carl Erskine #17

The Gansa Mishpucha

(The Whole Damned Family)

William Gralnick: my father's father. Born in Minsk, a member of the Carpenter's Union and so buried in Brooklyn next to his union brothers, who oddly enough was a clothing salesman. During the Great Depression, the family often didn't see him. He took the subway to the Long Island Railroad, and that train to Patchogue in Suffolk County. He returned late at night and left early in the morning.

As the Great Depression raged, the family's circumstances waned further and further until they lived in a three-room, sub-street apartment, the six of them—the girls in one bed, the boys in another (the middle boy both in bed and in age becoming a bed-wetter), and parents sleeping on a pullout in the living room. You could look out the window and see the feet of the passersby, but not the weather.

Willie, as he was called, was the apple of his second child's eye, Pauline, and was rumored to have had an affair because his wife Jenny was, well . . . difficult. He died in a bed in the hallway of a charity hospital before I was born.

Jenny Gralnick: My father's mother, a Mirer, was born in Romania. She was forever traumatized when the Cossacks rode through town cutting off the beards of religious Jews (pretty much meaning all Jews.) One missed and cut off a man's head in front of her.

She did not adjust easily or well to America, living initially with the family alongside the 'El', or elevated trains, in Brooklyn. Out of fear, she rarely left the apartment, except for Shabbat when she washed the floor, covered it with newspaper, and went out to buy a chicken.

Mildred Gralnick was my mother. Born before her time, she was a graduate of Douglass College, the teacher's school of Rutgers

5

University in New Brunswick, New Jersey. She had one brother, Howard. Her parents were divorced by fiat—fiat by my grandmother's sisters who scolded her that her roustabout husband was soiling the family name and she either divorced him or she would be banished from New Brunswick. Divorce won.

My mother was a bright, quick-witted, intelligent woman born of a time and married to a man when women were homemakers. She read copiously, sometimes a book a day. She smoked copiously, sometimes several packs a day and eventually drank copiously, who knows how much. She died of cancer at age sixty-one.

Abraham Gralnick, my father, became a dentist. He wanted first to be a violinist and then a physician, but he was the oldest boy amongst the five siblings. Dentistry was then a two-year shorter course and he had two other brothers who needed to be put through school. He was the first in his class to open a regional dental practice; in those days most dentists practiced out of their house and were the neighborhood dentist. He established himself in the Fox Building in downtown Brooklyn and was eventually driven out by Murray the K and his rock 'n' roll shows, the patrons of which scared the pants off his patients. So, he "moved on up" and became a Madison Avenue dentist. That made Mom very happy.

Highly neurotic socially, he had to have my mother plaster him with cold compresses before social engagements. Abe was mild mannered, everyone liked him, which used to PO my mother, whose usual response was, "You don't have to live with him."

Highly skilled as a dentist, he made everything he put into his patients' mouths, until he could no longer keep up with the volume. So distinctive was his work that one of his students at NYU Dental, working in my cousin's mouth on an aircraft carrier, recognized my father's work. When my father died, he was treating the fifth generation of some families.

Ever scarred by the Depression, he lived in fear that the dollar in his pocket might be the last the family would have. He pressured both his children to become "professional men" in charge of their own destinies. They both disappointed him.

He lived and died his dream. At eighty-seven, he went to work, during his sixty-seventh uninterrupted year of practice, came home, had a heart attack, and died. No hallways in charity wards for him.

Louis Feinstein was my maternal grandfather. He left the family in his mid-teens maybe a decade after they arrived in America. He sold hats and anything else that made him a buck.

A tough guy, he lied about his age to get into the Second World War, was assigned to the Red Cross relief as army liaison in Japan, and later turned his contacts into a job as an international toy salesman making him #1 on the grandfather hit parade. He was rumored to have been in a bar and knocked a guy off his stool for having made an anti-Semitic comment.

He loved taking me out to eat, making sure to tell the waiters that I was his grandson and had a hollow leg, so they'd best feed me well. A great grandfather, a lousy husband; who knows how he ever hooked up with my grandmother, who wore an "S" on her chest for staid.

Beatrice (Bea) Peshkin Feinstein came from a good family. She was one of four girls. She owned and operated a toy store and continued to do so for years after her leg was amputated because of cancer. Her greatest fear was that I, whom she loved dearly, would at three not recognize her the first day I saw her with one leg. Family lore has it that I ran straight to her, and jumped in her still enveloping lap, while tears were shed all around.

She died at about ninety-seven, in a home, although she was not aware of it. Ravaged by what is known now as Alzheimer's, she took to speaking only Yiddish because she thought the nurses were plotting against her.

A tough disciplinarian, she none-the-less loved me dearly. At the reading of her will, she had written, "To my favorite grandson, Billy. For his love I leave him a double share of my estate." She died penniless, but the emotion was worth more to me than the money.

Frieda Gralnick Rosenthal was the oldest of the Gralnick children. She was perky, fun, a "balabuster" as was said (real homemaker/mom/family-oriented person). Her bust line was almost the size of her height. Everyone loved her. She married Dr. Benjamin Rosenthal, a friend of her brother's, my father. Ben was a gifted physician who had with Frieda, three boys running the gamut of brilliant to not quite. All became, like he, ophthalmologists. Ben was charming, fun, intelligent, a driver to success for his boys, someone who whistled better than anyone I had ever heard, and who, against everyone's advice, made Frieda accompany him to a conference in California while she was having heart problems. On the return trip, she got off the plane and dropped dead.

Pauline Gralnick Pollack was number two in line. She was the oddest of the ducklings. Unlike Frieda, who was built like a bulldog, Pauline was tall and athletic, like a tennis player. She was also nutty as a fruitcake, which can happen when your fiancé jumps off a bridge. More pages are later devoted to her devotions and nuttiness, especially after her later and late-in-life marriage to the Welch lamp-maker, Isadore Pollack.

Irving Gralnick was the second of the boys and the fourth of the children. He too was a brilliant dentist, a crown and bridge man as they were called, but unlike my father, he never seemed happy doing what he did. My father's students at NYU loved him; my uncle's student's lived in fear of him. A poorly performing student could well be eaten alive by my uncle right there beside the dental chair.

Both my father and Irv were handball wizards, but my father would tell me with marvel that "Uncle Irv used to be able to throw a football 100 yards on a line!"

He married a beautiful woman and had a booming practice that started out on Madison Avenue (no Brooklyn for him).

They had three beautiful daughters.

He died early of an embolism, or aneurism, or one of those things that blows up inside and kills you immediately. One often wonders what happens when a dentist drops dead while working on a patient. Oh well.

My dad was now down a sister and brother as well as mother and father. He was an emotional funeral goer and both times had to be restrained from jumping into the graves.

Al Gralnick was the baby, the fifth and last of Jenny and Willie's shenanigans. Often the black lamb, then sheep, of the family, Al was at times a card-carrying communist and a lifelong socialist, a socialist who ended up building a private, psychiatric hospital for the treatment of schizophrenics that sat on about 250 prime acres in Westchester County, New York, the town of Portchester to be exact, famous for having the Life Saver manufacturing plant and his hospital.

I'm not sure why he was in Chicago when he met a Jewish dance hall girl named Ruth and married her. They were childless and adopted two boys, William and Daniel. Both became medical doctors. For a psychiatrist, my uncle's relationship with his children—it seemed to me—could have been a lot better. Neither was anointed by their father to become medical director of the hospital when he retired.

Ruth and Al divorced. Al had three more wives, actually two—one he married twice. Oh yes, and a mistress here and there. Leave it to a psychiatrist. Al and wife #2 had one natural-born child, Michael. Wife, Frances, came to the marriage with a son and daughter. The son saw no need to have a stepfather. Al invited him to leave the house or be banished. He apparently was prone to saying to my uncle, "You're not my father, so don't tell me what to do." My uncle was great with crazy people, not so much with the normal ones who hadn't had lobotomies or electro-shock therapy. The stepdaughter eventually left home too and never spoke to my uncle again, or most any of us, for that matter. She married a doctor and seems to have won the prize for living the most normal life of the bunch.

Then there was my brother, Jeffrey Charles Gralnick, who hated his name. Born in 1939, he was my hero. After managing to scrape through high school, flunk out of college, and get drafted, he grew up, and entered New York University night school. By his junior year, he was sports editor of the NYU Square Journal, a school newspaper that had a circulation larger than many mid-size American dailies. Great as a kid to have a sports editor for a brother who covered a team that played in Madison Square Garden and that had two potential NBA stars in the mix.

My brother, twice married and father of three, lit up the journalism world, and can be easily tracked in Wikipedia. While he blazed a path through TV News, he also blazed a path through sometimes four to five packs of cigarettes a day and died an ugly death at seventy-two. With him went my Star Ship shield for life.

Howard Feinstein/Fain was 6'2" tall. From whom he got that height I'm not sure. He was handsome, and a decorated war hero from being chewed up by a German machine gun, during the Battle of the Bulge. He was my mother's baby brother. He married by far the most popular Jewish girl in West Hartford, Connecticut. He built a thriving retail business, had one son and adopted a second. He was chairman of the West Hartford Chamber of Commerce, and became a real live hero for the second time, organizing a boat brigade to save lives during a massive flood, and was the toast of the town when he and his wife, Joan, got into their Woody (Mercury) station wagon, about as long as a freight car, or so it seemed, and went to play golf. He was an idol to both my brother and me. With the help of the US Army and the cigarette industry, he smoked himself to death at forty-one.

These are the A-team family players. There is more family, and there are more players, but let this serve as little reference manual as you ply your way through my life.

Story Time Tapas to Whet the Appetite

There are two reasons for this insertion. First of all, some stories, even in the right chronological order, stand better on their own. They don't quite fit right. The other is that some span the chronology; they cover years or decades, not happenings of a single hour, or even day.

So, I've let them stand alone. That way, you can get a taste of what is to come. I've tried to choose some of the best—mostly so that you'll get hooked and keep reading.

Enjoy the tasting.

"I was driving my 1959 Chevy Impala down King's Highway in Brooklyn with the top down, and I heard 'Oh! Carol' on three stations at the same time while I was channel surfing. I knew then that I made it."

– Neil Sedaka

Aunt Pauline the lady with the secret pencil factory.

Aunt Pauline

(The Pencil Lady)

"In a word, he was cheap. In two, he was very cheap."

Everyone has an Aunt Pauline, regardless of her name. She's that spinster aunt who loves you dearly but can't quite remember which birthday it is you're celebrating. She takes you places you don't really want to go and gives you things you don't really want, but she smells nice and means well. My Aunt Pauline didn't stay a spinster forever, but we're not there yet.

The second oldest of my father's five siblings, Pauline was sort of mannish looking, also prim and proper. Unlike her older sister, who was short, stout, and had a bosom that could confound a bra saleswoman, Pauline looked more like a tennis player. As the family was hit harder and harder by the Great Depression, Pauline became more and more "Papa's girl" as she worried about his long hours and financial struggles. This pattern became her life after her fiancé committed suicide by jumping off the Brooklyn Bridge during that Depression, something my brother and I as teenagers found inexplicably funny. When my grandfather died, she threw herself into the caring of her nieces and nephews, of which I was her favorite.

There were things she took me to that she was sure I would love, that I didn't—like the annual church bazaar on Eastern Parkway across from The Abraham Lincoln Apartments where she lived for decades. There were other things I hated then but came to realize were wonderful things to have done with her, like the Brooklyn Museum and concerts at the Brooklyn Academy of Music. The Museum had this amazing display about American Indians that

I remember to this day, and I heard Peter and The Wolf for the first time at the Academy. It remains today a seminal memory; I still have the 78-rpm with Basil Rathbone (real name!) narrating.

The thing about Aunt Pauline was that she was a little weird. She never forgot my birthday, but for years the number on the card was always a year or two off. And always too young. Maybe she didn't want me to grow up. Usually, her birthday presents were also off, more appropriate for the age of the card than the age I actually was, but her strange ways manifested themselves in, for-no-good reason, gifts of pencils and dollar bills.

Whenever we had the family over, Aunt Pauline would come in and whisper that she had something special for me. Each time, that special thing was a bunch of #2 pencils that she had used and sharpened back to a point. Thus, they were both used and of varying lengths, and bound together by a rubber band. What she thought I would do with them, especially after she'd already given me about a pound and a half of pencils, I don't know. But they just kept on comin'. The other gift brings us to the end of her spinsterhood.

My mom was the advisor to all the women in the family on whatever problems they were having, or whatever decisions they had to make. Years after Uncle Murray the Furrier died, Aunt Pearl met Harry the real estate maven, who asked for her hand in marriage. She was on the phone and then "at Mom's crystal ball" in record time. What to do? What to do? Mom said marry him. She did.

This is how it happened. It came one day that Aunt Pauline decided her dull, dark apartment needed a new lamp. She walked down the block a-ways to the lamp store and there she met its owner, Izzy Pollack, from Wales. Izzy was about the size of a gnome, had ears like Dumbo and was immediately smitten with my aunt. He sold her a lamp and then pursued her like a golden retriever puppy pursues its playmate—relentlessly. So, with mom's assurances it was the right thing for her to do, a marriage ensued, leading to one of the most hysterically funny nights in our family history.

It was a simple wedding conducted by a rabbi in the chapel. We had a reception at our home, and afterwards Iz and Pauline left to spend their wedding night together at the Abraham Lincoln Apartments. No honeymoon. Iz was, in a word, cheap. In two, very cheap. Lovely guy but . . . Both, I guess, in their fifties and sixties at the time, the tennis player and the gnome took their leave from all the well-wishers and disappeared into the night. At about 1 a.m., the phone rang. It was Pauline—screaming.

In trying to calm her down, my mother woke up everyone. When she finally got Pauline calm enough to understand what had happened, this was the story: All the cabinets in the kitchen, full of dishes and glasses and whatnot, had fallen off the wall in what must have been the likes of the cymbal crashes in the "1812 Overture." It scared them both awake and half to death.

Now they were faced with a disaster scene. Abraham Lincoln Civil War-like destruction was to be found in his namesake apartments in Brooklyn. Just no dead bodies. A brigade was needed. All hands on deck. We Gralnicks dressed and drove over there and, no lie, all the cabinets were everywhere, some smashed on the sink, some smashed on the floor, pieces of plates and glasses large and small, exploded over everything. You know, of course, what my teenage brother and I conjured up in our minds as we envisioned what the tennis player and the gnome could have been doing on their honeymoon night to shake the cabinets off their moorings . . . so we laughed until we almost wet our pants and our mom slapped us.

As I said, Izzy was cheap, so cheap that he made the proverbial Scotsman seem generous. Someone said, "He squeezes the nickel so tight, it makes the bull shit." For instance, eventually everyone in the family had new lamps, but Izzy's idea of a gift was a deal.

So now we come to the first of Pauline's gifts.

I think my mother had tipped her off that I had enough pencils to run an art studio and she could start throwing them out rather than wrapping them up. "Well," she asked, "what do you give a boy?"

"Money," was the answer, out of earshot of Uncle Iz of course.

Came the inevitable family party, and now Aunt Pauline has a husband, a cheap one. As usual, she greeted me with a whisper, "I have something for you."

Later in the day, I saw her scope out the room to see where Uncle Iz was located. When he was far enough away, Pauline pulled me into a corner and slipped something that felt like origami into my hand. It was a dollar bill, folded as many times as one could possibly fold it, then pressed into my palm with this admonition: "Now don't tell Uncle Iz . . . you know he loves you but . . . you know how he is."

Yes, I do, I thought—cheap!

And so, unfolds the story of Aunt Pauline—and her origami dollars—who lived longer than Uncle Iz, and I think ended up with more money than he had, and certainly more pencils.

"My family originally lived in Brooklyn. Our first apartment was a little place above my father and uncle's hardware store in Coney Island. Now, don't get the impression that we were surrounded by merry-go-rounds, roller coasters and Ferris wheels. Nope, this was a little side street."

– Gilbert Gottfried
Actor, Comedian

Uncle Murray the Furrier with back to window flanked by spruced up brother Jeff (the one who is half Uncle Murray's size).

Uncle Murray

(The Furrier)

*"When he yelled, 'Pearl!' the tub faucets
almost turned themselves on."*

He was a footnote in a medical textbook, I was told. But that came much later. In doing research on my family, I discovered we had an ostrich feather exporter who then became an ostrich feather importer. That was news to me. That we had a furrier in the family you couldn't escape knowing. My mother never lusted after ostrich feathers. No Paul Manafort was she . . . It was mink she wanted.

Grandma had three sisters. The second oldest was Pearl Peshkin. Pearl married Murray the Furrier. Murray Waranoff was one of those genuinely nice guys. He was the viola to my Aunt Pearl's fiddle—soft, gentle, and mostly quiet. My family knew several furriers. Most were like used car salesmen.

Not Uncle Murray.

Uncle Murray had two distinctions, both personal but very different. First, he liked quiet. Why he had three children was a bit of a mystery. The bathtub was the vehicle he used to meld together his two desires: a quiet household and clean children. When the decibel level exceeded his toleration level, he would shout, "Pearl! Give the children a bath!" Since they were two girls and a boy, that meant two baths and more quiet time. Nor was he fooling. When he yelled, "Pearl!" The tub faucets almost turned on themselves.

It is said that "Only the good die young," and so it was with Uncle Murray. He developed kidney disease. Not only was the transplant still a thought in some researcher's mind, there wasn't even dialysis that could sustain him. Both kidneys went.

In Mel Brooks and Carl Reiner's, *2000-Year-Old Man* routine, Reiner asked Brooks his secret to long life. He cited "nectarines (the best fruit in the world!) and the will to live." Reiner said, "You mean you had such a strong will to live you wouldn't die?" Brooks: "No dummy, Dr. Willtolive. What a doctor!"

Well, Uncle Murray must have had the same doctor. The predictions of his death were constant and incorrect. When you have no functioning kidneys, your body has no filter system and it poisons itself. Maybe some animal he was skinning had bitten him and gave him some kind of antidote. While he had to take to bed, and became weaker and weaker, thinner and thinner, the light wouldn't go out. The doctors marveled. Blood tests indicated levels of toxins that no body could withstand—except Uncle Murray's. Truthfully, I think Aunt Pearl was getting a little disgusted. Every time the doctor told her to get ready, it would only be a few days or a few more hours . . . they were wrong. Murray kept on truckin.'

Until one day he didn't.

I was told that he became a footnote in medical history mentioned in nephrology studies and a textbook. Who knows? What I do know is, here's a guy who spends his whole life as a furrier—and ends up known because of his kidneys. Go figure.

"You know, I still live in my neighborhood. I live in Brooklyn and the same neighborhood, so I don't really get star treatment like that. I'm still Vanessa from the neighborhood."

– Vanessa Ferlito, TV Actress

"Charlie Chaplin" Gralnick and wife, my mom, Mildred.

Open Wide—Wide Open

*"He didn't care what color you were, only
what color your teeth were."*

My father was a dentist, and for sixty-seven, non-stop years was my dentist, as well as the dentist for a lot of other folks. We thought we'd get him into the Guinness Book of Records but upon his death we learned there was some older-than-eighty-seven geezer still fooling around in peoples' mouths a day a week—which closed the book on that quest.

I heard "Open wide" a lot. I heard a lot else as well:

- I heard the story of my cousin being on an aircraft carrier, going to the ship's dentist and having him remark, "The only person I've ever seen do work like that was my professor, Abraham Gralnick."

- I heard dentists I used when out of reach of my dad say upon looking into my mouth, "I wouldn't put that much gold in my kid's mouth!" I had the pleasure of responding, "Well, I guess, my father felt differently about me than you do about your kids."

- I heard there was a line, like ants, between his office and the Brooklyn Navy Yard. He did his part for those who were going to do what he could not because during World War II he received an exemption, for some reason or another.

- I heard that my dad was the first to start a regional practice out of an office building—and he did that following graduation from the New York University Dental School, one of a few in the 1920s which took Jews. The point here is that dentistry in those days was neighborhood-based and practiced out of one's house. The building that housed my father's practice was the old Fox Theatre Building in downtown Brooklyn. The coming of rock and roll and Murray the K's raucous shows that wrapped lines of screaming kids around Nevins Street created a gauntlet his patients had to run. Later, and because of the many patients now coming from Long Island and Westchester, he moved the practice to Madison Avenue in Manhattan.

- I heard that until the 1960s my father made virtually every piece of dental appliance he put into a patient's mouth, and I saw enough plaster molds lining shelves in his office to think he could throw a dynamite Halloween party. Later, and when his workload required him to begin getting these dental appliances from dental labs, I listened to him curse the slow, shoddy, work of those labs.

- I heard (while listening to a late-night call from a patient) about a man whose son was being flown back from Europe on an ambulance plane. He had been in a horrendous automobile accident. There wasn't a dentist in Europe this man would let reconstruct his son's mouth—had to be my father—who in turn hopped into the ole Buick, headed for the hospital, and spent all night doing that reconstruction.

- I heard the old, vinyl records of my father's voice doing pro-fluoridation radio spots for New York State. In those days, fluoridation was seen by many to be a Communist plot to poison Americans, and one could get hurt, literally, by being one of its proponents.

- I heard that, at a convention in New York City, three of my colleagues had broken teeth. My father did all that work—for free. Every year thereafter, and until the convention moved to DC, colleagues during breaks would head over to Dr. Gralnick's for one thing or another.

- I heard that he treated every member of his immediate family: aunts, uncle, nieces, nephews, and their children—for free. He believed in family. He also believed that affordable health care was a right. He never turned anyone away because of money. He would agree to any payment plan, and didn't care what color you were, only what color your teeth were—all of which created more dust from my mother's molars. Thank goodness people in Brooklyn no longer raised chickens and goats . . . bartering would have given us a farm!

By the time he graduated, dentistry had gone beyond the hammer, chisel, and pliers mode of treatment, but I heard about, and saw, some of the equipment he used in those early days. You pumped the drill with your foot to make it go. Later there was a lever on a motor to hit with your toe. So, you were pumping or pushing while leaning in someone's mouth drilling.

There used to be a famous utility company sign in New York that read, "Dig we must for a better New York." It was Con Edison's (known to us all as Con Ed, or to some just as Con) rationale for screwing up the streets and traffic all over town at the most inopportune times—and in New York that's about nineteen hours of each twenty-four.

Dental digging and drilling in the old days was about like that—smoke, dust, noise. It wasn't until the high-speed, water-cooled drill came into use that the process became easier for both the dentists and patients. Then it just smelled like someone had lit a match inside your mouth.

So, I heard all this and was struck by a thought: I have a father who is part of the growth of American dental history. I'd never have known this if I hadn't been an attentive eavesdropper. Later in life, I developed two oral history collections for my organization and did some great interviews. So, the screen in my head lit up. It said, Interview Dad, dummy!

Soon after the lighted sign incident, I found myself headed to New York. I had my questions ready, my outline prepared. Dad always had a tape recorder on the dining room table. After my mother died, he could leave whatever he wanted wherever he wanted and that's where he wanted the tape recorder. In his office, he was a scientist—neat, orderly—and knew where everything and anything was at any given minute.

At home, fuhgedaboudit!

The absent-minded-professor he was. Wrote notes to remind himself and forgot where the notes were. Having prepared him for my version of oral surgery, we sat down, positioned the recorder, hit the button, and took a breath.

Nothing happened!

No click. No whine of the tape being spooled across the machine. Turns out not only had he not moved the tape recorder for years, he hadn't used it. The batteries were corroded—so corroded that when I turned the recorder over, I saw that battery acid had leaked onto the table. More batteries he had; another recorder he did not.

When I left, we made one of those "next time without fail" promises.

There was no next time. He realized his dream. He worked until he died—and we buried an amazing amount of history with him.

The only recording of his voice I have recounts a different kind of history. It is his answering machine saying: "You have reached 555-3629, please leave a message."

The message therein, dear reader, I'll leave up to you.

"If you've never seen people taking the pledge of allegiance for the first time as U.S. Citizens, it will move you: a room full of people who can really appreciate what I was lucky enough to grow up with, simply by being born in Brooklyn."

— Alexis Ohanian
Internet Entrepreneur
and Investor

"Oy Vey!" The OMG of Brooklyn.

The Legend of

Trapper Abe

"This was a real execution and we were the executioners."

An encounter with a squirrel in our backyard the other day brought memories of "Trapper Abe."

In the backyard of my childhood, squirrels were the nemesis of my mother's green thumb. She liked to plant things that grew from bulbs: crocuses, tulips, and the like. Bulbs are to squirrels what carrots are to rabbits. In would go the bulbs, out would come the squirrels, gone would be my mother's hope of neat rows of flowers.

My mother could be a cranky sort, and the squirrel thievery definitely ratcheted things up on the cranky scale. A solution was needed, so "Trapper Abe" rode to the rescue. Trapper Abe was my father. To him fell the decision of dealing with the bulb-filching vermin or dealing with St. Mildred the Cranky.

First, my father called the Parks Department. I think they laughed at him. He then turned to the hardware store. In the '50s, a hardware store was not only a place that had all manner of exotica one needed for household fixin's but was run by men who had knowledge about things most people—like dentists—had no clue about.

My father had two choices. One was "mole nuts." They looked like bulbs, and while designed to kill moles, they would work just fine on squirrels. There were three problems:

- As a family, we were anti-capital punishment, especially for robbery.
- No one wanted to be the undertaker.
- The mole nuts would work as well on our dog as on our poachers. Thus, a bad choice.

But the hardware maven, Mr. Title, had another idea—a trap. The trap was aluminum with wire sides and was about two-and-a-half feet long. In the center was a tray upon which one placed something succulent. The tray was attached to a spring that operated the doors. Squirrel touches tray, tray trips the springs, the springs trip the doors, and doors snap shut and trap squirrel.

We bought two.

Home we went. We chose cheese for the bait. Apparently, it was a good choice because it didn't take too long before we had, in fact, trapped our first squirrel. Clattering about in the trap, he looked a lot more frantic than guilty. So, there we were—mother the planter, father the trapper, and sons the snickering bystanders, all relating to someone's ancestral heritage. We had trapped an animal, but no one was going to skin this baby and make a stew. Short of that, just what did one do with a trapped animal?

Enter again the sagacious Mr. Title. "Drown it," he said. This genius said to fill up the bathtub; drop in the trap, and a short while later toss the dead squirrel into the trash.

That was not going to happen. Aside from the philosophy of capital punishment, this was a real execution and we were the executioners. No thanks. Besides, unless my father had a way of getting the bathtub out of the house, there was no way my mother was letting him bring the squirrel inside, no less drown it in the tub the family used to bathe.

Then one of us then got a brilliant idea: relocate the population. Who knows, maybe what biologists now are doing all over the globe with endangered species, we started right there on Waldorf Court, in Brooklyn, New York.

We lived about six miles from Prospect Park. My dad threw the trap and trappee into the back seat of the Buick. The beast was released in the park; everyone was a winner, and thus was born the legend of Trapper Abe.

There was, however, a postscript. If you're not going to skin and eat what you trap as part of day-to-day survival, the process gets old pretty darn quickly. There were countless numbers of stupid, cheese-addicted squirrels in Brooklyn, and only so much time for running to Prospect Park. Ten or fifteen squirrels into the game, my father decided a few less tulips would be just fine, and he could deal with my mother's crankiness.

The traps went into the garage. The squirrels rejoiced in the trees. The bulbs were left to fend for themselves. And so died the legend of Trapper Abe.

The Star of our show, Milton Berle (I told you he had no shame...)

Uncle Miltie

"If the show was too long, it just ended."

Odd it is that the need for escape can be cause for a light-hearted detour from the pressures of life. "Lawsy mercy," as Butterfly McQueen used to say to "Miss Scarlet," do we need a break from life's headlines right now. Milton Berle provided millions of Americans in the '50s and '60s with exactly that and did it in prime time. You didn't need to stay up until all hours to see funny stuff.

First, just the act of acquainting or reacquainting oneself with his kind of slapstick is cause for joyous relief. The most important thing to understand about Milton Berle is that he had no shame. There were no limits to the heights, or depths, to which his comedy would sink to get a laugh. He could do one-liners with the best of them, like "Mr. One-Liner," Henny Youngman (who often said most of Berle's one-liners were so funny because they were Henny Youngman's!).

In a suit and tie and doing standup routines with the likes of Phil Silvers, he was a master of comic timing. But he'd appear in drag, in clown costume, in anything that touched on the outrageous. If there was a laugh in you, Berle would get it out. I often needed that. Just like I can listen to Abbott and Costello's *"Who's on First?"* routine one hundred times in a row and laugh out loud every time, all I needed was to hear someone yell "MAKE-UP!" and I broke up because what came next was hilarity embedded in my mind before it even happened. Berle is in a chair or standing next to someone. Then, a lunatic from the wings, often sporting a fright wig, bolts onto the stage and hits Berle in the face with this gigantic powder-puff that sends white powder flying. Then Berle gazes at the camera with a look of disgust that is somewhat different every time it happens. Even if you groaned, Berle was happy. He had reached you.

In today's world of sensory overload, the simplicity of life with television in the '50s is hard to imagine or even describe. How does one understand watching a test pattern in anticipation of a show coming on when today one has access to dozens, and sometimes hundreds, of things to watch 24/7? Imagine a time when, at times, there really was nothing at all on TV.

How does one who didn't live through it understand the transfixing nature of a medium that it caused people to gather on sidewalks in front of television stores to watch "Uncle Miltie" and later *I Love Lucy* in whatever weather the good Lord was throwing down that day? Star-power is when some individual causes whole industries to create conveniences to make it easier not to miss these shows. TVs in stores that sold them were turned on and faced towards the street. Crowds gathered to watch and hopefully would come in later to buy one.

The food industry? They didn't call it an "instant dinner" or a "quick dinner" or a "frozen dinner." They called it a "TV dinner." And mostly, in those days, they were awful, but we ate them—in front of the TV.

Today, the "Berle Show" seems almost quaint. In those days, four, freshly scrubbed guys in gasoline service station uniforms that had never been spotted with grease came singing their way into our living room with the line, "We Are the Men from Texaco. We serve you from Maine to Mexico" and they seemed, well, entertaining. They opened their arms, swept them out, and introduced, "The star of our show . . . Milton Berle!" Vaudeville came right into your living room.

Berle invented the format we now know so well—the monologue followed by variety. Part of Berle's variety was a guy named Sid Stone. Bowler hat, striped shirt, sleeves pulled up above the wrists and held in place by armbands, Stone was the stereotypical shyster from which Johnny Carson later made half a dozen characters. Stone could sell ice to an Eskimo in winter and he'd do it with the line, "Tell you what I'm gonna do . . ." The "deal" was coming, and along with it a broad smile that stretched across America because everyone knew it. It was a *shtick* line employed ever since, the set-up line that people knew by heart, anticipated with glee, and then made part of their everyday vocabulary.

The greatest wonder of early TV was that it was live. That made it both "real" and really funny. It also provided us with the last generation of skilled and unschooled performers on television. A show was a certain number of minutes long. There was one take. The show had to fit, or it became a Procrustean bed. If it was too short, it had to be lengthened, and watching that happen could be painfully funny. If the show was too long, it just ended. Comedians tested their fellow actors. Men like Sid Caesar and Milton Berle took pride in being able to unnerve another actor in a skit, watching in glee as the person's face contorted, as he or she struggled both for composure and articulation. The early days of *The Carol Burnett Show* with Tim Conway and Harvey Korman are some of the best examples. The real benefit of it all was sitting in your living room and being part of it. I remember Charo dancing out of the top of her dress and I couldn't decide what was funnier, my mother's screaming, or the look on Ed Sullivan's face after it happened.

That kind of television and the people who made it—Berle, Caesar, and so many more—is virtually extinct, to be found only on late night television. It was a wonderful time with wonderful memories. No matter how bad the day, no matter how bleak the mood my "Uncle Miltie" would fix it—guaranteed. It was pure escapism for nights when escape was what I longed for.

The Merritt Parkway: First limited access highway in America meaning it had only entrances and exits but no interchanges.

Buddy, Can You Spare a Dime?

"Ships of great majesty and reputation."

Once upon a time there was no interstate highway system. That stroke of genius belonged to former General and then President Dwight David Eisenhower. It eventually changed America in incredibly important ways from demographics to economics. The real reason behind it though was the ever-chilling Cold War and Eisenhower's sense that we needed a system that could accommodate the high-speed transportation of mobile missiles and other articles of war.

In the mid to late '50s the famous/infamous I-95, the highway that stretched from Maine to Florida, or Florida to Maine, depending on which way you were going, was only partly finished. The slow death of small-town Route 1 tourist economies began. When I was in my middle school years, as you would know them now, and we wanted to visit my mother's brother and his family, we'd drive to New Jersey, through Brooklyn using the newly minted Brooklyn Battery Tunnel or the Goethals Bridge (no Verrazano Narrows Bridge yet either), hie on up to New Brunswick, scoop up grandma, turn around and head north.

As I recall the trip to West Hartford, it was really interesting, and that's something to be said when three adults and two kids are squashed into a car with no air conditioning in the hot months, or wearing heavy coats in an over-heated car in the cold months. The winter clothing could either be worn or taken off, but it took up cumulatively about the space of one additional passenger. If memory serves, the trip involved the Belt Parkway, which coursed through lightly inhabited parts of Brooklyn with lots of wide open spaces, then the West Side Highway (now gone, a piece of which is a Trump above-ground shopping development), the Hutchinson River Parkway, known to everyone who used it as "The Hutch" and finally the Merritt Parkway.

My favorite part of the trip was the West Side Highway and the anticipation of passing alongside of the then-famous Port of New York. There we'd see the great ocean liners of the day. The *Queen Mary* and *Queen Elizabeth*, the SS *United States*, the *Ile de France*—ships of great majesty and legendary reputation. If we really got lucky and it was fleet week, spaced before and after these huge liners could be destroyers, cruisers, even an aircraft carrier. It was a little slice of boyhood heaven.

"The Hutch" was no big deal—that is until you passed the startlingly big George Washington Bridge. To my eyes, it was a colossus. In the evening, it was a-light with millions of bulbs creating almost a surreal looking structure launching itself across the mighty Hudson River (known of course only as "The Hudson," never by its full name).

After leaving it in the rearview mirror, we passed Grant's Tomb, and the imposing, from another century looking Riverside Church. If you had a passion for close-in suburbs there were plenty of those too, each definably different as one neighborhood in New York usually was from another—Yonkers, Riverdale, Scarsdale, "The Hutch" had shown all it had to show.

The Merritt Parkway—known always and only as "The Merritt"—was a different story. Winding, twisting, and narrow, it sliced through the lush woodlands of New York and Connecticut. Sometimes we got to see deer, sometimes alive, sometimes dead and spread out as roadkill. For the driver, "The Merritt" was tension-evoking if the weather was anything but sunny and clear and the clock hands somewhere between 10 and 4 p.m. In rain or snow, or at dusk and sunset, it was downright treacherous.

These were still the days of whitewalls and non-radial tires. No such thing as self-sealing tires you could shoot arrows into and then drive on them for fifty miles. In the winter, one's car wore snow tires that, without snow, made road noise that could drive a passenger batty as their wide, deep, irregularly patterned treads gripped the road without wanting to let go. For a while, until the highway engineers of the day realized what they did to the roads, there came upon the market "studded" tires. These tires had metal studs punched into them that actually dug into the road surface. They were most popular in areas that had ice storms or were prone to runoff that turned to ice. On the highway, they made such a disconcerting racket that it was hard to talk over it. And let us not forget emergency chains. Everyone had a set in their garage, or their trunk, and always in the trunk once winter arrived because, if a snow emergency were called, whole areas of streets and roadways weren't open to cars without chains.

If your car had to do battle with real snow, there was nothing like a set of chains but talk about noise. On bare pavement, the noise was indescribable. However, one noise chain-bearing cars made was unmistakable and definitely describable: put two thousand pounds of steel and chrome on top of a set of chains and run that car at sixty mph on asphalt, building up whatever the friction quotient became, the link that held the chains around the tire might snap. Now you have a set of chains loosed from their bindings whipping around a small circumference at sixty mph. If I'd passed physics, I could tell you the calculation of the force.

What I can tell you is they only went 'round once, twice at the most. They'd hit the underside of the wheel well with whatever that force calculation was. Out of nowhere there came this tremendous THWACK!! THAWK!! THAWK!! If the driver didn't drop dead instantly of a heart attack, then he (in those days if there was a man in the car, the man drove) had to hit the brakes because the chains could seriously damage the car. Once off one wheel but still affixed to the others, a set of three could make the car unstable, very difficult to control. Not to say anything about the damage the unleashed chains flying down the highway could do to other cars. Mostly consisting of two lanes, an accident on "The Merritt" in bad weather, hot or cold, backed up cars for miles and miles of miserable waiting.

And came the final joy, fixing it. Remember, cell phones were still a military secret.

Thus one was either jacking up the car and trying to put on that extra pair of chains, or waiting for a state trooper to pass you by and call for help. Maybe a kind soul would see the problem and stop at the next rest stop and call for you. No matter how you sliced it, you could get killed in many ways. The car could slip off the jack, or actually be blown off it by the repeated gusts of wind created by cars speeding by, one of those cars could hit you and knock you into the next county, or you could drop dead from the exertion. Thus, most folks sat in their cars, hunkered down, and waited.

But assuming one avoided these various mishaps on "The Merritt," it also offered something heavenly—rest stops. From "The Belt" to "The Hutch," to the first stretch of "The Merritt," one crossed one's legs, if one had to go. Except, that is, for poor Grandma who was an amputee. You can't cross your legs with one leg. The physiology doesn't work. Oh, there are muscles one can squeeze but only for so long, especially once one is in one's sixties. To see the first rest stop, knowing getting into it involved being helped out of the car, being handed one's crutches and then making one's way across the parking lot (sometimes in the snow or on the ice), was, I imagine, like riding a camel and seeing the needed oasis in the distance.

"The Merritt" offered something else as well—tolls. Tolls are nothing new. The head scratcher is how many people believed the politicians when they said, "When it's paid for, you ride for free," which was the mantra for clearing the way for the Brooklyn Battery Tunnel. Bullshit. By the time the toll had gone from twenty-five cents to a dollar, it dawned on people that this was forever. Now, I think you have to write a check or leave a fender to cover the toll. I believe the Merritt Parkway began at one thin dime and by the mid-fifties was two thin dimes and a nickel or five pennies, because in those days you could, and many did, get rid of their pennies that way.

So, one bitter, but clear, winter's day we're tooting up "The Merritt." Steering wheels were not padded, nor was much of anything in the cars of the '50s. Nor, of course, were there seat belts yet. The front passenger seat was affectionately known as both "shotgun" and "the death trap." In some areas, it was "the suicide seat." I remember when I was in the front seat and my mother had to quickly hit the brake. Her arm would flash out like a safety gate across my chest to keep me from going through the windshield or running my head into the glove compartment. Physics again. I guess she didn't take it. Were she a world class weight lifter, even then her arm would not be able to contain the force of my ninety-pound body moving forward, if she had to panic stop, not even at thirty or forty mph. But back to that bitter, but clear, winter's day.

The steering wheel was cold, and my dad was driving with his gloves on. He usually kept the change for tolls someplace handy: either in the ashtray (yes, cars had them, and lighters too), or in a little indentation in the door designed for holding change. He never had to reach into his pocket for it, which was a good thing given his gloved condition that bitter, winter's day. We pulled into the toll booth, he rolled down the window (no power windows then either), scooped up the change, took a quick look in his palm, and then stuck out his hand and turned it over into the palm of the toll taker (no electric money counting basket and certainly no electronic toll passes).

Out we pulled and off we went—for about five minutes when into our consciousness comes a high-pitched sound. It sounded like a police car and then all of a sudden it was right on our tail, red light flashing, siren piercing our eardrums. My mother, the attentive one in the family, shouted, "Oh my God, Abe, he's after us!"

Since we hadn't pushed our behemoth Buick up past thirty yet, my father didn't believe her, pulled to the side to let the officer by, whence he pulled up alongside us, and out of a very unhappy looking face came the words, "PULL OVER!"

Now my father believed my mother. He pulled over, rolled down the window, greeted the officer, who said, just like in the movies and just like today, "License and registration please." My dad, ever mild mannered, asked, "What's the problem officer?" The reply? "You ran the toll, sir."

My father was flabbergasted. First of all, he truly would never do something like that. If there had been no toll taker, he'd probably stop and wait for one to show up rather than drive on through. He's the one who, at 3 a.m., with no traffic, stops at a red light and waits for it to turn green. Secondly, he knew he had reached for the change, counted it, and handed it over. As he handed the officer his license and registration there came a very audible but tiny "tink." In between the pinky and fourth finger of his left gloved hand had lodged one thin dime. As he spread his fingers a bit in handing over the documents, it dislodged, plinked off the window casing, bounced off the rounded, protruding door, and hit the frozen cement.

Oooops.

The trooper, having spent who knows how much time, energy, and money in catching us bad guys, leaned over, picked up the dime, said he'd return it to the state of Connecticut, and wished us a good day. Once again, we were West Hartford bound—and much better prepared for the next tollbooth encounter.

Section Two

Jeff's post Bar Mitzvah party at Waldorf Court.

Childhood Introduction

"Wonderible—an age both wonderful and horrible."

Childhood is a collection of ages when put together gets you to the next stage of life. A tremendous amount happens but most of it as a baby well before cognition. Years zero to three are so miraculous that they have been called, "The Magic Years." Think in terms of the span of life and how quickly a child goes from helpless to the "Terrible Twos," when its wants are so powerful the child becomes a veritable Vasco de Gama or Ponce de Leon, on a constant quest for discovery . . . That's why houses get baby proofed. That's why, in spite of a parent's best efforts, like mine, a child ends up sitting in, not on, a toilet bowl, for a fully clothed self-bath experience, or picks up a gallon can of paint in the nanosecond you weren't looking and pours it across the couch.

Sometimes you aid and abet disaster. Out of the corner of my eye I saw my two-year-old reach for a glass a waitress, who obviously didn't have young children, put on the table much too close to him. I was a second late realizing what was going to happen. Thirty-two ounces of ice-cold soda, with the ice that was making it cold, ended up tsunami-like in someone's lap. Oooops.

Bigger "oooops." Mother of child stops car in driveway and runs in the groceries. Three-and-a-half-year-old crawls into driver's seat and manages to find the one recall item on the car that hasn't been shared with owners. It is gear slippage. Car rolls backwards down sloped driveway, executes a turn on sloped cul-de-sac, picks up forward momentum, jumps curb onto very steep front lawn, shoots down lawn, and punches hole in front wall of neighbor's house. The stunning event is complicated by the fact that neighbor's super expensive collection of Lalique porcelain is on the other side of the wall . . . . Need I say more? Yes, God cares for drunks and little children. The child was unhurt. Insurance cares for the rest.

The "Terrible Twos," which, shockingly to the new parent, don't start at two or end at three are "wonderible." That's my word, a combination of wonderful and horrible. At this age, the child's reach, or wants, exceed its grasp. Thus, part of the time the child is frustrated and cranky, and part of the time is climbing bookshelves, sweeping things off tables, or pulling on tablecloths with no ability to realize what might be sitting on them. Also doing all manner of things that result in blood—sometimes copious amounts of it.

It is just after this period that scientists, at least some, agree that memory starts. It is here then when the stories start, so buckle up, put the key in the ignition and let's get going.

"We left my birthplace, Brooklyn, New York, in 1939 when I was 13. I enjoyed the ethnic variety and the interesting students in my public school, P.S. 134. The kids in my neighborhood were only competitive in games, although unfriendly gangs tended to define the limits of our neighborhood."

– Irwin Rose
American Biologist
Winner of Noble Prize

"In memory of Salty" by a little boy.

Presented here is K-9 Cigo who was KIA this year taking a bullet for his human partner.
A salute to him and thanks to the Palm Beach County Sheriff's Office.

Salty

"She was more pet and less protector."

It was an argument with no end, this one. My mother swore children could not remember as far back as I was remembering. "I was making memories out of pictures I had seen, stories I had heard," she said.

I volleyed back that the memories were clear. Seeing the pictures, I claimed, came after the memories.

I was born in Brooklyn Jewish Hospital, a sensible place for a Jewish kid from Brooklyn to be born. I was brought home to 1 St. Paul's Court, to an apartment with linoleum flooring and a view of the Prospect Park BMT subway station. There to greet me was Grandma with both her legs (to be explained later) and, I believe, Mrs. Curtiss, a white-haired woman with a stern temperament, who was paid to take care of the manse, such as it was. It was also the birth home of my brother, Jeffrey Charles Gralnick, who hated his middle name as much as his first, much preferred Jeff to Jeffrey, and had a five-year head start in life on me.

In about two years, we moved to the Neponsit section of Far Rockaway, Queens, or "The Beach" as it was known. We lived one block from it. The house, known as a bungalow, represented one of two times my father could have made a killing in real estate, and didn't either time. There we got a dog, a black and tan German shepherd named Salty. I remember her being furry and having a neck that was great to hang onto when she sat next to me. And I remember crying miserably when they came to take her away. But some memories come before that terrible day.

I, of course, remember none of this.

Writing about memories often triggers more memories. So, a brief digression for one. In writing this piece, I realized I had no earthly idea why this large black and tan dog was named Salty—salt, especially in those days, being white. Then the other night it hit me. House by the beach. Beach by the ocean. Salt in the air. Dog bought for house at beach by the ocean with salt in the air . . . Aha! Salty.

However, about that time, things kicked in, like the big, black pram I was walked around in. I don't remember what the floor covering was, but I do remember the feeling of sand on the floor as I crawled around in my diapers, and, of course, sand in my mouth, which is where everything eventually ends up when one is three.

OUCH! The clearest memory is of the first fright I ever had far enough from my mother's skirts to—well, remember it forever. As in many New York, and almost all big city Jewish neighborhoods, come once or twice a year the collectors for *Yeshivas.*

Yeshivas in New York "where your child would get a fine Jewish upbringing." *Yeshivas* in Eastern Europe "which are struggling to rebuild and survive the Holocaust, with the few Jews Hitler, may his name be cursed for eternity, didn't murder." Or, of course, *Yeshivas* in Israel "that will grow and flower like the new land, *baruch hashem* (blessed be God) and produce a new generation of scholars." Many of these rabbis, because of "angels on the head of a pin" theological arguments, wouldn't be seen in the same *shul* together. But they all had two things in common: black hats and long beards.

And so, the doorbell rang. My mother is in the back of the house, which isn't all that big, doing the laundry, and Salty is raising enough of a ruckus that my mother says something she'd never said before. "Billy, answer the door. I'll be right there!" I assume she assumed a kid answering a door with a huge dog by his side is a pretty safe bet. So, I did, and in the opening, looking down at me was this big, long, black beard topped with a large, black hat. Between the two was an extremely wrinkled face. Before the beard was able to release its sermonette on American, or European, or Israeli *Yeshivas,* I screamed, really screamed. I had never seen such a visage before. The door opened right into the living room so some feet behind me was a couch. I wheeled, ran, and half-jumped/

half-slid as far under the couch as I could get. And right next to me was my protector—Salty. I was well into my teens before the cold water that empties into the stomach when one is scared half to death stopped running.

Thus, in this story, we learn that Salty was more pet and less protector. That was re-enforced when my uncle returned from the Western Front, a decorated, wounded, captain in the Infantry and decided something must be done about this. He decided to dress up like a burglar—not that anyone in the family had ever seen one except on TV or in cartoons. Trench coat, muffler, floppy hat, scarf—a stealth outfit. He waited 'til night and began skulking around the house making a noise here and there as he skulked. He came to the back porch door, opened it, slipped in, and was confronted by our beast—whose tail was wagging so fast it helped support her as she stood on her hind legs and began licking this "intruder" on the face. My uncle yelled, "No! Bad girl!" The dog seemed to give him what I'd now describe as a screw you, I don't need this crap, I can play better games by myself look and walked back inside the house.

You might think this failure of character was Salty's end, but it wasn't. Allergies were. Not the dog's, but my mother's, also not to the dog, but to the molds that grow in wet areas. There's something about mold allergies and dog dander that I don't remember. I do remember sitting on the brick stoop, again, arm around her neck, when the folks from the Seeing Eye Dogs for the Blind came and took her away. For a while, I understand we got letters telling us of her progress and finally her placement. Eventually, I stopped crying. I don't give to the *Yeshivas*. But I still support the Seeing Eye Dogs for the Blind.

And the house? That bungalow couldn't have cost more than $12,000 in the '40s. Let's be generous and say my dad sold it for $15,000. Had he kept it as a rental, he not only would have made "oodles" of money, but thirty years later could have sold it, virtually unchanged, for nearly a million bucks.

"A journey of a thousand miles begins with the first step." Confucius

A Boy Named Wilhelmina

"It was once the name of a Queen."

With apologies to Johnny Cash and his ode to "A Boy Named Sue" that song could have been me. One day, in one of her many cross—a popular term in the '50s for "pissed off"—days, my mother was pining away at the awfulness of her not having had a daughter. That, of course, triggered a what's so bad about a second son feeling that overcame me. "In fact," she went on, "the only reason you were born was because your brother was a boy." I believed it. My dad had told me once that my mother was a high-strung, nervous mother. My brother had colic and one day it was so severe that he didn't stop wailing. It had gone on for hours. When my father came home from work, he found her in a state of hysteria—not the laughing kind. He pulled all of the tricks out of his dental psychology bag. None worked so he smacked her across the face (a popular remedy in the '50s). That worked.

Back to the story.

"If you had been a girl, you would have been named Wilhelmina," she said, as if she had said, "If you had been a girl you would have been named Ellen or Sue." But she didn't. She said, Wilhelmina.

WILHELMINA?!?! Egad! I had never heard that name—ever. It was weird and ugly. A life as a Wilhelmina would have been hell, even if I had been a girl. I did know a Willianna, but she was black and from South Carolina and already at least as old as my mother. I could sort of see her going through life unharmed as Willianna. Me as Wilhelmina? Uh-uh.

It was a mere accident of genetics that saved me, and the power of Jewish tradition that almost ruined me.

It is tradition in Ashkenazic Judaism to name a child after a deceased family member one wants to memorialize. Some say you start at the beginning of the line, someone who died the longest ago whose name hadn't been used or was of such family import that it would be re-used. Some say you begin at the end of the line with the name of the most recently deceased. Some say you don't have to use the actual name, just the first initial and still others say you can do it with the Hebrew name rather than the English one. What everyone says is there are no juniors or thirds—except, of course, the Sephardi Jews, and also that small number of Jews who so admire gentile social culture that they think having a Jr. or a 3rd in the ranks would be cool and also helpful to the child as he/she navigates the business world.

Of course, just to show you the pitfalls of generalizing about Jews, I did know a Schwartz who was a Jr. and conceived a 3rd. Schwartz is Ashkenazi—Jews whose roots trace from Germany and Eastern Europe. Sephardim are those whose roots stem from the great expulsion from Spain in 1492 (and you thought that was a year only Italians and Native Americans took note of).

Many went to the Middle East so Spain, Africa (yes Virginia, there were Jews in Africa—still are, and not all of them are white either), and the Middle East are the petri dishes for Sephardic Judaism.

But I stray. So, from whence almost came Wilhelmina? My dad was one of five: three boys, two girls. His dad, whom he called Pop, was named William or Velvel (its Yiddish equivalent). At least two of the brothers, my father being one, idealized Pop. They both wanted to name their kids after him, but Mamma died first, and my dad was the oldest boy. He had a boy as his first child, so he honored his mother, Jenny, by naming my brother Jeffrey, a name my brother detested, and I loved. The next male to come along was my uncle's son, so he got the William. Then it was my turn. I guess my father figured, "I'm the oldest, I put my brothers through school and set them up in their practices, screw it, I want to name my kid after Pop." So, he did. Hence, along came the second William. To keep peace in the family, and avoid confusion, the first William would be exactly that . . . William. I would be Bill (or for decades, Billy). If you called William Bill you might as well have called him Arthur, and if you called me William, I would look around to see if my cousin had arrived.

It took me until my late teens to announce that Billy had left the building. I would now be Bill. "Send out the memo," I informed my mom. Some got it, some didn't, but by the time I started work, I had pretty much shed it. As fate would have it, my first job was in Atlanta, Georgia, the south, where every William is not only Billy but Billy-Something like Billy-Bob or Billy-Joe or Billy-Ray. I thought life brutally unfair and considered shooting myself—or those who again raised the specter of Billy-dom.

I got over it, helped by a transfer to Miami in the state of Florida where it is said the more south you go the more north it comes. Once I passed Orlando, I once again escaped Billy-dom and by the time I hit Miami I was *Guillermo* (William in Spanish).

Now, to be fair, there have been many Wilhelminas, some even queens, the kind with crowns, like the Queen of the Netherlands. The name itself means "the great protector," fitting for a queen, and another reason the name didn't fit me.

In fact, in the 1880s, it ranked among the 215 most popular names. On the other hand, it hasn't cracked the list since 1950s.

There was one Olympic athlete named Wilhelmina, the late great Wilma Rudolph. And no one else since that I've ever heard of—to this day.

"Hey Kids, it's Howdy Doody Time!"

"Hey Kids . . . !"

**"The person who took me had the grace, charm,
and compassion of Nurse Ratchet."**

It's an old axiom, "It matters more who you know than what you know." It's probably grossly overstated, but at times it seems right. This is a story of when it was right. It is also a "careful what you wish for" story.

My parents had friends of long-standing, so long that I called them aunts and uncles because they knew me before I was born. Uncle Dave was a Public Relations agent, and a good one. Many of the stars of radio, TV, and stage were his clients. He often secured me autographs from them for my collection.

I was a loyal fan of *The Howdy Doody Show*. I would sit impatiently before the TV waiting for Buffalo Bob to grin his way into the room and shout, "HEY KIDS—WHAT TIME IS IT?" And all the kids in the "Peanut Gallery" would gleefully respond, "IT'S HOWDY DOODY TIME!!!"

While mildly inconceivable, it is possible that one of you readers has no clue what this is all about, so excuse me to the others while I educate the unknowing. Understand first there were only three television channels in most places, four in New York. There was often nothing—and I mean nothing at all. If you turned it on during those times and waited for the dozens of tubes, large and small, inside the large box that held the small screen, usually twelve inches, you would eventually see what was called a test pattern. It said to you, "Don't worry, when something does come on, your TV is working, and you will see it." Some people could be put into stupors watching test patterns and listening to the hum of the TV that went with them.

Even when there was something on, there wasn't a lot of it. There were eventually enough shows that they could be grouped into categories. Kids' shows were one. John Gnagy (his name was pronounced Nagy), the artist. Rootie Kazootie (honest!), *Buck Rogers*. Later on, came *Captain Kangaroo* and *Mr. Rogers' Neighborhood*. One of my favorites was *Kukla, Fran, and Ollie*. It featured a goofy alligator hand puppet with a snaggle tooth that had a terrible crush on his show-mate, Fran—along with me. It wasn't until my seventies, when we began to patronize a Greek Restaurant with our niece that I learned that *Kukla* was Greek for cute or cutie-pie.

But my all-time favorite and the reigning king of children's shows for years was *The Howdy Doody Show*, whose star was a marionette—with reddish hair (you didn't know that from TV because broadcasting was in black and white), dimples, freckles, a permanent smile—dressed in cowboy clothes. The sidekick of the show was Clarabelle the Clown who communicated à la Harpo Marx, with a big horn, and made his presence known by squirting everyone—even the kids in the Peanut Gallery—with his bottle of seltzer. To me, that was entertainment at its zenith.

One day, Uncle Dave said to me, "How'd you like to go to *The Howdy Doody Show* and be in the Peanut Gallery?" There was nothing in the universe that could have excited me more. He had procured tickets from a client, and a few weeks later, weeks filled with anticipation, my mother and I set out in the Buick to go make a dream come true. This part is as good as it got. It was all downhill from there.

It was hot as blazes. Cars as yet did not have air-conditioners, seat belts, sunroofs, or even passenger side-view mirrors for that matter. I shared a trait that my mother said came from exposure to Salty who had the same trait. That trait was carsickness.

It was a long, sweaty drive to the studio, with sweat and anxiety pouring off of me, and my mother intoning, "Billy, keep your head out the window. The air blowing in your face will help you feel better." It didn't, but I arrived there, green but functional.

We took our tickets to the entrance and something unanticipated happened. They took me from my mother. It had never dawned on me that I had only seen "peanuts" in the Peanut Gallery, no walnuts, or macadamia nuts or any nut larger than a peanut, and nary a parent. The reason? Only peanuts were allowed in the gallery, no parents. I was terrified as some stranger took me to the gallery and another escorted my mother to a holding pen of sorts. The person who took me had the grace, charm, and compassion of Nurse Ratchet. I was unceremoniously plunked into a seat amidst a sea of unknown peanuts who were screaming their heads off.

The crew was scurrying around. Clarabell was half made-up and bell-less, also without her (really his) horn, for that matter. Buffalo Bob was storming around annoyed about something and looked nothing like that smiling face in my TV set. Worst of all, I saw my hero. Child-sized on TV, in real life Howdy was an eighteen-inch-high marionette hanging on a hook by his strings. That was the reality. It was awful. But it would get more awful.

As we got closer to show time, the pace became frenetic. We were told to quiet down. I had to go to the bathroom and was told quite sharply, "Not now—hold it!" Then the stage and camera lights went on. The temperature went up to about 250 degrees. Rivers of sweat soaked my clothing.

Buffalo Bob, who by now had found his smile, came center stage, and called, "Hey Kids . . ." For the answer, the camera swung to the Peanut Gallery and, at that moment, I threw up . . . on national television.

Within seconds, some lady, who came out of nowhere, snatched me from my seat, grabbing me like a field mouse is snatched by a hawk. I didn't get to answer Buffalo Bob, nor did I get to sing the "It's Howdy Doody Time" song. I missed Mr. Bluster, Flub-a-Dub, and Princess Summer-Fall-Winter-Spring. I was handed to my mother like a sack of smelly garbage to be tossed out as quickly as possible. To say I was despondent on the ride home doesn't come close. Nor was Uncle Dave too happy to hear about the fruits of his labor going rotten.

Fast forward about fifty years to one birthday or another. My wife handed me a present the size of a shoebox. With enough little boy left in me to be excited, I ripped off the paper, yanked the lid from the box, and came face-to-face with a smiling, dimpled, freckle-faced, red-haired museum edition of my hero and pal—you guessed it, Howdy Doody. He stands happily on a shelf in the den, his smile reminding me that in the end, some things do turn out all right.

"I was born in Brooklyn, delivered by a Chinese doctor on a table in a boarding house on Sept. 23, 1920."

– Mickey Rooney
Star of Stage, Screen,
TV, and Multiple
Marriages

*Fashionable mom holding baby with "grasa pulkies"
(big thighs—either on turkeys or kids).*

Immigrants

"Like dwarfs with lights, we entered the basement."

One of my brother's biggest bitches in life was that we were like immigrants. We did move a lot but since I was five years younger, it had less disruption for me than it did for him.

We lived at 1 St. Paul's Court when Jeff was born and when I was born. I don't think there was an in-between. From 1 St. Paul's Court we moved to Neponsit, back to 1 St. Paul's Court in less than three years, and then to 500 Ocean Avenue where we stayed, I guess, about four years. That is a lot of moving.

From 1 St. Paul's Court, I have early memories: hunting rats, eating Milk Bones, Tom Bassknight, and two "let that be a lesson to you" accidents, that fortunately did not involve me.

Across the street from us was a large, old, dark church rumored to have rats in the basement, which was kept locked. We had a true immigrant family in the neighborhood, Germans who had left Germany during the war; how, I didn't know. What I did know was that the boy was several years older than me, wore weird shorts with suspenders, sandals with socks, spoke with a very heavy accent, and kept telling me it was okay if I was a Jew.

The biggest in our small group, "Helmut" or whatever his name was, decided to organize a rat hunt. He told us to take flashlights from our apartments and meet by the church at the appointed hour. There we gathered, all shaking in our proverbial boots but for our commander, who was clearly up for this, and in charge wearing his sandals. He knew that, previous to us, someone, or someones, had worked on the locked gate and little people like us could easily crawl through. Damn! Such luck . . . So, like dwarfs with lights, we slowly entered the basement.

It was pitch-black even though it was only about 2 p.m. We skulked around ready in an instant to jump out of our skins but found nothing. Well, not exactly nothing, we found a half, or whole step, down into a half basement, even darker than the first. Hugging the walls, we slinked down the steps. Suddenly, there was a sound. I don't remember what kind of sound because I had flown up the stairs, ducked under the gate, and burst outside before the full sound had managed to get to my eardrums.

Oh, did I mention the screaming?

After that, the commandant abandoned me. One word he knew in English was chicken and he used it correctly.

The dog biscuits were a dare. The son of my parent's friend, a retired army colonel named Albert (I think it was Col. Albert, but it could have well been Albert Simons or Schwartz or Greenberg) dared me to eat a dog biscuit. So, I did. Actually, they weren't bad. Long on crunch, short on taste. Milk Bone, of course. I went through a phase for about a week of having them for my afternoon snack, until one day my mother spied me carrying around the Milk Bone biscuit box. The answer to one direct question from her and that was the end of that snack.

The names of movers in those days were usually from friends. "Oh, I just used so and so, and they were the best." Tom Bassknight, black as night, was someone else's best, so we hired him. I remember he smiled a lot, which was disconcerting. I'd never met a black person up close and he was very black, and when he smiled his teeth were so white, they seemed to explode out of his mouth.

He had an odd sense of humor too. He and a mate had picked up a long dresser that I was on the wrong side of, the wall side not room side. They slowly, but certainly, moved the dresser towards the wall giving me less and less space to maneuver, until I was flat up against the wall with the dresser pressing against my chest. I must've had an I'm gonna die expression on my face. They thought it was the funniest thing they as movers had ever seen. I didn't agree.

Now come the lessons. Parents, especially my mother, are never at a loss for making sure their kids didn't miss the obvious lessons of life that surrounded them. One kid in the neighborhood shot out someone's eye with a BB gun on the Fourth of July, another blew off his own finger with a cherry bomb. When I was a parent, my children had neither. "Lesson learned, Mom!"

So, we turn to the next to last move as a family, to 500 Ocean Avenue.

Family and BFF's with Jeff center rear. "Our" Colonel is
the one with almost no hair, no uniform, or any chicken
. . . who lived at 1 St. Paul's Court when we did.

500 Ocean Ave

"A few became few too many."

We left the beach and moved back to 1 St Paul's Court. Nothing in my memory bank tells me why the building was graced with such a name. I can only assume that since the building business in those days was heavily Italian, and Italians were heavily Catholic, it was named accordingly, and so on . . . It did, however, have a courtyard between the sidewalk and the lobby. So, the pieces of the name fit neatly into the puzzle I created about them. It was a low-rise, brick building maybe two or three stories high. Close friends lived one block away in a cookie cutter look-alike building.

To move, one needed a moving man. Of course, you needed moving men and a moving company, but the phrase was always the moving man. Tom Bassknight was once again on the case, with his old dresser trick again. He'd grown older; I'd become smarter. Why on earth would I remember his name? Because the first time I saw his truck, which was the biggest thing I'd ever seen in my life, his name, which I couldn't read, was emblazoned across it. Secondly, my exposure to him and his crew was my first to black men, big ones. I remember being amazed. At what? That they were black.

So Tom, et al., took us about a thousand yards. Diagonally across the street from 1 St. Paul's Court was a high-rise apartment building.

This time we were "movin' on up," literally and figuratively. We moved up one block, over and up five stories into a recently built apartment building. Its newness was marked by the red of its bricks compared to the brownish red of the much older 1 St. Paul's Court.

500 Ocean Avenue was a marvel to me. It had a balcony that looked down on a very busy street, Ocean Avenue, so there was

always something to see. In the hallway, it had this trapdoor in the wall called the incinerator. You could throw things down it to feed the furnace, making that little door have a very ominous meaning to me. And before Tom would show up for the third time, 500 Ocean Avenue provided three very different stories.

At five or six, a balcony from which one can see the world below, if standing on tippy-toes, one gets a totally different perspective on life. Ocean Avenue was always a-buzz with traffic on the four-lane two-way street and people on what always seemed to be too-narrow sidewalks. Once or twice, due to accidents, things went in reverse. Cars took over the sidewalk and people used the street to skirt around them.

If I stretched my neck and looked out to the right, I could see the trolley cars on Church Avenue, and watch, fascinated by the sparks thrown off the lines, as the cars switched tracks. I was entranced by the ever-so-distinctive "clang, clang, clang," yes, of the trolley car, so distinctive that those very words were a line in a popular song, *"Clang, clang, clang went the trolley."*

At one particular time, someone really special would show up: the organ grinder. He was a small man, dressed the part, with a little monkey. I begged and begged, "Mommy, take me downstairs, take me downstairs." Only once did I get the timing right with the man and monkey in sight but yet to be on our block, my mother's mood receptive to do it, and the elevator with no one using it so no time was lost waiting.

It was everything I hoped. The man was from Italy; I'm assuming the monkey was not. It looked Chinese, which I thought was really funny. Later, I learned it was a Capuchin monkey. He had on this little cap and excitedly ran to and fro on his leash jumping in one fell swoop from his master's shoulder to the ground and back again. Then he ran up to me and held out his little paw. My mother had to be properly prepared with a coin. He took it from my hand, put it in his mouth and bit on it (the humor of which I didn't understand 'til years later), then hopped up on the man's arm and dropped it—clink—into his cup. What fun! Of course, I wanted a monkey but not everything of interest was down below. Some nights an unholy racket came from above. My dad would look up at the ceiling, and say, "Slapsie Maxie's at it again." Apparently, a well-known boxer, well past his prime, nick-named "Slapsie Maxie," I think from being a little goofy from getting hit a lot, lived above us with his wife. In his day, he was a middle-weight of some championship caliber, and an oddity because he was Jewish (Max Rosenbloom), boxing not being a sport that drew a lot of Jews into the ring. Betting, yes. Owning fighters, yes. Gambling illegally, yes. Getting smashed around a ring, no.

Periodically, he and Mrs. R. would have at it after one or the other of them had a few and then a few more, until it was a few too many. Then they got into these screaming matches. Following the screaming came the noises, noises like someone was moving heavy furniture. It sounded like that because that's what it was. When Maxie was mad enough, he'd start pushing around the furniture. Why? Do I know? Probably to mess with his wife by re-arranging everything. The noise ceased, being followed by a slamming door that rattled the walls, followed by the hum of the elevator, followed by Mrs. Rosenbloom starting the noise up again by moving everything back. It made for some long nights, fortunately mostly on the weekends.

Then there was that aforementioned trapdoor in the wall, the incinerator. Here we take a detour. Cute or not, a monkey was out of the question and Salty was gone. One of my aunts had given me a life-sized Persian cat as a present. Here sadly, and never to be forgiven, came together the story: the cat and the incinerator.

The cat became for me what Linus' blanket was for him. Unfortunately for me, the cat had joints that blankets don't. After a year or more of carrying this poor, stuffed creature around, his neck crooked in my arm, he split a seam. In those days, stuffed animals were stuffed with straw and it wasn't long before my mother began finding bits of straw here and there: in the bed, on the rug, under the dining room table. She made a unilateral decision that the cat had to go. The decision wasn't that the cat had to go to the seamstress to have its neck sewn up. The decision was the cat had to go into the fires of hell. It was to be dropped down the incinerator.

With me wailing at her heels, she marched my precious cat down the hall, opened the incinerator closet door, snatched down the handle protruding from the wall, and with unceremonious dispatch dispatched my cat. Screaming as I was, I was lucky I didn't follow it down the chute courtesy of my mother.

Murder it was and in the first degree. Premeditated at that. And as I said, a crime for which there never came forgiveness.

"I grew up in Brooklyn, and my parents were Holocaust survivors, so they never taught me anything about nature, but they taught me a lot about gratitude."

– Louie Schwartzberg
Award Winning Producer,
Director, Cinematographer
Best known for Time/Motion/Stop
Frame Photography

The BMT (Broadway Manhattan Transit subway line) running above ground.

On the Road Again

" . . . those really were the days."

Not that it matters, but I don't remember how long we were at 500 Ocean Avenue. Within a few years, I guess the Rosenblooms got the best of my parents and it was Tom Bassknight time again. We loved the excitement of Church Ave. where there was a little luncheonette my mother would get her favorite—BLT on toast— and I was treated to mine, a cherry vanilla ice cream soda. This move didn't take us very far in distance, maybe five miles, but it was dramatic in difference.

We moved into a house, not an apartment, and a big one, at least to me. Another difference: a dead-end street with no traffic instead of the four lane Ocean Avenue. Rumbling above ground were the subways that on occasion blasted out their WATCH OUT! I'M COMING! horns to replace the clanging of the almost at end of their run trolley cars. There were neighbors in the real sense, there were no elevators and no incinerators; there was a street with no traffic and lots of kids to play with on it. Yet there was that "would I fit in?" anxiety that comes with a new neighborhood. As Tom and his team emptied the truck and filled up our new house, I stood out on that street, alone, looking around, knowing that kids who already lived there were looking out the windows at me and being told by their parents that it wasn't polite to stare. Would this be fun? Would there be more to do than hunt rats? Would there be more friends, and would they like me?

As I lay in my bed that first night, feeling the whole house shake as the night trains went by, these were the thoughts that stood between me and sleep.

The next day would be the first day of ten years of answers to those questions. It would also bring with it the reality that I had to go to a new school. Not only would I be a new kid on a new block, I would be a new kid in a new school, even though it was an old school, a very old school. PS 217 would bring untolled stories beginning with my first day in third grade, with Mrs. Kimmel. So, let's get to it.

"From the year of his birth in 1914 until the outbreak of war in 1941, my father lived in a mostly white, mostly working-class, mostly Irish Catholic neighborhood in Brooklyn, New York."

– Tim O'Brien
Irish American Novelist

#12 Waldorf Court—Home, Sweet, Home
Photo courtesy of George Marks Photography

The Neighborhood

*" . . . the Robin unpacked and announced he
was here for the spring and summer."*

"A group of houses and businesses located in an area that is localized." Basically, this is what the dictionary calls a neighborhood.

It is a definition that doesn't come close to what "the neighborhood" means to a kid from Brooklyn, and probably kids from many other places.

A neighborhood in Brooklyn began one step off the front porch. That one step landed me in my own *Brigadoon*. In writing this, I came to realize that it wasn't so much what was in the neighborhood. What mattered is and what was in my mind. That's what makes this neighborhood so special for me, but also will make it special for you because the stories will re-open your mind to those things that happened in your own *Brigadoon*, no matter what the neighborhood was called.

Waldorf Court was one of a series of tree-lined, dead-end streets that opened into Rugby Road (E. 14th Street) in the Midwood section of Flatbush, Brooklyn. The streets ended at a large, iron fence behind which ran the BMT (Brooklyn Manhattan Transit) line of the subway that was still called the "subway" in the neighborhood, even though it ran above ground. Go figure. The streets were 110 yards long. We knew that because we measured. How do you claim victory in a foot race if you don't know the length? Really.

Waldorf Court was flanked by Wellington Court on one side and Glenwood Road on the other. Glenwood Road added to the mystique of our *Brigadoon* because it had a footbridge over the tracks. On the other side was another neighborhood through which we walked to get to Midwood High School. Walking over the bridge was like leaving *Brigadoon* and landing in someone else's.

But the neighborhood, as referred to here, began at Avenue H. There, one found the local stop on the subway and the late-night newsstand. Tucked under the always ominous, always dank smelling subway underpass, was where my parents picked up the first edition of the Sunday Times late on Saturday nights. That came after a run up to Avenue J to Junior's to pick up lox and bagels.

But the heart of that one block of Avenue H was Lou and Al's Candy Store. Much of life that was not lived on Waldorf Court was lived at Lou and Al's, which seemed to major in selling everything—not just a lot of candy—and offered three ways to escape the neighborhood without leaving it and, at least in my mind, endangering one's health. One was a bank of phone booths when calls were a dime for three minutes and a nickel every so often thereafter. I once spent more than five hours on one phone call speaking to a girlfriend, so long that the operator said, "Okay kid, forget the nickels, the rest of this marathon is on me."

Another was at the shelves lined with the latest comic books. Escapism at its best. There I longed for the new 3-D comics. They were fifteen cents, then a quarter while the regular comics were but a dime. My comic books collection, the sale of which could have put my kids through college—if my mother hadn't thrown them all out when I went off to college—was my refuge.

The third was a real, old-fashioned soda fountain where one could sit and dream endlessly for a 10-cent Cherry Coke, or 15-cent Lime Rickey, or an egg cream—that famous chocolate drink made with neither eggs nor cream. Yet, let it be said that once past Wellington Court, the approach to Avenue H produced within me the kind of sensation a dog feels when it approaches the invisible electric fence buried around its yard. It was a sense of warning. A buzz. Not quite "Uh-oh!" but definitely "all systems on alert." Why? It was the end of our neighborhood and the beginning of another, one whose most notable feature was that it just wasn't our neighborhood. It was someone else's.

That same sensation was palpable going the other way. Once I passed Glenwood Road that unease would rise up my spine. The houses were bigger. The numbers of children were smaller. And my parents didn't know anyone who lived there. That feeling ended at Foster Avenue. It was no man's land until Foster Avenue, but Foster Avenue, car-lined instead of tree-lined, was wide and open and familiar. It was part of the neighborhood, though detached by a street or two.

To the left a few blocks down would be Coney Island Avenue, so named because it indeed did run all the way to the famed amusement park of the same name. And the neighborhood movie theatre, The Leader, with its fearsome matrons dressed in white, to prevent 'hanky-panky' in the balcony. To the right, across the street, was the neighborhood's shopping mecca. The Title Brother's Hardware Store; Mrs. Goldstein's notion's store; Bohack Supermarket, still at that time with sawdust on the floor and where I got my first job; Joe's, the Italian immigrant's fruit and vegetable market; a little sandwich/deli shop; the butcher; the pharmacy run by "Cockeye" and his brother; and the Leprechaun Bar and Grill, which appeared to me through furtive peeks in the window to be everything one would conjure up as an Irish bar in Brooklyn. No matter what time I happened by, someone was sitting on a barstool, drinking.

The centerpiece of the neighborhood was not at its center. It came after one passed the Leprechaun. There to the left opened up Newkirk Plaza, the subway's neighborhood express stop. This was the pulse of the area. The station and its newsstand were in the dead center. The Plaza sat above the station, which was below ground level, but open-air. Standing on tippy-toes, I could look over the wall down onto the tracks and watch the trains pull in and out. Rows on both sides contained a variety of stores: the Kodak shop; Holiday House Gifts (where my brother got his first job); the dry cleaners; the Post Office; the Dime Savings Bank; Grillo's Seafood store and restaurant; the place where my mom got her hair and nails done; John's Barber shop where my dad, brother, and I got our hair cut; and another hardware store, the one we never went into because we were Title Brother's customers.

Around "The Plaza" however, was also that invisible fence. Next to the Post Office was a short tunnel that led to a side street. Entering that tunnel set off the alerts. Only twenty-five or thirty feet long, it opened onto a street where rough guys on trucks off-loaded supplies for the stores and restaurants, where one might on occasion see pieces of fish or meat rotting in the street after deliveries, cats fighting over them, where the "homes" were not houses but were older, shabbier apartment buildings whose tenants somehow just didn't feel like they were "us'uns," and who sat on the sidewalk in folding chairs often speaking in other languages and smoking cigarettes. It was a little scary. Or so it seemed to an eight-year-old.

At the far end of the Plaza was Newkirk Avenue, a wide, less commercial street, tree-lined with cleaner, newer apartment buildings and some beautiful, old homes. It led to the neighborhood where *Sophie's Choice* was filmed. 1818 Newkirk Avenue, Apt. 5-H with its balconies that collected copious amounts of city dust from the air and snow in the winter, would become my parent's home after I left for college, but until then it was foreign territory.

The major reason, however, the alert system went off at Newkirk Avenue, was that when one left the neighborhood via the Plaza, one entered the Erasmus Hall High School district, and for us, those ticketed for Midwood High School—Eramuses' arch rival—that was not the "right" neighborhood to be found in. One had a clear feeling of "I don't belong here." That same feeling arose when one crossed Coney Island Avenue into the heart of St. Rose of Lima parish and its lower middle-class neighborhood that belonged to the Irish.

But what was it about these localized six or seven city blocks' houses and businesses that made them able to produce so many stories? It, of course, was the people who were in them. Let's meet some of them. The names have been changed to protect the innocent—and the not so innocent.

THE WAR of the ITCHY BALLS

As one turned off of Rugby into Waldorf Court, my house, #12, built around 1906, was second on the right, distinctive because it had a front yard, an iron fenced, raised porch, a bright red front door, and on the driveway side, an elbow that jutted out of the stucco house making the garage a challenging destination by car. Maybe that's why we stored things in the garage and parked in front of the house. Like most of the houses, it had a basement, an attic, and two large floors for living. The house had a den, a formal, mirrored living room, a formal dining room, a kitchenette, and kitchen. There was a bar tucked under the staircase. And a half-bath off the den, the den having a picture window onto the street. Upstairs there were three bedrooms and two full baths, and more upstairs were two large rooms used, before we moved in, as living quarters for the owner's elderly grandparents. It had a small but adequate kitchen and running water, as well as another full bath. The basement was similar except larger, and it could only be accessed from the driveway. The door opened onto a set of stairs. At the bottom, across the little hall was, on the left, the apartment, and on the right the laundry room. In sum, it was a great place to grow up. Lots of space inside and out, in which one could pretty much always find space away from one's parents.

The first two houses on the street were the largest. In fact, they were not on the street at all, having Rugby Road addresses. In one lived the Gardens: a family of four, a bit wealthier than most. They had two sons, one my age and one several years younger, and a mixed breed Spitz dog named Tuffy, who wasn't. They were a small family, actually diminutive, he being barely 5'5" and she—well, she often had to sit on a phone book in order to see over the steering wheel of their Cadillac. Truth! In those days, the days of phone books, the ones in New York City were huge, probably 6-8" in thickness. She needed every inch of them. The Mrs. was a wannabe Broadway star and rarely was there a bar mitzvah or another event where she didn't sing and dance. It was expected, and actually she was good. They also had a live-in maid named Martha who took it upon herself to give some of us an idea what we were missing because of the dearth of sex education in the '50s.

Facing the Garden's at the street's entrance were the McTurnip sisters. My brother called them the "weird sisters." Older, heavy, not much to say, with a semi-severe attitude, they chose to emphasize that they belonged on Rugby Road not Waldorf Court.

Next to the weird sisters were the Cohens. They had three children: two girls, one my brother's age, five years my senior, one my age; and a son about the age of the younger Garden boy. It was a very artistic family. Poppa was an old-fashioned cabinetmaker, everything handmade, hand finished. Mom was literate, articulate, sweet, and long suffering. (Poppa was a better craftsman than businessman.) The older girl made a name for herself in ballet and arts. Later in life, she could be found in the Times in stories about dance, and later still the redevelopment of Times Square from seedy to almost proper, and live outdoor theatre in Central Park. The middle child struggled in the shadow of her sister and ended up marrying an Israeli and moving to the Negev desert where she finally flowered, while the son, who was an extremely talented toymaker in his own right as an adult, was best known in his younger years for having the temper tantrum of the decade, lugging a bale of peat moss to the second-floor bathroom, locking the door and throwing handfuls at anyone who attempted to talk him down.

The temper tantrum was probably my fault. It was probably caused by brain damage, or so I thought. He was my first babysitting job and the first night I sat for him he split his head open running headfirst into the glass top of a piece of his father's handiwork.

The most interesting thing the Cohen's had wasn't theirs, and it wasn't in their home. It was in their garage. It was a 1905 Willys-Overland automobile owned by my next-door neighbor, Mr. Mash. It was on his front porch that I received my first kiss from someone who wasn't a relative. But I digress. The Mash family, three children—boy, girl, boy—was most interesting. Mr. Mash kept a compost heap in the garden which produced such copious amounts of worms—some big enough for Japanese horror movies—that during a rainstorm they would escape drowning by worming their way into our driveway, pounds of them, which I'd scoop up and throw back over the fence into the compost heap. In their basement were rows and rows of fish tanks. Mr. Mash bought a motorcycle that within days put him in the hospital for weeks. Mrs. didn't adjust too well to the new Chrysler Imperial's power steering and turned it into tree a good twenty feet from the turn to exit the street. They yelled at each other a lot, but they took ballroom dancing together. He was a taciturn sort, but for the coming of spring.

There are many hints in the north that spring is in the air. The crocuses poke their purple and white heads up through the snow. The squirrels chatter as they look for mates, and eventually that first robin shows up, unpacks, and announces he's here for summer and fall. The bells of the Good Humor man's truck sound, as does the voice of the drover on the horse-drawn flower cart. Heard for blocks around, he'd bellow, "Hey fla-wahs, fla-wahs, fla-wahs. Hey fla-wahs hey . . ."

For us, though, the sign of spring was Mr. Mash throwing open the door of the Cohen's garage and beginning the annual tune-up of his pride and joy. Even in the 1950s when cars by today's standards were primitive, this was amazingly so. The windshield wipers were operated by hand. The engine was started with a crank that on occasion kicked back with such force it could break your arm. "Stand back! Stand back fer Chrissakes! Y'er gonna get killed!" Mr. Mash would yell at us as we crowded around while he tried to muscle the car into life. There was a choke on what would later be known as the dashboard, and the gears were a slide gizmo on the steering wheel. It took a fine touch to coordinate them all into producing combustion. But after the choking and backfiring and bucking, that old baby began to purr (with a motor probably no more powerful than a motor scooter, it certainly didn't roar), and that meant we could line up and be taken for a ride. The top was down as I recall because there was no top. The air was crisp, clear, and cold. Everyone on the streets would wave and stare. We'd wave back and holler. What a hoot!

As one worked one's way down the block there was story after story, everyone more innocent than the next. We had the kindly,

Irish drunk who made daily post-work use of the Leprechaun Bar and Grill before he went home to his wife and four girls. We had the new kid who lived two doors from the trains in the haunted house. There was a schizophrenic—another boy with mild cerebral palsy—who eventually earned a PhD in English, a bunch of teachers, two principals, lots of dogs, and as I recall, nary a cat.

Oh yes, there was an element in the neighborhood one needed to avoid. They belonged to two gangs. One was the "Amboy Dukes" made famous in the movie *Blackboard Jungle*. The other was a local group of toughs whose gang, named after its leader, was ironically called, "The Slaughter Gang."

This was the stock from which came the stew of my life. Sit down and enjoy the rest of the meal.

"And when we used to play and fight in the streets in Brooklyn and I would get hurt or something, my mother would always come out and save me. So that sort of postponed the inevitable about getting a good beating, without having somebody to come and save you."

– Sanford I. Weill
Computer Entrepreneur
former chairman of IBM

Waldorf Court, the 110 yards from Rugby Road to the subway tracks.
Photograph courtesy of George Marks Photography

The Cast of Characters

"She took off her shirt and I was looking at more than biceps."

Every neighborhood has its characters. No matter what defines normal, these are the folks who don't quite make the cut. The reasons were different neighborhood to neighborhood, but characters they were regardless of the measure. I will fudge the names, so the lawyers will be able to relax.

Waldorf Court itself had its own characters. Because it was a dead-end street and every house had a fenced-in back yard, very few of the adults associated much, or even knew the adults on the other sides of their yards. We were almost as insular as we would have been if there had been a wrought iron fence at the head of the street like the one that fenced us off from the train tracks.

The street was a perfect rectangle. There were the same number of houses on each side of the street and each directly faced the one across the street. Yet, there seemed to be a dividing line halfway down the block. Most all the houses in the front half were owned by Jews, and those from the middle down to the tracks were owned by Gentiles. One doesn't need the real estate acuity of Donald Trump to figure that the closer you got to the tracks, the lower were the prices of the houses, so I assume the divide was as much economic as it was religious. Being a character, however, knew no dividing line. We had Jewish characters and Gentile characters.

The isolation of the neighborhood was both good and bad news. It was good because it was safe, had large groups of youngsters, male and female, in three groups each about three years or so apart. There was always something to do with someone you knew well. The bad news was that the isolation kept us from becoming very streetwise and one subject that was absent—at least in my life—was sex. It wasn't that there weren't opportunities. There were. It's that I was clueless in recognizing them.

On my side of the street, down at the end, abutting the subway tracks was an Irish Catholic family with a basket full of girl children. The last—whom I believe was a year or two older than I—was born with a birth defect. She had a withered arm and walked with a limp. That, and the fact that she went to Catholic School, and was "below the divide" on the street, kept her out of the mix of kids I was in. She was a sweet girl and on occasion we talked. Every so often, I even walked her down to her house, which brought disapproving looks from her mother, one of those mothers who had a catalogue of disapproving looks for most any situation.

Her name was Jean, and frankly I have no idea how we got into a conversation about having children (not she and I, but people in general). It may have been that someone in her family had just given birth, not unusual for an Irish Catholic family in the '50s. Talk went from the hospital to the delivery process. At that point, she said she knew where babies came from, not that I had asked. It just seemed to pop out, not the baby but the information. Close enough to the content, but almost a *non sequitur*. Always looking for useable information, I asked her where and she said, openly, honestly, proudly, "the ear." All I'm going to say is this: I knew enough to know that she was wrong. I also knew enough not to correct her. But truthfully, I didn't know enough to be sure.

Jean had an older sister, also named with a J. She ran girls track in high school and had long, toned legs, long hair, a cute nose, and penetrating eyes. She made me feel like a young moose that knew it was time to rub the moss off his antlers but didn't know why.

You see when it came time for sex education my mother gave me a book. Thank God for older brothers, but he hadn't gotten to that part of my growing up yet.

The girl's father, Mr. O'Tool, was, for want of a better description, a happy drunk. Better said, he was, I'm sure, an unhappy man who was happy when he was drunk. Every day at five, he'd get off the subway at Newkirk Plaza and stopped at the Leprechaun Bar and

Grill, knock down a few, and then weave his way the five blocks to Waldorf Court. Then, as he passed each house on the right, if there was someone outside, he'd tip his hat, saying nothing, until he had weaved his way home.

Then there was the girl across the street. She was naturally lithe and athletically built and, for an eighth-grade girl who did no noticeable exercise, had amazing biceps. At the drop of a suggestion, she'd flex them for us. They created a sensation within me without which I had gone unconscious of to that point.

It was a quiet day on the block. Most everyone was elsewhere, and she and I found ourselves the lone occupiers of the street. She said, "You want to come over and see my room?" I said, "Sure." I was so naïve, the suggestion created nary a flutter in my gut. Since both her parents were principals, they had not come home yet so, unquestioned, we went upstairs. There she did something amazing. She took off her shirt and I was looking at more than biceps. Now I had a flutter. She said, "Okay, what do you want to do?"

My response? "Let's play Cowboys and Indians." Now you could be thinking, "That sly boy. He couched this pubescent sex thing into an innocent cover. He would be the Cowboy, she would be the squaw and they'd dive into the teepee together—so to speak."

You would be wrong. The big game at that age on the street with boys and girls was Cowboys and Indians. To me, it was a logical suggestion. Somehow, she knew instantly I was hopeless because we ended up back outside—playing Cowboys and Indians. That turned out to be a good thing because shortly thereafter her older brother arrived home and then her parents. Yet, it was years later before it dawned on me why we had so little contact after that fateful unveiling. "Hell hath no fury like a woman scorned . . . ." Even when she's not yet a woman.

Then there was the girl with the high hair. She was high school mature by the seventh grade. She was one of many girls in my life who I just knew "couldn't possibly be interested in me" and about whom I would be wrong. In one of those stupid beginning of the year "let's go around the room, tell stuff, and get to know each other" exercises, I mentioned that I had a two-room attic in my home which was mine to use. I explained that in one room I had created a major league Lionel Train set-up. It really was something and I was really into it, especially the gizmo that loaded and unloaded a cow into a cattle car and that my engine both whistled and puffed real smoke. The other room had my war scenes made of models I assembled and painted. The rooms were separated by a small hallway; each room had a door.

A few days later, this girl, who wore very short, tight jumpers and had hair bee-hived higher than the length of her hemline, sidled up to me, and said, "I love model trains. Can I come over some day and see your set?" Honest to God, that's what she said. Again, nary a flutter because, after all, it was all about showing off my trains. And her name was Rosenbaum. So, she came over and I followed her skintight skirt up three flights of stairs, turned to the right, flung open the door, and displayed my greatness. An hour later, when she said she had to go home, I followed that skirt down the stairs, showed her out the door, and was left to digest this very quizzical look she gave me before she turned and left the block. I only had the rest of the year to ponder why she never spoke to me again about trains, or much of anything, because she was in a different high school district and was gone from my life.

Then there was the little, Gentile girl from Avenue H. Dear me. My first crush. I would see her at the candy store. She was really cute. But even without her cross, I knew she wasn't Jewish. It's just something you know when you're from New York. Mostly it was about the shoes. Jewish girls didn't wear her kind of shoe, black slip-ons that cut just above the arch line and looked more like a slipper than a shoe. Mostly they were black, patent leather.

She presented a new problem for me. The Gentile girls on the block were neighbors. The Gentile girls not from the neighborhood were *shiksas* and *verboten*. This could be a long story, but its impact was such a shock that it works better short. I invited her to come over and see my train set. She rang the doorbell one day. I was expecting her. This time I did have a flutter. Even just as an invite,

I felt I was doing something "wrong" and therefore something exciting. I ran to the door, swinging open the inside foyer door, the outside red door, the storm door and held it to usher her in when this Valkyrie in the form of my mother swooped in from behind, took one look at the shoes and the cross, said, "Billy has to do his homework," and actually shut the door in her face.

You know, she and I never had another conversation either.

Not all the characters could help themselves. One of ours was a schizophrenic. This is a sad story. It is sad for the boy, a few years older than I, who would harmlessly walk up and down the street talking to his own characters. Sometimes he'd get up in your face, to use a today term, invade your personal space, and often be quite scary. Then there were the times when he would flip out, become well . . . crazy, violent, and have to be hospitalized.

It was sad for his parents who were both educators and dealt with this when electro-shock and institutionalization were the only medical recourses. Imagine doing that to one's child, even if the then current wisdom was that it was the right thing to do?

It was sad for his younger brother, a very bright, gifted, athletic kid whose job was his brother's care when his parents weren't home. His brother became his Scarlet Letter and separated him physically and emotionally from the rest of us. I imagine the scar is still there because some years ago I tracked him down. I found him at an important corporate position in Germany. I was part of a group of us trying to link the "old gang" from the block together. He wanted no part of it. Never answered.

And it was eventually sad for us all. One day after a particularly horrid episode, we found out he died. Exposure to him and contemplation of sins towards him, even if mostly minor, made us grow up a lot, at least in one corner of our hearts and minds.

Another character was the boy who wasn't ill but seemed to find his "happy place" acting like it. He walked around bouncing on his toes saying, "Mouse! Mouse! Mouse!"

Don't ask. I don't know.

His family had a really nutty, Irish terrier, which they kept in the back yard. They ran a metal line from the back door across the yard to the garage. You could put the dog out, snap his leash onto the line and he could run back and forth like the lunatic he was. One day our young man decided to imitate the dog's life, put on his collar and leash, snapped onto the line and jumped off the back steps. Fortunately, someone was home to unleash him . . . .

His dad installed the first, automatic, garage door opener in the neighborhood. One day he decided to push the button in the house and race the door, seeing if he could slide under it into the garage before it shut. He couldn't. By the way, first generation automatic garage doors didn't have electric eyes and safety retractors. He almost lived the rest of his life with an indentation across his back from the door mindlessly trying to hit the cement, which his body was keeping it from doing.

Finally came the proverbial doghouse, occasioned by the brother's prized fancy guppies that he bred and sold

In his basement were his brother's prize guppies. In the '50s, fish keeping was a lot trickier and more complex than it is today. Modern chemistry has made keeping fish alive a lot easier. If one kept fish, especially ornamental guppies, one had to put a lot of time and effort into maintaining them. That included appropriate diet.

When children grow up with pets they usually want to play with them and pamper them. Guppies are not ideal for such activity, but a child's mind acts . . . well, like a child's mind. One hot summer day came the jingle jangle of the bells on Dave's Good Humor truck. The basement was hot and humid. What was a special treat on hot, humid days? Why Good Humor Ice Cream, of course.

We can collapse the story here into the purchase of a half-gallon of vanilla ice cream, the holding and individual feeding of the ice cream to the fish, the melting of the ice cream into the fish tanks, and we can assume the passing to a better place for many of the imbibers.

What happened next my prying eyes couldn't see. So, take your best shot and figure it out for yourself.

Then there was Gordon of the "Mystery House."

On the left side of the street, second to last house, lived a boy a few years older than me. He came and went quickly leaving only one memory, but it was one worthy of a movie.

Unlike most all the homes on the block, this one stood out because it was never well kept up. The sidewalk was cracked. The house needed painting. The exterior was dark and foreboding. We not only had never been in it, we never went near it. Had I known more then, I would have described it as 'Hawthorne-esque'. Then "spooky" was the term of choice.

One day, the family that occupied it moved out and a new family moved in, and within days we would see a boy standing on the cracked sidewalk, just sort of hanging around. This was Gordon. His lineage was Scottish, so he was well placed on the Gentile end of the block diagonally across from the Irish Catholics.

Gordon seemed to have a very restricted range. He never came up the block. I don't ever remember playing with him. In fact, given that fact, I have no idea how the pieces came together for this story.

One day, I was down at that end of the block, probably doing what we did during idle time, which was figuring out how to get our Spauldeens back from off the tracks after they had gotten to the end of the street before we did while chasing them. Anyway, Gordon was there, and said, "You know, I live in a haunted house." Now that's a show-stopper, Spauldeen hunting or not.

"Waddaya mean?" asked I.

"My house has passageways, and moving walls, and hideouts and makes lots of noises," he answered.

"Gedouddahere!" I retorted.

"No really. Wanna see?"

I did.

This was one of those houses that was dark with the lights on. And everywhere you stepped, it replied with a squeak. Some were short, some were soft, some were long, and some were loud. It was very disconcerting, and we hadn't even gotten past the living room.

The layout is long gone from my mind except for a few places. One was the library. It could have come right out of a Hollywood murder mystery set. Dark furniture, dark walls, dark shelves and a wall of books. That is a wall of books that if you pushed, moved about two feet and opened into a passageway, very dark, that led to a staircase, even darker, that led to the basement. And the basement made the living room and library seem like brightly lit playrooms. How spooky is that?

It was, yes, dark and dank, and it too had a magic passage that led to a sub-half-basement. I have no idea what was down there because I had no desire to know. My curiosity was quickly coming to an end. Something told me that before I began seeing what was behind pictures on the walls if we went to the second floor, that I should hear my mother calling me, even if she wasn't. I thanked Gordon and split.

One day I noticed I hadn't seen Gordon at his post for some time. I walked down the block. The house was empty. The family had evaporated. My thoughts ran to moving walls, hidden rooms, and sub-basements. Could the house have kidnapped them? I decided I didn't want to know. I turned around and went home where nothing that wasn't supposed to move did.

Of course, there was a Halloween scare-you-to-death house as well.

Not all the characters in the neighborhood were on the block. We've met the weird sisters, and the good Rev. Chadwise shows up on these pages. Two doors down from him was another character. As it was said in those days, she was a spinster lady. Speculation was rampant that she actually was dead in the house because no one ever saw her. She apparently had no use for neighbors and particularly children. I learned that the hard way the first Halloween in our new house.

This was time the time of Dick and Jane morality. Came Halloween, no one worried about their children being given candy with pins in it, or poison, or the like. Mostly we got tons of candy, sometimes pennies, occasionally dimes, and every so often word would spread like wildfire that a certain house was giving out dollar bills.

My mother wasn't a trick or treat person though she did get me a costume. It fell to my brother to have me tag along with him. Since I was eight, I didn't have to go with the little kids during the late afternoon. Eight p.m. was when we started, and we were out until past nightfall. We'd go methodically from house to house, up one side of the block, down the other, and then around the corner to Wellington Court. I don't remember turning right and doing Glenwood Road. Too near a different neighborhood. We knew from the others, since this was our first outing, to pass by the good Reverend because he was nasty and stingy. And while Halloween was technically All Hallows Day, even though he was a rock-ribbed Baptist, he would have nothing to do with it. But no one told us about the spinster lady.

Some houses in the neighborhood stuck in one's mind, like Gordon's. Hers was another. These homes were built in the early 1900s. The ones facing the through street, Rugby Road, were on a grander scale than the ones on the dead-end streets. I suspect they were built first. They were wider, most with house-long front porches having wide, wooden steps. Her house was gray. It had heavy drapes that covered the windows. If the lights were ever on, you couldn't tell unless you were inside, and inside that house was not a place anyone of us wanted to be. But a heart of some sort must have beaten within Mrs. Spinster because while she didn't open the door, she did put a skeleton on it, which faced the supplicants as they marched up the stairs, goody bags in hand. She also had something else. And it was that else that did me in.

An unusual feature of this house was that the windows that looked out over the porch were higher than normal. At that point in my life, I was shorter than normal. When no one answered the bell, my brother said, "Look in the window!" Whatever my brother said, I did. But I couldn't, too high. Nor did I want to. But an order is an order, so I put down my bag, grabbed the window ledge, and pulled myself up, quaking with anxiety, to see what there was to be seen. What there was to be seen scared the living hell out of me.

Mrs. Spinster had bought the largest pumpkin I had ever seen in my life. It was carved for maximum fright impact. It sat on a table, in a dark room, and had a candle at its center. It was this face that met mine, nose-to-nose hole, as my nose passed the window ledge. For a moment, I froze. The sun had gone down. It was chilly. I had to go to the bathroom, and I was gripped with terror. But only for a moment. I let out what in Yiddish is called a *gahshri* (gah-shrye), a scream from the guts, dropped off the ledge, whipped past my brother, took the stairs by twos, and was home before he could get the questioning words out of his mouth—or so it seemed.

It wasn't until decades later when I had to take my own sons trick or treating that I was able to face down a well-carved pumpkin. Curse you spinster lady!

The girl with the biceps had a brother, Arnold, who had even bigger biceps. He was born with a birth defect of some sort that left him with a speech impediment and what we'd call when he wasn't around "the droolies." He had a hair-trigger temper, always had to win, and was always angry about something. In any game that involved guarding, i.e. basketball or football, he'd jump up into your face wave his fist like he was going to punch you, and yell, "Yaaaaahh!!" Sometimes it was effective; sometimes it was ridiculous. All the time, it left you wishing you had windshield wipers to clean away the spray. But to show that people do change, he ended up with a PhD in English, something you don't get by threats and yelling, "Yaaaaahhh!!" in people's faces, and when my brother died, he sent me a letter of condolence and some reminiscences. One of the most amazing ones was his memory of the baseball player's name inscribed in my Wilson baseball glove. I mean why?

Another was "Peanut," who proved that the offspring of very short parents are going to be very short, and his older brother, Sanford, who later in life moved to Florida, married and had a son, tried to equal his father's real estate success in New York, drove to a motel, wrote a letter, and committed suicide. Ouch.

So, these were the players, some bit players, some stars of our stage and screen called "the neighborhood." Some left small impressions, some large. But all left some.

"The ten-block radius around my house in Brooklyn has been my whole world. When I walk on the street, I feel like I've rediscovered my childhood innocence. I love it because nothing has changed."

– Lucas Hedges
Young American Actor,
break-through work was
Manchester by the Sea

Grandma after the amputation with her loving grandbaby, me.

Cockeye and Joe
(A Microcosm of Living in the Neighborhood)

"He'd hold it up at a 45-degree angle, so he could read it."

I never knew Cockeye's name, nor am I sure that his brother's name was Joe. They were the corner drug store/pharmacists in a world before political correctness and rarely found in America anymore. Every necessity a person needed in the 1950s and early '60s could pretty much be found in the neighborhood. Rarely did one drive to the store, one usually walked and carried home, often with children in tow as grocery Sherpas. Nor did anyone ever say they were going "to the stores" even though I can't ever remember just going to or being sent to just one of them. Well, I can but that will come later.

It was only when my parents were on vacation and my grandma came to stay with my brother and me that I ever went to one store instead of several. Grandma was the last of the great penny-pinchers and she bought only what was needed and only bought it a moment or two before it was needed—like stockings and therein is a Notion's Store story. Grandma was an amputee; she had a leg removed because of cancer. Talk about advancements in medicine. The cancer was on her heel and they amputated her leg almost to the hip! But it worked. She lived until ninety-seven. Because she had one leg, she wore only one nylon stocking. Nylons, as they were called, never stockings or nylon stockings, were sold however in boxes of two. She was a stubborn and certain woman, my grandma, so on her command off I would go to Mrs. Goldstein with instructions to buy one nylon stocking, and back I would come with the answer from Mrs. Goldstein that if she sold one she'd have no use for the other and back I would go to buy the box of two.

More amazing than her patience was her knowledge of her stock and her customer base. If someone needed three 3-holed green buttons—no problem. She knew just where they were. Mother-of-pearl beads? Second aisle from the front, fourth box. It was like she had everything anyone might have a notion about because I never heard her say, "I'll order it for you." And customer service? When my mom walked in, Mrs. G. was already up on the ladder pulling out the right box of whatever shade nylons my mom wore the same way the Starbuck's barista starts my wife's tea as soon as he sees her in the parking lot.

And a word about the vegetable man. Clearly his job was to sell his fruits and veggies but . . . if you picked something of which he didn't approve, he told you. "Atsa not ripe. Donta take atta one. This-a-one, she's a better." And did he know his melons. First off (Brooklynism!), he carried melons I'd never heard of like cassavas. I learned from watching him how to pick a ripe melon—smell it and then gently push the circle where the stem was cut off. It should give— not a lot, not just barely, but, well . . . after a while you just knew.

But back to Cockeye. He was so-called by my father because he was seriously cross-eyed. How he got through pharmacy school was a mystery re-enforced every time I went to pick up a prescription. In order to double-check that he was giving me the right bag he'd hold it up at about a 45-degree angle to his shoulder so he could read it. My assumption was that his brother did the pill counting and liquid pouring, or so I hoped. It was decades until it dawned on me that it must have been a huge challenge and therefore a great triumph for him to have gotten through school.

Cockeye was the garrulous one. He loved to chat up the customers. Between their medication changes and artful listening of their running mouths, he knew most everything about everyone. Privacy laws? What fun would they have been? None.

Joe was "just there" the studious manager carefully overseeing things making sure that small visitors, hard to see over the counter, kept their hands where they were supposed to be and left the candy and such where it was supposed to be.

And so it was back then. Waldorf Court, my street, was its own little "Lake Wobegon." It was always a quiet week on a block where "all the men were handsome, the woman beautiful, and the children above average."

That was about as true for the neighborhood as it is for anyplace, including "Lake Wobegon."

> *"I LOVE IT!!!*
> *AND REMEMBER IT WELL!!!*
> *YOUR BEST WORK—QUIT WHILE*
> *UR AHEAD!!!"*
>
> – Dan Zipkin

The Life and Times of
Willie Anna Harris

"My brother and I cringed every time my mother lifted the bell."

One day she just showed up. She was slight, short, sweet, and from South Carolina. Her name was Willie Anna Harris, and she was black. I wasn't aware that my mother decided the house was too big to take care of by herself, or why. I had no idea she was interviewing people. It just could have been that in the '50s and '60s, the wives of professional men were supposed to have what were then called "maids." Willie Anna was a wonderful cook, a lovely person, and I assume a competent housekeeper. There was only one drawback. She was a "live-in." That meant I lost one of the hideaway playrooms on the third floor because that was where Willie Anna lived six days a week.

Now we'd done this dance once before when I was a very little boy. That woman's name was Mrs. Curtiss. She was short, round, and decidedly not sweet. She was also white and didn't sleep in. Go figure. It seemed to me that Mrs. Curtiss' role in our family was to teach me manners and what went with them. I could make a bed like a marine. To this day, every time I lift a soup spoon towards my mouth first, instead of to the back of the bowl and then forward, I can feel her glare. I can eat noiselessly. I know how to set a table with a formal setting of three sets of silverware implements: one atop the plate, one ranging out from each of its sides—I can still tell you the purpose of each. I know where the napkins go too. But to tell the truth, I often forget whether my glass went to the right or left. Yet and still, over sixty years later, I'd say she did a really good job.

Willie Anna was old school, old line 'Southern Negro'. She wouldn't call a white person by their first name even if given permission. She was deferential to a fault. She could fry chicken like nobody else. And her accent could substitute for dessert; it was that delicious. She loved me like her own, and she had an amazing tolerance for my mother.

There was the time my mother decided it was unladylike during dinner to call out Willie Anna's name to come from the kitchen to the dining room to clear the dishes for the next course. The two rooms were approximately ten steps apart. So, she bought a little, antique, brass dinner bell and at the end of each course, or at any time of need, she'd tinkle it. When not cooking, Willie Anna sat in a chair in a nook maybe four feet from my mother's chair. Basically, the whole thing was ridiculous. My brother and I cringed every time our mother raised the bell. To Willie Anna, it was no worse than a dining room in South Carolina and had the added advantage of not coming with any overt, or even self-recognized, racism.

Then one day she said goodbye. The call of the South became irresistible. It wasn't until I went to college that I learned about reverse migration. In the '70s and '80s a fair number of Southern Blacks who had answered the siren call of the industrial north learned that there weren't jobs for everyone, just like the Jews learned the streets of America were not paved with gold. The Jews couldn't go back to Europe; they learned how to spin straw they bought from someone else into their own gold. While African American's weren't about to go back to Africa—but for a tiny few—they could go back to the South, take advantage of the early changes in civil rights law, rejoin their extended families, and push for greater industrialization of the South, along with continuing movement in civil rights law. Tens of thousands did. And while I got my room back on the third floor at a time in my life when I really needed a hiding place (I was not a happy teenager), there was many a day when I regretted the trade. You see as she loved me, I loved Willie Anna Harris back, and miss her ways to this very writing.

Section Three

PS 217 last 8th grade graduating class in Brooklyn. That's lil ole winemaker me right hand side, fourth row up, fourth boy in.

PS 217 Introduction

It was a long walk for short legs to get to school. About a block away, I heard the hum. It sounded like millions of bees hiving together. I gripped my mother's hand—tightly. We approached the schoolyard, which opened up to a sea of bodies from which that hum was coming. I'd never seen so many kids in my life. The schoolyard was wall-to-wall children—literally—with some adults thrown in. And I knew not one. The sidewalk seemed to turn into wet cement; it became more and more difficult each time I put a foot down to pick it up again.

There were signs everywhere. It looked like the political conventions I'd watch with my parents on TV. Each sign, rather than announce the site of a state delegation, was a grade and class. My mother, quite good at such stuff, found my place all too quickly, said her goodbyes, and let go of me or tried. I stuck to her like a suction cup to a board and cried like, well, like I'd never see her again. But, unlike me, she was made out of strong stuff, pealed my hand off hers, hugged me goodbye, and disappeared into the human ocean. It's amazing how isolated one can feel amidst hundreds and hundreds of bodies. The terror I felt was only slightly ameliorated as my class, now lined up and moving like ducklings, followed the teacher into the red brick building with massive metal crime deterrents covering the enormously tall and wide first floor windows. So, there we were, thirty small bodies with a kindly, excited, young teacher, Mrs. Kimmel.

And education began.

Rumors abound in school, many "fake news," to scare the new kids. One at PS 217 was that you never wanted to get sent to the principal's office. She was, it was said, at least at old as the school, dressed in black, hard as steel, and had this stare that nailed the 'staree' to the wall. She was part of a distinguished, New York City family of educators whose influence on the school system began shortly after the colonists arrived. Not really, but such was the hype. It wasn't long before I would be called to her office. I found that Miss Bildersee had earned her reputation well.

The reason I was there was not shared with me. Someone opened our class door, went to the teacher, and the teacher announced, "Billy Gralnick, report to the office." My heart stopped. I was given a chunk of wood, "the pass," and led by the executioner's assistant to "the office." I was seated on a bench that gave new meaning to "hardwood" and looked like it had been installed right after the doors were first opened. There I waited. And waited. And waited some more until a woman appeared from the office to announce, "Miss Bildersee will see you now." Jell-O that had taken my shape moved into the office and then to the inner sanctum.

What I saw and what was actually to be seen could not have been the same. What I think I saw looked exactly like the rumors, but more so. I remember what appeared to be a small, stern woman dressed like a Sicilian or Spanish mourner, all in black, complete with a black veil over her hair.

Through the veil came a voice that inquired, "Are you Billy Gralnick, the one summoned to death by my hand?"

I replied, "Yes, Ma'am."

The voice said, "Your record says that once a week you will be late for school for a doctor's appointment. Is that correct?"

I replied, "Yes, Ma'am." "What is wrong with you?"

"Aaaa-llergies, Miss Bildersee." Pause.

"That will be all. And don't forget to take your pass and give it back to Miss Kimmel." "Yes, Ma'am."

I trembled my way back to class, sat down, realized I still had the pass, had to get up, walk to Ms. Kimmel's desk with thirty pairs of eyes on me, return it and walk back to my seat. I felt the eyes shift position in their sockets as they followed me.

School, it seemed, was not going to be fun.

"I didn't appreciate Brooklyn until I left it."

— Rosie Perez
Actress, Comedienne

The First Day

"There's a reason my school memories
start here—it's called trauma."

I vaguely remember going to a pre-school. It was in a brownstone and downstairs. I have no memory of grades one and two. I must have gone to them because I do remember beginning grade three and I couldn't have done that without having gone to grades one and two. Right?

By the time I was school age, we were for the second time near Prospect Park and then around the corner at 500 Ocean Avenue. When we moved from '500', we went into a different school district and that put me into PS 217, one of the oldest elementary schools in Brooklyn. Its size was imposing, though almost anything of size is imposing to a third grader.

It was a big building whose front, with steps and columns, was on Newkirk Avenue, but only visitors used the front. The other three sides of the building were hemmed in by cement schoolyards, each with a door leading into the school. One faced Rugby Road. That's the entrance I used either through the gate or when no one was looking, through the arch that was artfully snipped into the fence by some kids so that you could play in the yard after school hours and on weekends. The other playground faced Coney Island Avenue.

The building was red (or once was) brick and had huge windows that had to be opened from the inside with long "window poles:" they had a circle at their business ends that hooked into a metal hook at the top of the window. Some you pushed and they opened on a diagonal; some you pulled down on and they opened like, well a window. All the windows had full-size metal grates on them from the time that the Board of Education realized that budget was more important than esthetics. Air conditioning? Hadn't been invented when this school was built.

There is a reason my school memories start here; it's called trauma. On the first day, my mother drove me, and again for several more days. We had to park aways from the schoolyard. I could hear the din of line-up before I ever saw the school. It was a hum or maybe a buzz. And it got louder as we got closer. We crossed Foster Avenue, continuing on Rugby. There were, on the school side, several older houses. Across the street was a large apartment building directly facing the schoolyard and side of the school building. When we passed the last house leaving nothing between us and the din but a chain link fence, I almost croaked. With nothing to block the noise, it turned into a low roar and it came from a sea, a veritable ocean, of kids who were intermingled with teachers yelling, "Grade whatever, Mrs. So and So over here." Some also had signs. It looked like a miniaturized labor rally. Into that mass of humanity, I was to go, stopped at the gate by a teacher who said something like, "Okay, Mom, say your goodbyes. I'll take it from here." She politely asked me my name, and I impolitely burst out crying and almost ripped off my mother's dress as I grabbed for her. Kids remember stuff like that.

Never did a desk feel so safe. While the teacher called the role, I imagined how this person looked who went with the name. I also read the etchings put into the wood over the years. None of them said, "RIP." I figured if the previous occupiers of my seat had survived, so would I.

Day one was in the books.

"No, I ain't a star—I'm just a kid from Brooklyn, living his dream."

– Astro, Hip-Hop Star

"Before being taken over by artisanal cheese and ironic beards, there was ... Brooklyn—large enough to be America's 4th largest city. If Brooklyn lore wasn't part of your life, it can be now, thanks to Bill Gralnick.

"Good luck with it—and please know your Brother's memory lives on, in me and others, every day—in the words we write and the pictures we choose."

– Brian Williams, NBC News

And Education Begins

I wonder what it feels like to step in wet cement.

It wasn't long before I realized that all those pairs of eyes that were looking at me from within their homes on our moving in day, would be part of bodies that would walk with me to school. It was an easy walk, maybe seven blocks to the schoolyard that, day by day, became less and less intimidating. On rainy mornings, my mother drove me; on rainy afternoons, I came home wet. There came one day the challenge of the age-old question, "If you are confronted with a situation that you know isn't dangerous, but you know your mother would be very unhappy about, and even so, if you lost your senses and fell prey to, 'I always wondered what this would feel like,' of course you would be driven to find out. One day I found out.

I was on the way home from school. There was a sign that said two things to us, only one of which was written on it. What was written was, Caution! Wet Cement! What was not written was: This will probably feel really weird if you step in it. So, I paused. Of course, in every group one person carries the devil's voice. That person, Neil, said, "Go for it!" So, I did. Plonk! My foot didn't stop descending until the cement oozed up past the top of my shoe and into it.

Then it got worse.

Sidewalks were made of cement boxes. Every three feet or so would be a line where the wood beams held the cement in place. What I didn't notice was that these beams ran halfway up the block. As fate would have it, one of the paver-men came 'round the corner from working on another street and saw me ankle deep in his art work and bellowed stuff I'd never heard before. I bolted like a frightened deer galloping straight ahead—plonk, plonk, plonk—down the entire length of the paved sidewalk.

From there, I only remember this: I could decide, would it be better to get home fast before the cement hardens me into a podiatric foot form and get the hell beat out of me, or find a spot safe from the enraged paver-man, sit down, and try scooping most of the grey goop off my shoes. That way I might slip into the house and wash the rest off, escaping my fate. Memory fails here. My assumption is, whichever plan I chose, it was the wrong one.

But what I do remember is how that cement felt, and I can describe that to anyone who asks. I await the cocktail party where someone asks, "I wonder what it feels like to step in wet cement?" I'm still waiting.

"I remember being very young and going to AA meetings with my father in Brooklyn. I thought it was fun because they served hot chocolate and cookies."

– Rochelle Aytes, Actress

The Matriarchs

Wet Pants and Muffins

To open that metal box and smell those muffins—ooh la la.

I have to preface this by saying this is a really true story. Everything I'm telling you, dear reader, is true but some are more believable than others. So, I emphasize—this is true. Here goes . . . I once failed "bathroom." Now you might wonder why such a category would be on a report card. Me too. But it was. And I got a "U" (as in "unsatisfactory"). I must have had prostate problems in elementary school. There were days when I just about made it home. In those days, there was no such thing as a latchkey kid. Moms were home to open the door, except for mine on this one day.

It came on me suddenly. I felt like I was filling up, turning into a water balloon. Why, when one has to pee, does he walk like a shackled penguin? I don't know, but it seems a common thing regardless of age. I waddled faster and faster and faster. As I turned the corner and our red door came into view, I thought I had it made it. However, for reasons I don't understand, the rule was to enter the house at the back door, not the front. Those were the rules. Those few yards extra this day portended disaster.

Had my mother been in the kitchen, or even downstairs, there was the possibility . . . but she wasn't. She was upstairs. I pounded on the door. I was even yelling for her in the forbidden Brooklyn pronunciation: "Maaaaaaaaaaaaaaaaaaaaaaaaaaaa!!" (My mother once said, "We may have to live in Brooklyn, but we don't have to sound like it. If you want a goat yell "Maaaaaaaaaaaaaaa." If you want me, Mom is what you say." That too is true. By this time, my legs were entwined like I was Gumby in a leg twist. Finally, she opened the door. She began, "WHAT ARE YOU YELLING—" as I took one step across the threshold. Big mistake but no other choice was available except the bushes and now Mom was there to watch. Unwinding my legs was like turning on a spigot. Warmth filled my pants—tan chinos as I recall—so the wet stain was obvious to a blind person.

Children must have bladders of size disproportionate to their bodies. It was remarkable how wet I got, and how quickly.

Mother: "What is the matter with you?!?" Me: "Uh . . . I had to go to the bathroom."

By the way, I didn't get the "U" because my teacher thought I had a bladder problem. Shall we say, she thought I had a hormone problem? It wasn't for urinating that she gave me the U, but for what other stuff she thought I was doing in the bathroom, stuff frankly I hadn't yet learned about. But that's probably more than you need to know.

The back porch was not, however, routinely a place of disaster. We had a lovely backyard. When I came home it was to birds singing and squirrels playing. The treats, though, were the days I came home and the Duggan's man had made his delivery. Regrettably, this is a short-lived memory because it wasn't long before milk, eggs, and muffins all came from a shelf, put in a box, went into a cart, got packed in a bag, and were toted home. But to open that grey metal box on the back porch and smell those fresh muffins . . . Oooh la la. My favorites then, before I became a chocolate addict, were raisin bran muffins. The raisins were big as Maine black flies and they were juicy. The outside of the muffin was firm but take a bite and it all came apart as it reunited on the taste buds. Yum!

In the morning, came milk and eggs. The milk was actually in a bottle, and most of you my age, regardless of whether your milk is from a cow, an almond, or a cashew, still say you're going to pick up a bottle of milk. The glass bottle had a distinctive shape with a long neck, a paper insert with a little tab pressed into it, and it was covered by a tin foil wrapper. One slipped the forefinger under the wrapper to dispense with it and the fingernail under the tab. That you kept because it snapped back onto the top of the bottle after each use. But best of all, between that cap and the milk was about an inch of cream, real "stick-in-your-arteries-cause-a-heart-attack-fifty-years-later" cream. And since my parents didn't often use the cream, just poured it off, I would open the bottle and drink it. Statins came just in time.

Writers are warned about clichés, but you know . . . those really were the days!

"I think of myself as a girl from Brooklyn."

– Barbra Streisand

Walking to School

*"The teacher . . . sent the Inspector Clouseau
of the teaching corps looking for me."*

I don't ever remember it raining when I had to go to school. In six years, it must have. It got dark and threatening at times. Sometimes, it was a race to school or home before the skies opened. I don't remember ever getting wet, but for one time that we'll get to.

It was a fairly bucolic walk from my house to the schoolyard. As I've described, Waldorf Court was a dead end that opened onto Rugby Road, E. 14th Street. It was a side street artery lined in my area with graceful homes most built around the turn of the century—the twentieth century, that is. They had front yards (with a lawn split by a walkway to the porches), and backyards. The streets were tree-lined. It was unlike the areas not far from it. I had only to walk up one block to Glenwood Road, the one with the pedestrian bridge over the subway tracks and divided down the middle by an island of trees, shrubs, and dog crap. Litter bags and "pick up after your dog" campaigns hadn't yet dawned on the city's leaders. It would be the route that I'd go to high school. For elementary school, I turned left.

It was an easy walk. After a few weeks, I could have done it blindfolded. There was one traffic light at Foster Avenue, and there was a cop or school guard there. Rugby Road was also lined with private homes—all the way to Foster Avenue. There began the apartment buildings.

On a daily basis, it was boring, but much could go on in reality and fantasy when little boys have nothing much to do but walk and think. An elm tree could be stately one moment and frightful the next. A shadow in a window could portend evil waiting to bound through the door, down the porch steps, and attack. Bigger kids with no interest in you at all could become bad guys; little kids could be nasty. Bucolic didn't mean safe, even when it did.

Things happened. Sometimes the dog crap wasn't always on the island, and you either went to school or went home smelling like a kennel that hadn't been cleaned in a week.

Sometimes a big kid did give chase and the bucolic walk turned into a mad dash.

Sometimes a creepy, old person would pop out from behind the front door. The purpose was to get the morning paper, which might or might not have ended up on the porch that morning, but your mind screamed ALARM! ALARM! RUN! RUN!" and you'd take off leaving a very puzzled old person in your wake.

Sometimes, you were daydreaming and didn't notice what you should have, and as noted, end up standing in wet cement.

To tell the truth, other than the cement, I liked the walk. It was solitary and usually uneventful. I was a nice kid and a good student, so my teachers liked me, and I was rewarded with good grades, until one day I came home with a report card full of "A's"and "B+'s" and one big "U". Grades came in black except for "U's". They were in red, so you couldn't overlook them. They were your Scarlet Letter. Later would come another, but it was written in disappearing ink.

In those days, report cards had about fifteen things where you got graded. Some were subject matter, and some were behavioral issues. Remember from the previous chapter, one of the categories was Bathroom. But this becomes even stranger because Mom went to school to see the teacher.

A "U" was not a grade to be brought home to my house, nor was anything below a "B". I didn't have a clue why I had gotten a "U". The teacher seemed to like me a lot and I her. I was not looking forward to my mother's return from school. But she said little. And when my father came home, she said nothing to me, but had a whispered, dramatic conversation with him. "What do you think it means? Isn't he too young for that?" Do you think we need to take him to the doctor?"

As I recall, it was a year or more before the grand secret was revealed to me. I must have had an undiagnosed urinary tract infection, and for that quarter of the year, I was asking for the pass a lot. First, they thought I was smoking, but I was way too young, and besides, kids like me didn't smoke, even though my mother smoked like a chimney. Then the teacher thought I was fooling around with someone in the halls or the bathroom, and actually sent an Inspector Clouseau of the teacher's corps to follow me. Finally, they decided that I was doing something I'm not sure I even knew the meaning of at the age I was supposedly doing it—masturbating. That often?

Years later. When I learned the word and the act, I contemplated that "U" and thought, gee—I wish they had been right . . . .

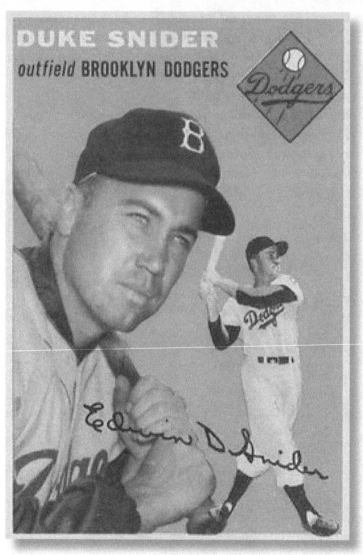

"My Hero"

The Worst Thing I Ever Did

"Every so often, the devil wins . . ."

I was a good kid, almost boringly so. But I was also a good kid who on occasion did bad things.

I filched chocolate from the Whitman's Sampler when my amputee grandmother couldn't see. I didn't realize, of course, that one day she'd want a piece herself and notice that the box was nearly empty. I got clubbed for that one.

Once, I grabbed a buck from my mother's pocketbook—and got away with it.

You'll read about my escapade with the BB gun (spoiler alert) and shooting out the neighbor's garage windows. You'll also find out why my brother got a beating for that instead of me.

Something I really could have gotten in trouble for was the short but intense period of shoplifting from the Russian's candy store. The store was well-placed, only two doors off the route to PS 217. A detour didn't take much time, and for pulling a caper you could quickly blend into the crowd of kids, most who looked just like you, funneling into the schoolyard.

The thievery was confined to Topp's baseball cards and the unbelievably bad chewing gum that came with them. Sometimes, the gum was so old that if you hit it on something it almost atomized. More amazing was how long the cards themselves retained the scent of the gum—months, at least, especially if you kept the collection in a box. This clipping of cards continued until Max, the owner—who was missing a finger for reasons he'd never divulge but making him a spooky fellow to elementary school kids—saw me.

He came within an arm's length of grabbing me by the collar. It was so close a call I must have slipped through the space in his fingers. Words in several languages trailed me out the door. They all sounded bad. We made an unspoken deal. He didn't call the cops, and I never went back into his store. Actually, I did, but it was some thirty years later with my own kids in tow. Somehow, along with growing older, he had gotten much smaller, just as Waldorf Court had shrunk in my absence. I introduced myself and my kids. He didn't know who I was and really didn't care either.

But the worst of the worst of things I did was at the movies. We had two movie theaters in the neighborhood, both within walking distance. One was the Leader Theatre and Bowling Lanes, the other The Kent. The Leader catered more to families and kids. On Saturdays, they'd have afternoon specials. You could see a dozen cartoons, newsreels, and a double feature—first for a quarter, later for a half buck. Parents could send their kids to the movies at 11:30 a.m. for the noon show and know they were out from underfoot, especially on a rainy day, until five. And, with candy and a soda, it was about a dollar a kid.

The movies could be scary. First, they were dark. Then there were the movies themselves. I remember my brother taking me to see movies like, *The Thing* and *Godzilla* and spending a fair amount of time on the floor under my seat, hiding. We had an active gang in the area. If memory serves, it was an offshoot of the Amboy Dukes, famous Brooklyn troublemakers. While my brother was rustling up some popcorn, they surrounded me and covered me with threats, but as eerily as they had shown up, they disappeared. I guess beating up an eight-year-old was no big feather in a gang member's cap. Breathe with me a big sigh of relief.

The Leader was the movie house of choice for mothers who needed time off from their kids, it had something The Kent did not—matrons. Matrons were not uncommon in movie houses of the day. In more upscale places, they acted a bit like ushers in a theatre. In places like the Leader, they were enforcers. Enforcers of what? First of all, they patrolled the balcony. It was in the balcony that the older boys nestled with their honeys and made out. *Verboten!* Secondly, they were always on noise patrol. How one expected a movie theatre full of kids who were either laughing at cartoons or shrieking in terror from the latest Japanese horror movie would, or could, be quiet is a head-scratcher. But making noise—*verboten!*

Thirdly, they were air raid wardens. For reasons I can't explain, the most common pre-movie activity was to reach into one's pocket that had earlier been filled with paper clips and a sturdy rubber band. The clips would be shot at the screen. Each clip provided two missiles because you had to break them in half in order to hook them on the rubber band, thus weaponizing them. Over the din one would hear a "dink" and then a few more "dinks" and if the matrons weren't on their toes, volleys of "dinks." The theatre looked like newsreels from the front lines, missiles from the launchers flying at their targets.

For the movie theatre, this was serious business. An errant clip could put out someone's eye. Enough people concentrating their firepower could put a hole or holes in the screen. Replacing a movie screen was expensive, especially once the Cinemascope era began. Fifteen- to thirty-thousand dollars expensive. And that at fifty-cent admissions. That's why in some neighborhoods the local movie theatre had a screen with patches of tape here and there.

Then too, if enough clips were on the floor, someone could slip on them. Lawsuit! I suppose the matrons picked them up for that reason, as opposed to collecting them for forensic evidence—a science that really hadn't been invented by then to any great degree.

I tell you this because this is what one day turned good boy Billy into a "baaaad" boy.

The stable of matrons was varied. There were usually two, always dressed in white uniforms like nurses. One was I guess a utility matron. Often, she was someone we didn't know and who didn't know us, but the Sergeant Major of the Matron's Corps was a woman who was large, very large, about as wide as she was high. When she grabbed two lip-lockers from behind whilst they were lovin' on each other in the loge, she could scare the hell out of you. Two ham-sized hands swatting the back of your head—ouch! If you were running down the aisle, also *verboten*, and she grabbed you by the arm it felt like she was ripping it out of your shoulder. This nameless barge was a personage with which to be reckoned.

I don't know what came over me. I was, as I said, basically a good boy. Yet every so often, the devil wins. An opportunity is put in front of you that is so indescribably, deliciously tempting, so excitingly opportunistic that you can't resist it. And that's what I was presented with.

My seat that day was upstairs. I don't know why. I was neither with my brother nor a girl, just a bunch of us goof-offs from the neighborhood. Upstairs, if you were there to watch the movie, really gave you a better look at the screen. That may have been the reason. What happened that day just happened. There was no forethought, though there was plenty of after-thought. It was a scene that just unfolded before me, and I was drawn into it.

I was sitting in my seat. My weapons of destruction had not even been drawn. Big Momma Matron was on patrol and making her way towards the screen. Then something caught her eye and she bent over, presenting me with a target that was so big, so wide, so tempting—well, I couldn't resist.

Now it takes a while for so much girth to bend over and a while more for it to be raised, like a drawbridge. During that time, my hand, on its own, went into my pocket, pulled out the rubber band and a clip, broke the clip, slipped it onto the band, and stretched that band 'til it was taut to the breaking point. Then "Zing!" Away it went. I had nothing to do with it; it just happened.

The devil's aim was as accurate as a cruise missile. I don't think I've ever seen that much pulchritude straighten itself up in so little time. I also never got out of a seat, run down a flight of stairs, and fled any place as fast as I did that day.

I don't remember what I told my mother about why I was home so early, but I can still to this day hear the sound of the scream that followed me down the stairs and out the door. I see it encircled in a comic book balloon—EYOWWWWWWWWWWW!!

Bad boy.

*"Brooklyn was a famous team.
I wanted to play for the Dodgers."*

– Roberto Clemente
Pittsburgh Pirate
Hall of Famer

"Some things never change . . ."

When Teachers Were Teachers

". . . waiting for you was the assistant principal—with a canoe paddle."

PS 217 was an historic place, sort of. It was the last eighth grade school in Brooklyn. Everyone in my district who came after me went to junior high school, attending PS 217 only for six years. It was a lousy system, soon discredited and replaced with the middle school concept, but let me tell you for true, from grades three through eight, I had some real teachers.

These teachers knew their stuff. These teachers were not social workers. They were not police personnel. They were not your friends. They were your teachers, and you respected them or you went to see Ms. Bildersee, and if that didn't work, you went home with a note, and if that didn't work—again, honest to God—during Assembly your name was called, you rose from your seat, and did a perp walk in front of the entire school, marched up the stairs to the auditorium stage where waiting for you was the assistant principal—with a canoe paddle. That usually worked.

I remember them all, that's how amazing they were, but some were more amazing than others like Miss Diehl, Miss Nelly Ennis, and Miss McNulty. One taught social studies, one English, and the other math. It wasn't however what they taught, it was how they taught it. And then there was Max Proshan, a character unto himself, who taught general science. And let's not forget music, or shop . . . which get their own story.

Miss Diehl:

Like most of the teachers in school, Miss Diehl was short, stocky, and had gray hair. She was tough as nails, hard as steel. There was one way for things to be done: her way. She liked having "pets" and it was definitely best to be her pet and not in her doghouse. Pets clapped erasers, made sure the garbage was in the can, and most importantly, were exemplary students in every way. Susan Dickey was her pet and my first schoolgirl crush.

Aside from being adorable with dark hair and freckles, always impeccably dressed, Susan wore Mary Janes, black patent leather shoes that gleamed like tempered steel. Miss Diehl loved them. Ms. Diehl loved her.

"Snooty" would be a good descriptor for Susan, and clearly, if I was going to even be looked at, I needed to be a young version of an Eversharp razor commercial: I had to look sharp and be sharp. Looking sharp, albeit for a somewhat goofy lookin' kid, wasn't easy. That was my mother's job. Being sharp? I was on my own. I had to shine in class just like Susan's shoes. Then came my chance.

I was always a good reader, ahead of my grade. I read fluently and clearly. My handwriting was atrocious, but what came out of my mouth off the written page was another story—usually.

Just not in this story.

We were reading about the agricultural history of America and the invention of the cotton gin. As the reading assignment went from one student to the next, up and down the rows, I would count ahead to see which paragraph mine would be. While others read, I practiced in silence. I was in the middle of the last row by the window. Miss Diehl would call out each student's name with a sharpness that was bracing. The student had to stand up, straight of course, face the class, and read in a loud, but not too loud voice, enunciating clearly. As I stood, I was facing Susan whose scrubbed face must have blinded me.

Suddenly, I was nervous. I did not get off to a good start, but I was in there, moving towards the groove, when disaster struck. I had come to the inventor's name, Cyrus McCormick. In my clear, not too loud voice I proudly enunciated "Cries McCork."

And Miss Diehl cried out, "CRIES McCORK?!? William Gralnick, who on earth is that? READ IT AGAIN!!"

I did. Perfectly. But the damage was done. Smoke poured from Miss Diehl's furnace and there was a smirk on Miss Shiny Shoe's face, a smirk that lasted until eighth grade—and this was only fifth.

Miss Ennis:

I don't know if any of these women were married, but we addressed them all as Miss, so I guess it wasn't any of our business if they were. Miss Ennis was to English as Miss Diehl was to social studies. The only difference was, instead of gray hair, hers was yellow, like corn.

The New York City School System, in its infinite wisdom, had decided that students no longer had to learn how to diagram sentences. The only problem was, they didn't ask Miss Ennis what she thought of the idea. Her thought? That such a ruling was just short of insanity, the ruination of future culture and civilization. "Students not knowing how to diagram? She never added another sentence. Furor took over which produced a "Harumph!" It didn't take too long for people to stop asking what she thought.

Her second pet peeve was pronunciation. Her students had better know where the accents went in a multi-syllable word, or there was a payment to be exacted. The payment was a look of grave disappointment, like you had let her cat die because of some failing on your part. The other payment, of course, was on your report card.

To this day, I remember the student who had in her class the same experience I had in Miss Diehl's. The word was grimace. Today it is acceptable to everyone, except me, to pronounce that word exactly as it is written, "grim'ace." Back in the day, the accent was on the last syllable: gri-mace'. But to this very day, I can only say it that way and when I hear someone say "grim'iss," I honor Miss Ennis's memory by making a gri'mace.

That's what I call a teacher having a lifelong impact on a student.

Miss McNulty:

"Bones" McNulty was in a category by herself. Miss McNulty taught seventh grade math. She had gray hair, but she was so terrifying to look at, her hair could have been puce and I'd not have noticed. Miss Nulty was about five feet eleven inches tall. She looked to weigh about fifty-three pounds. Her fingers were as long as yardsticks, all boney with protruding joints, and blue veins coursing along her skin. When she wasn't happy, she pointed a finger at you and lightning flamed from its tip burning holes right through your shirt into your chest. She was often not happy. The only thing I learned in seventh grade math was to duck.

Mr. Proshan:

With the accent after Pro, he was a sad but almost comic figure. A veteran of WW II, he was, in the parlance of the day, "shell-shocked." The manifestation of that was when he heard a sudden, sharp, loud noise like the backfire of a car he would blurt out "Woo-woo!" and then go on teaching as if nothing of the sort had come out of his mouth. The science classroom window overlooked four-lane Newkirk Avenue. Need I say more?

Mr. Proshan had a closet full of brown suits or just one. In either case, that's what he wore every day. And the same near-sighted tailor made them all. His pants were too short, and his sleeves were too long. The shirt was of no consequence. And he either had worn the same socks every day or also had a drawer full of them too. The sleeves, however, were another story.

These were the days of blackboards and chalk, erasers, and dust. By late in the day, the tray under the blackboard would be full of chalk dust. Mr. Proshan was a short man, and invariably, after writing on the board, he would sweep around to face the class, and in so doing, scoop up copious amounts of chalk dust between the jacket sleeve and his shirt cuff. At that point, you could assume one of two things would happen. He'd either point to a student as he turned, or a car would backfire; he'd throw up his hands and go . . . well, you know. Either way, he would suddenly be enveloped in a cloud of white dust. Now, clearly, for dopey eighth graders, this type of daily comedy sketch was bound to test the restraints not already tightly laced into that age group.

One day they broke. It was report card day. Everyone was nutty with anticipation. I had been doing very well, and was expecting an A. I didn't get it.

Poor Mr. Proshan was hit with a double whammy. While he was collecting chalk dust in his cuffs, a truck backfired. He spun around, and what happened next seemed to be in slow motion. His sleeves, like Mickey's in the Sorcerer's Apprentice, billowed out. His "woo-woo!" seemed to hang in front of his lips where it was enveloped in the growing cloud of white dust. There was a gasp, a moment of silence, and then some thirty-five students just fell out. It was mass hysteria. Tears rolling down cheeks, palms slapping desks . . . Had we been the audience for a comedy, it would have been wonderful. We were not.

Mr. Proshan went crazy. He turned a color I had never seen on a human being before. Roman candles shot out of his eyes and ears, and very un-teacher-like phrases exploded from his mouth. My best recollection is something like, "Laugh at me, will you? I'll show you, you little bastards." He scooped up all the report cards, a red pen, and proceeded to flunk the entire class. Having handed out the last card, he said, "Now get outta here and go home!"

A "U" in bathroom was one thing. Going home with an "F" in science was not a good thing. My mother sat me down in the kitchenette and stone-faced listened to my story. She then turned the same color as Mr. Proshan had with similar pyrotechnics to accompany the twisting of her face into a contortion of anger she didn't match again for years. *The Exorcist* comes to mind. She was looking at straight A's except for this work of communist-red art in the middle of the line. "HOW DID THIS HAPPEN? WHAT ABOUT THAT PROJECT MR. COHEN HELPED YOU WITH??"

I explained as best I could. She was fuming, but fortunately not at me. She was sputtering mad and sputtered all night 'til morning when she said, "Get in the car!" Not only had she hardly ever driven me to school, she rarely ever saw numbers on a clock before ten. Now this same lady who, in a previous chapter, verbally assaulted a gang and promised to call in air strikes if they didn't get off our block, parked her car and was headed missile-like straight for Mr. Proshan's door with me in tow.

"HOW COULD YOU DO THIS? THIS IS A STRAIGHT A STUDENT! YOU COULD RUIN HIS ACADEMIC AVERAGE!! DON'T YOU KNOW THAT THIS F WILL FOLLOW HIM THROUGH HIGH SCHOOL?"

While this tirade was going on, I was under a desk somewhere wrapping myself in humiliation, or wishing I was.

The bell rang, she left, I went to class and awaited with dread, seventh period. I walked in and sat down in a now deathly silent classroom. Mr. Proshan called on me and asked me to give the report I didn't give on F-bomb day. He waxed rhapsodic, took back my report card, which had to be turned in with a parent's signature, scrubbed out the star-spangled "F" and over it put a big blue "A+", however with no asterisks.

And the other students?

Let's just say it was a good thing it was the end of the second semester and the next year I'd be in the Midwood building. The greater numbers protected me from being assassinated by the kids whose grades weren't changed.

We learned later, though, that Saint Mildred the Mother wasn't the only complainant, only the most threatening. The principal investigated the "grade slaughter" and mandated all the grades be re-evaluated and re-posted. We heard through the grapevine the following year school was Proshan-less; he had retired.

Mrs. K:

Sweet Mrs. Keiselbach—who, until I went away to college and saw Blaze Starr in a strip show, had the biggest chest I'd ever seen in my life—was a music teacher. She wanted to be an opera singer. The Great Depression did that to people's plans. My dad wanted to be a concert violinist. He couldn't afford the time it took to become one, and neither could Mrs. K afford opera costs. She was a sweet woman who loved to sing, her only problem being her voice. Coming out of that chest, it wasn't meant to be contained by a classroom. Loud. Very loud!

And she was a prayerful woman. She was my homeroom teacher in the seventh grade. We began every morning with the Lord's Prayer. And, truthfully, even though I am an ardent supporter of the separation of church and state—it didn't hurt me one bit.

Now we come to shop. Turn the page.

"My 'act' was schoolwork. I was your basic, garden-variety, ambitious, upwardly mobile, hard-working Jewish boy from Brooklyn. I was bound to go beyond my parents. It was simply the way things were."

– Clive Davis

Shop

". . . everything looked like an ashtray."

If asked about Jewish kids taking shop, Jackie Mason would have replied, "Don't be ridiculous. Jews don't make things; they buy them. Jews don't fix things; they hire people." This was especially true in my house. With a father who was a dentist, a stray blow from a hammer, the removal of a layer of skin on a hand or finger with a chisel could mean a long time on mac and cheese for the family. Daddy didn't make or fix stuff unless it was going inside someone's mouth. That he did superbly. Thus, as you might imagine, my acuity for shop was not great. In those days, Jews still bought homes that had kitchens, so the girls I grew up with took 'Home Ec' while we boys took shop. The girls were a lot better at cooking than we boys were at hammering and sawing.

I have no idea what my shop teacher's name was. I remember he was a solid guy about five-eight with a pencil mustache. He wore a thinly striped, blue and white shop apron and always had at hand a steel yardstick.

Remember that, it's important.

Unlike high school chemistry, where one could really do some damage—like when one of my classmates blew the windows out of the 'Chem' lab—eighth grade shop never rose to a danger level that couldn't be handled by a Band-Aid.

The first half of the year we learned how to survive in shop without cutting off a finger or shocking ourselves badly enough for our hair to stand on end. We used this kind of saw or that. I'd tell you which, but frankly I don't remember their names, and haven't used them since. We also did some ceramic work. We made an ashtray that had a groove to hold a cigarette—times have changed.

There's no more shop class, but if there were, it wouldn't include making ashtrays. We made other things that were not ashtrays, though my creations always seemed to look like they could be, but for their lack of grooves.

There were basically two kinds of students in class: one group was handy because their fathers were handy; one group was not. My mother would no more let her husband the dentist pick up a saw than she would have sent me to truck driving school. In fact, her vision was probably that if my father picked up a saw and had an accident, we'd all have to survive by her then sending me to truck driving school. So, shop for me was a break from the classes, the grades for which my parents cared about. It also had a fascination for me. Watching someone turn a piece of clay or wood into something both recognizable and useful, was actually interesting.

Then it was my turn.

The second half of the year was dedicated to making something that was supposed to be both recognizable and useful—a lamp. This was a multi-phase project. The lamp had to have a base. It had to have a post. Both base and post had to have a hole for the wires to run through. Affixed to the top of the post would be a light socket. The bulb and shade were to be bought and brought in. But this was not all.

The base had to be filed and sanded so that its edges were rounded. It also would have an indentation about three inches square to hold things. You might ask, "What things?" I asked the same question. Its depth might accommodate paper clips, or a little lake of water or coffee if someone spilled something on it. And when done, it had to be stained, a process that sent many of us home with more color on our hands, arms, and clothes than on our lamps.

My lamp was not quite a work of art, but it was recognizable as a lamp and it did work. There were some variations on the plan. Somehow, my base wasn't flat, so the lamp had a bit of a wobble to it. My indentation wasn't quite uniform, nor was it quite square. The reservoir wouldn't hold much coffee. The socket atop the post was a bit askew, so the bulb and shade didn't point exactly at the ceiling. But it was mine, made by me, and I kept it I believe through high school, in my room, until I went to college, when mother "Mildred the Trasher" threw it out along with most everything else of mine that either wasn't taken to college, hidden in the attic, or nailed to something immovable.

But none of this is the point of the story. Remember that ruler? That's the point of the story.

As I had children of my own, I began to realize that middle school teachers should be given medals every three years and, in some cases, every three days. Kids, in what then were the sixth, seventh, and eighth grades, are weird. They develop at different rates. Some are short, and some are tall. Some are shy, and some are performers. Some think beds are for sleeping and yes, some think beds are . . . for other things. It is the season of hormones.

One of my shop mates was a body full of raging hormones. His name was Mark. Why I remember that, I don't know. Mark used to wear baggy pants and it seemed everything he looked at in shop—a saw, hammer, light switch, a water faucet—made him horny. He'd get an erection and would be immensely proud, so proud that he'd alert his bench mates who would pass the word around. Check out Mark, he's grinning again.

This was a big secret we all kept, or so we thought. Apparently, Mr. Pencil Mustache was on to us and wouldn't let erection-making trump lamp-making. He had a plan and it was wicked. Corporal punishment was still allowed in New York City schools, so you can surmise that teachers had quite a bit more leeway in discipline than they now do. In fact, today, Mr. PM might have gone to jail for this one.

Mr. Mustache had taken to walking about shop (never called "class") with his metal yardstick. Sometimes he'd use it like a walking stick, sometimes he'd tuck in under his arm the same way a British Colonel would tuck his crop. If a group wasn't paying attention, he hit the desk with the flat side of the ruler. The resulting CRACK! got everyone back in focus.

Mark had taken to being less careful and bold about his new-found talent. When "grinning time" came around, he would push himself up to the shop desk, stand on his tippy toes, and place the clothed protrusion in his baggy pants on the top of the workbench. How one could have thought the teacher was unaware only attests to the stupidity hormones can bring down upon a young man. Necks craned at all angles depending on where one's workbench was located. Clearly, no one was looking at the teacher. Grinning time was Mark's time. One day though, "Wipe that grin off your face" was given new meaning.

The word had gone out. Necks craned. Thirty eighth graders were grinning like Cheshire Cats. Not one person was aware that Mr. "PM" was stealthily moving across the shop. When he was about 32" from Mark, I seem to remember seeing a glint of light, a flash, like a strike of lightning. It was his 36" ruler. The air parted with a "whoosh!" The "whoosh" was followed with a "thwack!"

The "thwack" was followed by a sound. "Oooooooooooooooooo" and the "oooooooooooooooooo" was followed by the sound of a body sliding down a shop bench into a lump on the floor.

And so ended the grinning in shop class.

"I grew up in the projects in Brooklyn, and I consider myself lucky and blessed to be where I am—just working."

– Tracy Morgan
Actor, Comedian

This "Dick and Jane" like Health Department warning would have been more effective if it had a picture of my face on it.

Life Without Vaccinations

"Part of my childhood was spent coated with calamine lotion."

I had every childhood illness known to the Western Hemisphere, or so it seemed. Kids today, and their parents, just don't know what they are missing by getting vaccines that rob them of these experiences. I had German measles, regular (American?) measles (for a month, thirty full days!), mumps, rheumatic fever, chicken pox, and my all-time favorite, whooping cough.

In the days when "home schooling" was something one read about as done on the prairie when the one-room schoolhouse was too far away, pre-vaccination childhood could give one a real taste of it. School was the great breeding ground for everything. Once something hit, whole pieces of the student body would disappear. Parents today only get a taste of it when they take their previously completely healthy baby and put her or him into pre-school. Within weeks, the child is sick for the first time because some selfish do-do bird of a parent wouldn't, or couldn't, stay home with a sick child, sent it to school, and got everyone else's kid sick. And then, of course, Mom got sick taking care of her kid, and gave it to Dad. By that time, the siblings were sick as well. My mom used to say the worst colds she ever had, she got from us as kids. I pooh-poohed it—until some do-do bird got my kid sick, who in turn got me sick, and so on.

Part of my childhood was spent coated with calamine lotion, so much so that its mere mention instantly brings the smell to memory.

It is permanently embedded into my nose hairs and smell receptors. I was painted pink for weeks at a time.

Part of childhood, I spent high on a cough medicine I think is now outlawed, or should be, called Elixir of Terpin Hydrate with Codeine. A worse tasting concoction was unknown to children— yes, worse than cod liver oil—and 120 proof grain alcohol was the only thing since I've ever tasted that came close to how it felt going down. Fire water. But, oh, the feeling ten minutes later . . . It wasn't that it stopped the cough. It stopped you caring about the cough, or anything else.

First came the mumps. It was a bad way to start because it wasn't so bad. True, I went from having swollen glands to looking like a squirrel that thought winter would never end, and therefore had stored so much food in its mouth that the lower face took on the semblance of a pumpkin. Fever, sore throat, hard to swallow. No big deal.

Then came the measles. That one, folks, was a lollapalooza.

It started, as it always does, with a rash and low-grade fever. Trusty Uncle Ben, in his Buick, carrying his black bag, showed up after dinner one night to make the diagnosis. Measles everyone knew about. We had no clue however what "Billy's measles" were going to be all about. My virus fell in love with my body, and there began a long, miserable, love affair, thirty full days long. If there was a place to have a 'measle', I had it. Top, bottom, inside, outside. In my hair on my scalp, all over my butt, even in my stomach, so I couldn't hold down food. In my ears too, which made me want to scratch a tunnel through my head. They were in my eyes, so I couldn't see.

I knew I wasn't supposed to pick them, but I couldn't wait to be left alone so I could devise ways of touching them that wouldn't leave scars but would give me the tiniest sense of relief. My scalp became a road map of bumps. My chest and back looked like a modern art painting. And everywhere were either wet splotches of calamine lotion or dried ones flaking off into my bed, both with bits of cotton ball hanging from them. The dried ones were hateful. If I pulled them off, the dry lotion would crack, and there would appear yet another 'measle'.

I missed four complete weeks of school. Yes, my classmates made me get well cards, and after the first two weeks, teachers sent over assignments. My life was confined to either the couch in the den downstairs in front of the TV, or in my bed listening to soap operas and mysteries on the radio. Listening to radio voices was like drinking warm tea with a lot of honey, and usually had the same effect on me as taking Terpin Hydrate. I slept most of the month. I did get better.

But it was "the fever" that won the prize for sleeping. One morning, I woke up with a fever and it didn't stop. By the time it got to 104 or 105, I was getting alcohol rubdowns and it was time for Uncle Ben again. The short of it was at close to 107 and feeling a way I can only describe as weird, I overheard him say "maybe rheumatic fever" and "hospital if . . ." But then it began to subside. I was, as Grandma used to say, "Weak as Hector's pup" for days. About the only other thing I remember was that I got to watch Joe DiMaggio and the Yankees on TV. That proves I was really sick because as a Brooklyn Dodgers fan, I hated, with a capital "H", the Yankees.

By the time I got the German measles I was a pro. They were "nuthin'" hardly worth writing about. But the whooping cough. Now that was "sumpin!"

Whooping cough gets its name from the ghastly sound one makes as one coughs—and coughs—and coughs. To say the cough comes from way down deep doesn't do it justice. It is as if someone sticks their hand down your throat to somewhere below your intestines and pulls the cough up with it. The repetitions leave one in a cold sweat that goes nicely with the warmth of the fever. You could hook up an IV of Terpin Hydrate and it wouldn't help. "Wrung out" is how the coughing jags leave you, when it leaves you. Then you start again. It truly can be a killer cough. I would have them all again except for this one. For this one, thank God for vaccinations.

Stickball—the anyplace, anytime game of the Brooklyn streets.

The Greatest (Stickball) Game Ever

"I leaned into a fastball and 'Holy baseball, Batman,' I hit it."

I only needed to see it once and I was hooked that day when an eighth grader about the size of an NFL guard swung and hit this pinkie (a.k.a. rubber ball) in a high arc. It flew over the schoolyard fence, over the street, and landed on the roof of the five-story apartment house facing "left field." Transfixed by that feat, thus began my obsession with stickball—an obsession so long-lasting that many years later, I took my boys back to the schoolyard for one last game. Those results later.

Stickball was an anybody sport. Needed were a broom handle, a piece of chalk, and a Spauldeen, making the cost next to nothing. That was particularly true when the broom handle came from a broom that somehow "just disappeared" one day from the garage, the chalk disappearing from a classroom—and the ball itself costing a quarter. If you really wanted to go whole hog, electrical tape was wound around the bat handle—but that was it.

One drew a batter's box on the wall and/or a plate on the ground. In a two-boy game, there was a pitcher and batter. In a three-boy game, add an outfielder. And much like baseball, it was a mental duel between batter and pitcher.

Most games were won with a Wee Willie Keeler "hit 'em where they ain't" strategy, and others with a mammoth homer foretold immediately by the thwack produced by the ball compressing as it hit the bat dead-center. Unlike a baseball, a Spauldeen compressed when hit and it literally flew off the bat.

Stickball could be organized with teams, but in my neighborhood, it was *mano a mano*, all for individual bragging rights. And that's what it came down to one fateful, late fall evening.

I can see my opponent, but I can't remember his name. We had met over the summer, played some stickball, and quickly got into a rivalry that was to be settled back in Brooklyn at the schoolyard.

On that evening, we walked down the street to the side entrance of PS 217. The fence, of course, was locked, followed also by, of course, the fence being cut. The shape of that cut was a giant beehive—and continually patching it became foolish, so the custodian just stopped.

We used the yard facing us because with the building there, balls hit over the fence were retrievable. Hit one over the fence in the adjacent yard, and it ended up in the middle of four-lane Coney Island Avenue, shortly to be hit by a passing car and knocked halfway to Coney Island. Even at only a quarter a pop that became expensive.

Facing the fence was the red brick wall on the north side of the school. Just above where the batter's box would be drawn were heavy-duty iron grates over the first-floor windows. Thus, there was no chance of getting a "gimme" call on a ball that was high. It hit the grate and ricocheted away, cutting down on a lot of arguments.

Thus the game began, not at high noon in the O.K. Corral, but at about five p.m. when few, if any, kids would be in the yard. He was a flame-thrower. I was a junk pitcher—sneaky fast when needed, augmented by a really good curve ball. A Spauldeen could turn someone with strong fingers into the Clem Labine of the neighborhood. You could put such spin on it that it curved about sixteen feet—well, not quite, but you get the idea.

My foe was the Yankee's power hitter, Mickey Mantle. I was the Dodger's scrabble ball hitter, Pee Wee Reese.

First inning, I didn't come close to catching up to his fastball. He, in turn, looked like a corkscrew trying to hit my curve ball. So it went for three or four of the first "regulation" seven innings. Why seven? No idea. Then lightning struck. I hung a curve and he smacked it.1-0.

Inning after inning progressed toward the fateful 7th. In the 7th not so mighty Casey—me—came to bat and sure enough patched together a few scratch hits to tie it up.

The 7th came and went. So did the 8th and the 9th. They were followed by the 10th, 11th, and 12th. It was fall. The sun was setting, and it was getting chilly. It was also getting hard to see, creating a batter's nightmare. But the trash talking became more and more intense—and even if we had to play by the light of the green, Art Deco looking streetlights, this was not going to end in a tie.

By the way, there's a reason why good baseball coaches don't let kids throw curve balls until well into their teens. To throw a curve ball, the wrist is snapped to rotate the ball. This also rotates the forearm, which twists the bicep, which is attached to the shoulder.

Suffice it to say that by inning thirteen, my right forearm felt like hot lead was flowing through it, and also felt like it weighed more than my entire body. I went to the fastball but even if it was getting dark, it wasn't fast enough.

Then one of those things happens which causes a belief that God really does love you.

In the top of the 13th, he hit another one. He was working his mouth pretty good; all seemed lost. The cement turned into mud and I sank into it. I could barely hold the bat much less swing it. But swing it I did and on the first pitch, I blooped one over his head.

Man on first—actually, imaginary man on imaginary first. Then I whiffed twice. Need I go on? Surely, I must, even though this is the stuff of sappy movies.

Down to my last out, and only able to see the ball because it was new and still very pink, I leaned into a fastball and "Holy baseball, Batman!" I hit it.

Thwack!

The ball didn't rise to great heights and disappear onto the roof; rather it flew like a bullet shot from a rifle. A rising line drive, it barely cleared the fence and bounced off the roof of a parked car.

I won and carry that triumph over Mantle in my heart (or ego) to this day.

And my boys? Years later, we played in the other yard. I wound up and threw my oldest, maybe ten, a high, hard one, or the kind of high, hard ones father's throw to their ten-year old sons, and he hit it. Hit it but good. Another rising line drive, it cleared the fence and bounced into Coney Island Avenue. It was before automobile air conditioning was common, so everyone drove with the windows down.

The ball? It hit the street and bounced—right through the driver's side window space and onto the front seat of a passing Oldsmobile.

Lost forever—unlike the memory.

"An independent Brooklyn probably would have built a new stadium for the Dodgers, so today there might be not just baseball but also the only football team on this side of the Hudson."

– Pete Hamill
Columnist, Author

Duncan Yo-Yo's—magic in a box (for some).

Who You Callin' a Yo-Yo?

"TV was a salesperson that lived with you in your house."

There was a time in '50s that unless you didn't have fingers, you had a yo-yo—probably a Duncan. For a quarter or so, you could have two round blocks of wood held together by a peg around which was wrapped a string at whose end was a knotted circle for one's index finger. Oh, for sure, there were all kinds of others, many as gaudy as a rhinestone cowboy, including the one embedded with multi-colored rhinestones, or another model with actual blinking lights, a whirling rainbow it was. But they all did the same thing, the same way. The loop went on the finger, the wrist was snapped downward—except for the experts who turned their wrist upwards and snapped the yo-yo downwards over their finger (show offs!)—the yo-yo descended the string and then magic things happened—or didn't.

I wasn't very good at this. More often than not, down would go the yo-yo and up it would come sideways, like it was fighting to get off the string. Sometimes, I couldn't even get it to go straight down. Not infrequently, it went down and just stayed there with a "screw you" attitude being transmitted up the string to me.

For me, an accomplishment was up and down two or three times in a row. The few times I actually did "cat in the cradle," one of the beginner's tricks, it was a miracle. But that didn't stop me from admiring the skill of others or, more importantly, paying such homage to Mr. and Mrs. Duncan, that I believed that the very next yo-yo I bought would work better than the last, or if I bought a heavier, more substantial (read expensive) yo-yo, I'd have better results. Ah, marketing, making me a real yo-yo.

The yo-yo folks were no yo-yos at marketing. Since the optimal market for yo-yos was the fourth or fifth grader through the eighth grader, once you were in high school you were seen as a yo-yo, if you were still playing with one. That's where the marketing was concentrated. While there would be ads in comic books, and on occasion on TV, the yo-yo folks knew nothing sold yo-yos like great lookin' guys and girls who could do phenomenal things with them right in front of your eyes. You could see what was possible and never thought possible but just not by me. Mind you, that's possible, not probable. Thus, every so often timed with the letting out of school, standing right in front of the school, backed up by blaring dance music, were these great lookin' guys and girls doing amazing things with their yo-yos.

Let us step back a bit so we don't get bopped in the face by one of the masters of maneuvering and remember from whence it all 'cameth'. A Philippino raised in America is credited with the invention of the toy. His name was Pedro Flores and he started a craze, like the crazes that periodically overtake American kids and make their inventors a fortune—hula hoops, pet rocks (remember them?), or those little creatures made out of yarn with big feet and googly eyes? They weighed an ounce and were no more than an inch in diameter. The profit on each was probably 1000%! The word yo-yo itself is Philippino (Tag-a-log) for, (would you believe?) up and down.

Often it is one small stroke of genius that takes something that has been around forever and makes it into a hit, and Mr. Flores had such a light bulb go off in his head. Instead of knotting the string on the post between the two wooden circles, Mr. Flores used a slipknot. This enabled the player to do things such as make the yo-yo "sleep," (spin at the bottom of the string, until it was yanked back up).

According to Wikipedia there are about fifty standard tricks that were popularized with the yo-yo. Remember any of these?

- Sleeper
- Throw down
- Breakaway
- Forward pass
- Flying saucer
- Loop the loop\double or nothing
- Over and under
- Walk the dog
- Man on the flying trapeze
- Rock the baby waterfall
- And, and, and . . .

On average, I could do none of these, or the dozens I decided not to lengthen this story with.

So, there they were, the yo-yo wonders, the epitome of what every boy and girl in school would have a crush on. They looked cool, acted cool, and had magic hands. It was eye-popping to watch. It was like a multi-media show. Yo-yos flying straight out at you, yo-yos blasting off into the sky, yo-yos walking around sideways, yo-yos walking on the sidewalk, yo-yos swinging back and forth/in and out of intricate finger-created designs, under the legs, over the arms— we were not created with enough eyes to watch it all. And when it was over, of course there were packets to be sold containing "the very same yo-yos you just saw the instructors use and instructions for all the tricks that will make you as good with them as we are."

Right.

At the height of the craze, there were national competitions. Sometimes there were special demonstrations—today's equivalent of concerts—at dusk or at night that featured lighted yo-yos. The winners appeared on the popular TV variety shows.

Frankly, it was all designed to amaze, and it did. It did . . . until like many things when you got it home you couldn't get it to go. That feeling followed one through the teen years just like when you realized you could get killed trying to do double or triple jumps with ropes or wished that the hula-hoop was designed to twirl around one's knees or ankles, which is where mine invariably ended up.

For me, though, it was entertainment with a lesson. Not only don't believe everything you read; don't believe everything you see. Madison Avenue was more than a street, it was a heartbreaker. TV was more than entertainment; it was a stationary salesperson that lived with you in your house.

Life's lessons.

But if reading this gives you a flash of nostalgia, you can act on it. The yo-yo is alive and well. Rescued from near oblivion, sales falling to about a half a million nationally, by an old-time, old-fashioned salesman who had retired in the '80s from a lifetime of marketing yo-yos. Sales are now back in the millions for these still made-by-hand, $2.75 marvels. Your grandchildren, or children, are seeing a barrage of yo-yo ads on cable TV children's shows, so now they will relate to the stories you tell them about your yo-yo days. Then you can run down to Walmart, or most any place that sells toys, and have an intergenerational experience scooping up a few different editions that are made and work just like the ones you used.

Now that's a happy ending—until you try a "walk the dog" or "cat in the cradle."

"I don't think people realize how much I love basketball. A lot of people think because of this idiotic comment I made that I love baseball and don't like basketball. Baseball came first because if you grew up in Brooklyn in the 1940s, that was the No. 1 thing. But if you have more than one kid, you love them both."

– Jerry Reinsdorf, Owner,
Chicago White Sox

The Good Humor Truck. It speaks for itself.

When There Was Nothing to Do
We Ate Ice Cream

"The truck was driven by a man with one name—Dave."

It was the sound of bells that not only heralded spring, but which later would be remembered as among the best times of life.

Six bells jangled in unison on the front of that Good Humor ice cream truck. The truck was driven by a man with one name—Dave. We grew up with Dave. He was there spring through summer, until we went to college. Actually, he was still there; it was us who weren't.

There was always money on the table with instructions from Mom in case she missed the Good Humor man (never the ice cream truck, never the ice cream man—always the Good Humor man.) Dave had such a hold on us that eating anyone else's ice cream seemed like it would be a personal affront to him; indeed, taking food from his family's mouths. I guess that's one of the several guilty pleasures of ice cream.

This refrigerator on wheels had two seats and a running board, and while printed boldly on both sides and in the cab was the warning: "No Passengers Allowed," Dave was a sly one and knew how to cement loyalty when a few of us met him at the head of the street. He'd say, "Hop on," and we'd ride down to the end of the block, or until his first customer came out. It was a little thing, but Dave understood that it had a big impact.

Then it was time to make some money. The small, very thick doors would be pulled open and a puff of iced air whooshed out. Depending on whether you wanted a pop, cone, or quart, he'd rummage in one compartment or another and never once did he say, "Nuts, can't find it!" Or, "How 'bout trying this one?" Dave knew his customers and he stocked accordingly.

On one college spring break, I again heard those bells. I was, of course, by then too cool to race down the stairs and beg for a ride. I instead waved to this much older man, now with many fewer teeth, well-yellowed from age (no super-white, super-clean toothpastes yet on the market, no less little strips to hug your teeth into whiteness), and his white always sharply creased Good Humor man uniform seemingly much the worse for wear. Dave would not be long for offering up the joys of spring. Almost all "his kids" were now grown. The neighborhood wasn't the fertile field of drooling mouths it used to be. The spirit was still there; the flesh, however, was giving out.

We reminisced for a bit about what he hoped would be his rise to an eternal spring. We discussed who ate what and how much and where they were now. And he told me how good the spring and summer of the Waldorf Courts of Flatbush Brooklyn were to him. Dave had put four children through college on my insatiable urge for chocolate and my mother's totally incomprehensible addiction to Toasted Almond.

> When the spring came, even the false spring, there were no problems except where to be happiest. The only thing that could spoil a day was people, and if you could keep from making engagements, each day had no limits. People were always the limiters of happiness except for the very few that were as good as spring itself.
>
> ~Ernest Hemingway, *A Moveable Feast*

Dave, the bringer of spring, was one of those few.

"I could do nothing but Brooklyn shows for the rest of my career, and I could die ignorant."

– Anthony Bourdain
Internationally famous
"foodie" and food reviewer

"I knew what the Dodgers uniform represented as a kid growing up in Brooklyn."

– Joe Torre

Says Who?
(The *Bar Mitzvah*)

"Someone actually gave me a Bible . . . can you imagine?"

You will find several directives throughout to whip out a copy of a textbook by Sigmund Freud. This would be a good time to grab one. When I finished the content for this book—I realized nothing was said about my *bar mitzvah*.

For you uninitiated, the *bar mitzvah*, or later in time, the *bat mitzvah* for girls, and the *b'nai mitzvah* for when the ceremony contains two people, is the rite of passage from boyhood to manhood. Most kids read too much into that. They think it means what it says. It doesn't. Even in the 1600s no one in their right mind thought a thirteen-year-old was a man—entitled to the rights and privileges of manhood. Not even the law thought that let alone a mother or father. Yet, traditionally, one got a fountain pen, a slap on the back, and was told, "Today you are a man."

I still haven't figured it out. "Says who?"

Actually, the *bar mitzvah* is more about obligation than entitlement; it's a religious obligation. Now the celebrant is expected to know the commandments and follow them, to study the *Torah* and *Talmud* and put them into the living of one's life. It would be easier for the celebrant if preparations all started with a simple explanation of a *bar mitzvah*. It means son of the commandments. *Bat mitzvah* means daughter of the commandments. That doesn't sound like freedom or entitlement to me.

About 90% of American Jews begin *bar/bat mitzvah* study eighteen months in advance of the date being set. About 10%, roughly the number of Orthodox Jews in America, begin study around three, or sooner if you count environment. The student learns history, culture, Hebrew, and how to read the *Torah* with an emphasis on the portion the child will read on his/her big day. Frankly, unless you begin at three, to use a little Brooklyn vocabulary, learning Hebrew is a ball-buster, and most kids end up reading a transliteration, Hebrew written in English.

For the grandparents, there is real meaning in this rite of passage. For the kid, it is a payday with a party. I know of, and have attended parties where, the costs exceeded six figures, some by a lot. In Miami, a Cuban Jewish father rented out the gone-but-never-forgotten Orange Bowl Stadium, and at the end of the ceremony, had hundreds of white doves released into the air. A bit much, if you ask me.

On the other hand, Groucho Marx said his father bought one suit for the first *bar mitzvah* and each of the following four boys wore it. But Gentiles had Sweet Sixteens and Hispanics had *Quinceañeras* (Sweet Fifteens), and at Mafia weddings there was the "envelope," so Jews had to have something. No? The party was to bring the family together in celebration of this child who couldn't wait to get the service over with.

And that included mine. Like most second-generation Jews, my dad was brought up Orthodox and ended up marrying someone who wasn't, so he was an Orthodox Jew who read Hebrew by rote without understanding much of what it meant, and attended the liberal, Reform synagogue that was socially a much better fit for his wife.

My brother's *bar mitzvah* had much more meaning to me than my own. His rabbi had contracted Multiple Sclerosis and by the time of the ceremony was so crippled by it that his insistence on running the service was heroic. The guest speaker was a rabbinic firebrand who really spoke to my insides about human rights and Jewish law.

I, on the other hand, became *bar mitzvah* at one of the most liberal synagogues in Brooklyn. Architecturally, it was grand, outside and in. It had, I believe, five floors, and on one of them it had—

get this—a swimming pool. In my time of study, I never got to the part of the *Torah* that spoke about swimming pools, unless maybe I missed some underlying meaning from the Great Flood, but I'm pretty sure Noah was told to build an Ark not a pool.

It did make me giggle because a popular comedian of the day, Myron Cohen, told the story of his friend who hit it big in business, bought an estate, and on it built three swimming pools. When asked, "Why three?" he replied, "Some of my friends like to swim in cold water, so in that one I've got for them cold water. In the middle, is one for my friends who like to swim only in warm water. That one's got only warm." "And the third?" asked his friend. "Well, some of my friends don't like to swim at all, so that one is for them."

Ba da boom.

That pretty much tells the story of the synagogue swimming pool. Excess.

There was in New York a law that gave us religionists a special place in school life. It was called "released time." For students taking religious study who could not get to their house of worship by the time class started, their teachers were instructed to release them early. Hence, released time. I had to take two trains to my swimming-pooled synagogue and left school an hour early on Wednesdays.

Like everything in Brooklyn, you had to find a way to game the system. In Hebrew school, it was becoming a go-fer. Anytime the teacher needed something, like "AV" equipment, you wanted to be the one to get it. In doing so, you always managed to make it take a little longer than it should, then it had to be set up, and of course someone had to return it. You could miss a fair amount of class that way.

I went Wednesdays and Sundays. In a total of four and a half hours, I learned five thousand years of Jewish law, history, culture, and this very foreign language that went with it.

Not.

Came the first Saturday in March, we all woke up to a snowstorm, the kind where the flakes are as big as sheets of paper and weigh more. My dad was afraid the car wouldn't make it to Temple; my mom was afraid the guests wouldn't make it to the party. Both worries were unnecessary.

All I remember of my *bar mitzvah* was the end where the rabbi blessed the celebrants. He intoned how a student as good and serious as I would surely know the importance of continuing with his studies and taking confirmation class. I was giggling. It was over. The party was booked in the ballroom (if it had a swimming pool, the synagogue certainly would have a ballroom, no?) and everybody showed up. I got two special presents along with mostly checks and savings bonds. One was neat, the other . . . well, I'll tell you.

My party had a real distinction. My accordion and piano teacher also played in, and booked, bands. Making a living just from teaching kids like me wasn't making much of a living. A few days before the *bar mitzvah*, the saxophone player got sick. It seems that my teacher, Sam, had done a very famous sax player a very big favor that put him on track to become very famous. His name was Stubby Kaye. He was on Broadway and in Hollywood movies. Stubby, his nickname, fit him marvelously. On his fourth finger on his right hand he wore a serving platter. Actually, it was a ring that said, "Stubby" on it, but it was big. Thus, through the influence of God and Mother Nature, everyone was able to go home and tell their friends they had been in the presence of greatness. And they didn't mean me.

The other present? Someone gave me a Bible. For my *bar mitzvah!* Can you imagine?

*"I was bused to a school in
Gerritsen Beach in Brooklyn in
1972. I was one of the first black
kids in the history of the school."*

– Chris Rock, Comedian

"Brooklyn was the most wonderful city a man could play in, and the fans there were the most loyal there were."

– Pee Wee Reese

Murder!!

"Some mistakes you don't get to make twice."

Some kids are bad seeds, they just are. In my neck of Brooklyn, we had fewer than one might find in other parts. Here is a stark example about someone whose name I'm not sure I knew even back then. Why? He came literally and figuratively from the other side of the tracks. He wasn't the kind of kid that my kind of kid should have known well enough to know his name.

One day, I was out on a hall pass. I was returning to class and I passed him in the hall. He did not have a hall pass; I did not mention that to him. For reasons I can't imagine though, I said to him, "Where ya headed?" because he seemed to be headed towards the door and school wasn't over. I tried to make it conversational as opposed to adversarial. To my surprise he responded. To my greater surprise was what he responded.

"Goin' home to shoot my mother." He said it matter-of-factly, pushed open the door and vanished.

The next day in the size headline the *New York Daily News* or *Mirror* was famous for was an article that headlined, "Student Kills Mother." I was amazed. Now, I'd been angry at my mother many times for many things; you've already read that. It never once crossed my mind to shoot her; we even had a rifle in the house. Who shoots his mother? Well, according to the article, he did.

He left school early to assure that he was home before she returned from work. He moved the couch so that the seating-area faced towards the front door. He set up behind it using the hard back of the couch as a gun mount. She walked in the door and he shot her. Just like that. Bang, you're dead! Why? Who knows? I guess he didn't like her.

This was a long time before anyone routinely shot people in our neighborhood. A 'Columbine' hadn't happened, so there were no teams of crisis counselors who rushed to school, no private rooms for anyone to talk out anything. The next day we all just went to school.

Same thing after one of our teachers hanged himself. He was a very popular social studies teacher who was a Korean War veteran. Frankly, I really liked him and developed my love for the subject matter because of the way he loved it and presented it. I could have used someone to talk to about how I felt, especially the first day after we were told he was no longer there, wouldn't be again, and we were met by a substitute. Looking back on it, it was treated like "one of those things." We had a moment of silence, and then it was, "on with the game."

Another example? I've talked much about the subway at the end of the street. I've mentioned that every so often a Spauldeen would beat us down the block and roll through the iron spikes onto the tracks. Every so often we didn't have a replacement, or a quarter to buy one, so we'd go get them. One of us would watch to the right, another to the left, and a third would mount the fence, drop down on the other side and get the balls. It is hard to describe being somewhere you shouldn't and knowing a misstep could be fatal. Nervous and alone are two words I'd choose. Scared is another. We were schooled in "third rails," so we knew where it was, what it looked like, what it could do to you, which was fry you like a potato, and if a ball was under it to leave it be. The excitement of doing something really dangerous, and something we knew we'd get our heads handed to us at home if anyone saw us was a real adrenaline rush.

But that wasn't the only train. About five blocks up Rugby Road, just past Avenue H, was "the cut." It was where the Long Island Railroad freight line ran under the street. At that point the subway rose up and the freight tracks dropped into a track-lined cut in the ground about thirty or forty feet below the street. One could stand on the sidewalk and look down at the network of tracks, the overhanging electric power lines, the steep embankments from behind homes and apartments down to those tracks littered with debris—and the bold, unmistakable, red, DANGER signs that warned KEEP OFF! Watching the sometimes hundred-car freights roll by, making the ground rumble, pulled by double diesel locomotives, feeling the warning horns rattle your ribs as the train rumbled underneath you, you knew you were facing a powerful monster that made the subway seem like a toy train.

And yet, every so often someone would take the dare, defy the signs, and work his (always guys) way down the embankment to the tracks. Why? Probably the same reason as the chicken crossed the road. It was very gutsy—and very stupid. Again, came a headline this time announcing that three students, whom we all knew, but didn't know, again for economic and geographic reasons, had decided to become legends. Did they ever.

Knowing that to slip on the embankment and pitch forward uncontrollably unto the tracks could mean certain death, they decided to use a stick to plant into the ground with each step to steady and brace themselves. But it wasn't a stick they chose. It was a long piece of rebar separated from blocks of cement that had been thrown down the embankment who knows when. The middle boy held the "stick." The other two, flanking him, held on to him for dear life. They did their best imitation of mountain goats, jumping from this spot to that, trying to clear the piles of obstacles on the embankment.

Holding on for their lives caused their deaths.

Suddenly the center boy caught a toe on something. As he pitched forward, two things happened at once and happened in an instant. He reflexively threw up his arm for balance. The other two grabbed him tighter. The arm holding the rebar struck a power line sending tens of thousands of volts of electricity, enough to power a freight train, through him. And through him to the others. The papers described that their shoes shot off their feet and their clothing burned on their bodies, along with their skin.

If memory serves, one died. The other two were burned horribly and were in the hospital for months. They eventually returned to school—in wheelchairs, as multiple amputees. Again, no counselors. We had to draw our own conclusions. One was: Sometimes you need to believe what you read. Another was: Some mistakes you don't get to make twice.

"My life! That's a long story, too. I was born in Brooklyn, New York, like half of the world, I think."

– Erik Larson
Journalist and Author of
Non-fiction Books including
Five *NY Times* Best Sellers

NYU Dental Class preparing for charity work.
Uncle Irv is dead center, my father is lower right.

It Wasn't A Very Good Year

My catching career was over—at twelve."

Some things just aren't funny, or even cute. These two qualify—momentous but not in the least funny.

Let me start in the middle. It was a fastball. I was the catcher. My pitcher threw incredibly hard for his age, twelve. The batter took a good rip. I can still hear the "tick" of the bat just catching the ball. The next thing I remember was my head feeling like it wasn't atop my shoulders. My mouth felt funny, not funny ha-ha but odd, warm, and sticky. Dazed, I stood up, looked down and saw a torrent of red spread out across my grey uniform. I just stood there. Nothing seemed to work; I couldn't move. I was a bleeding cigar store Indian. As I looked around the infield, I saw my teammates pointing and yelling. I heard nothing. The third base coach was racing towards me. As he reached out, my knees gave way.

Now let's start at the beginning. I always thought being a catcher was cool. I knew those who wore the so-called "tools of ignorance" were usually the smartest baseball minds on the diamond. And one of my all-time, favorite ballplayers was a catcher, Roy Campanella ("Campy" to his mates and fans). As wide as he was high, he moved with the speed of a large tank, except behind the plate where he was as quick as a cat. He had a rifle for an arm, the accuracy of using a sniper's scope, and when he swung at a ball with his considerable rear end behind the bat, the ball travelled with the trajectory of a pistol shot—flat and fast. Campy also could curse with the best of 'em. He could string together epithets faster than most people could move their mouths, but he could also calm a pitcher like a horse-whisperer quieted a restless stallion.

I was the camp team's catcher. We had a good team. One of the advantages of having made the team is we got to travel, in the style of the lowest ranking minor leaguers, to other camps. Except one day, that day—the day of the blood—was different. We were playing a charity camp located on an island in the middle of Lake Winnipesaukee, one of the largest lakes within the borders of a single state in the union. The bus took us to the boat. The boat took us to the camp.

Other than our gloves, we didn't take much; the home team provided the equipment. The counselors didn't make the connection—charity camp, economically disadvantaged kids, they provide the equipment? Uh-oh. I walked out of the dugout with a chest protector about three times as thick as my sweatshirt, and a catcher's mask that wasn't for baseball. It was for softball, meaning that the space laterally across the mask was much wider than it would have been for a baseball mask, a softball being about three times the circumference of a baseball. The mask was also twice as old as I was. It seemed to be held together by spit and a prayer.

Both failed.

There was a man on, two outs. I called for a fastball, good ole number 1. My battery mate launched it. The batter swung, the ball hit the mask exactly in the too-large space forcing the top half upward, the bottom half downward. With little loss of momentum, the ball hit me square in the mouth, and as the metal came apart, a piece of it sliced open my lower lip inside my mouth down to where if it went any further it would have come out through the lip above the chin. All this I learned later. Right then as I said, I was too busy bleeding to bother with play-by-play analysis.

There are two key factors to remember. The first: we are on an island. The nearest hospital was a boat ride and car ride away. The second: my father was a dentist.

I recall towels, lots of them, packed with ice, turning red like someone was pouring Home Depot's red paint shelf on them. The ice looked like the ice one would see in the old-time butcher store, red with blood. There was no stretcher. Two counselors grabbed me under the armpits and walked/ran/stumbled me along the path to the lake. They lay me down and the next thing I felt was the thrust of the boat. It shot away from the dock with such force that I thought I was going to roll out the back into the lake. No such luck.

An ambulance was waiting on shore and I was whisked off to the emergency room. By now, ice notwithstanding, my face was blowing up like a balloon, and what wasn't red was turning black and blue. They took X-rays. My jaw wasn't fractured. But they didn't stitch me up, saying it was more likely that the wound would become infected if they did. The result was that as the wound began to heal and pull my lip pieces back together, I couldn't open my mouth very wide and was on a liquid diet pretty much for the rest of the summer.

I was the camp hero.

Lincoln used to tell the story of the reporter who offended the political powers in town. He was tarred and feathered and run out of town on a rail. Another enterprising reporter interviewed him at the end of this happening. "How was it?" The response was, "Well, except for the notoriety, I could have done without the experience." That pretty much covers how I felt about my hero status.

The next day, I was taken to the town dentist. He X-rayed my mouth and said all was well. Remember #2? Daddy was a dentist. The camp had called my folks immediately and they jumped in the car and made due haste to New Hampshire. He was handed the X-ray by the camp director, held it up to the sky, and began sounding more like Campy than Dad. Without the X-ray, in just the sunlight, he could see the crack in the tooth and the coming need for a root canal when my face healed. How did the 'townee' miss it? He didn't. Well, he did, but apparently, he was paid to.

Daddy was a dentist not a businessman. He was outraged at the ethical violations and hired a lawyer to make a point beyond almost eating the dentist for lunch when he finally got to confront him. He settled for $5,000, which in the '50s I guess was a lot but even in the '50s, that tooth probably could have paid for college.

I am left with a scar on the inside of my lower lip, an implant front tooth behind my upper lip and a not too funny story to tell about both. Oh yes, and I was never able to squat behind the plate without turning blue with fear. My catching career was over—at twelve.

That same year, something began that made me think my life might be over. It started with a small acne-like pimple—except in was on the tip of my right forefinger. It was painful, hot, and quickly on the move up (down?) my finger towards my wrist. Off to the doctor we went.

He didn't like what he saw. He did a culture; I had a staph infection in my blood. He had to operate leaving me with a gauze drain hanging from the front of my finger that had to be soaked religiously in hot saltwater while I took copious amounts of antibiotics—which did not work.

Within months, my right thumb showed the same symptoms, only this time I ended up in the hospital because the entire nail had to be removed surgically in order to clean out the infection. I was again left with my own SOS flag hanging from a finger. It was now determined that because the infection was in my blood there really was no way to know when and where it would pop up. A different round of antibiotics was prescribed. They too didn't work. A few months later, the symptoms showed up on my lower lip. Early teens were not a good time for my lower lip.

I am not sure why what happened next had to happen. I needed emergency surgery because the one pimple on my lip became two, and three and then four. My lower lip was so full of puss it hung down making me look like a Ubangi tribesman. The medical team was afraid to inject the area with Novocaine because if it leaked into the wrong place it could travel to my brain. That would leave me senseless, a state my mother often said was natural for me. Nor could they put an ether mask on me because well . . . they had to operate on my mouth. A horror movie could have been filmed from what came next.

Two medical personnel held me on the operating table by my arms. Another pressed down on my shoulders while my father restrained my head. The surgeon then proceeded to slit my lip from end to end and then squeeze out a totally amazing amount of green and yellow shit while I screamed and writhed in excruciating pain. This time I was left with four drains. Hanging from my lip, they made me look like a miniature flag football team that had put the flags on the wrong side of the body.

I needn't walk you through all dozen or more operations. My favorite, again done in the hospital, was the one just above my knee. It was so deep that when the drain came out, I could see my leg bone. It was finally decided that the only way to stem the tide before one of these pimples would pop up in a dangerous or even lethal place was to culture the infection and make "The Gralnick Vaccine." This was pretty cutting-edge stuff for the late '50s. It was an exciting day when the call came that the serum was ready. We went to the surgeon's office and he injected me with myself. And son-of-a-gun—it worked!

I was a footnote in some medical journal and like Lincoln's story told above, except for all the happy doctors, I could have well done without the experience.

"I came up in Brooklyn singing doo-wop music from the time I was 13 to the time I was 20. That music served a purpose of keeping a lot of people out of trouble, and also it was a passport from one neighborhood to another."

– Richie Havens
Musician, Singer

Section Four

The Gralnicks, a Fain, and a Feinstein after Jeff's Bar Mitzvah.

Free Time Introduction

"Did they do good things . . . ?
Did they do bad things . . . ? Yes. Yes."

One doesn't go to school all the time; it only seems like it. There are weekends, holidays, and the summer. We can extract summer because for one part of life that was spent with the family. The other summers were spent going to summer camp.

Summer camp, for those lucky enough to be able to afford it, especially eight weeks of it, comes when two realities arrive at the same time. The first is the parents' reality that another 365 days straight of parenting is likely going to result in something bad happening. The second is the child's reality that another 365 days straight of being parented is likely going to result in something bad happening. The search for a summer camp arrives. Because it can be such a unique experience, it gets its own section.

Here we deal with free time. What do kids do after school, besides homework? What occupies their minds? In the days when the only things that were electric were appliances, what did kids do with their time? Did they do good and productive things? Did they do bad and unproductive things? Yes. Yes.

Read on.

A Red Ryder BB Rifle—every boy's dream.

Red Ryder, Red Ryder

"Suddenly we realized that all the preacher's garage windows were gone."

Ah, the days of so-called yesteryear, when the must-have holiday or birthday present was the Red Ryder BB gun. Yes, there were pretenders to the throne:

- Duncan yo-yos.
- GI Joes.
- Lionel trains

But a "real man" wanted a Red Ryder. Red Ryder was a marketing machine:

- Ads were in every comic book.
- Cowboys hawked them on TV shows.
- Large newspaper ads showed up prior to the holidays.
- And what better gift than a rifle for a generation that revered cowboys, loved cowboys using rifles to kill Indians, and that played "Cowboys and Indians" in the streets for hours on end?

Red Ryders were touted as gateways to hunting, an easy and safe way to learn to shoot and even bag a few small critters right there in the backyard. Everyone wanted one, including me.

A lot of kids got one—not me.

Actually, in Brooklyn, BB guns weren't such hot items. "Bad kids" sometimes had them, but BB guns were more a country thing than a city thing. In Brooklyn, you saw more real guns than BB guns.

Then one day a BB gun came to Waldorf Court. It caused such havoc in such a short time that the parents who gave it to their kid, in turn, unceremoniously "ungave" it, and it was never to be seen again.

For the first few days, my brother and his friend, George, the bad boy recipient of this bad boy gun, could be found in George's driveway lying prone on the cement and target shooting at makeshift target-holding boxes. In retrospect, the fact that the targets were in boxes was something I should have internalized but didn't.

A BB exiting the muzzle makes an unmistakable sound. There is no bang; there is no pop. There isn't even a whoosh of air. The sound is *thit, thit.*

The other unmistakable sound is made by the BBs themselves rolling up and down the muzzle holder when the angle of the gun shifts. That clattering, as the BB soldiers march up and down waiting their turn at immortality, is a universally recognized sound.

But let's be honest. How long is target shooting going to hold an adolescent's attention?

Not long.

Sure, one can shoot prone, off of one knee, or standing. But after a while, thit and the sound of the BB hitting the target became, well . . . boring. More and greater targets had to be found. George and my brother found them.

First it was beetles, large bugs, birds, and squirrels. The first two were also boring because if you didn't put the muzzle up to the bug, the chances of hitting it were about zero. Birds were boring because they just sat in the tree and laughed at you as the errant steel balls flew high and wide, or bounced off of intervening leaves and branches. The air currents would override the power of the air gun and the BB would sail like a knuckle ball. But it was sad when, on that rare occasion, a bird was hit and injured. The worst was the one or two times a bird was actually killed. That's when people began to talk, and also the thrill began to wear off.

There's no one more annoying, or who drew more suspicions about secrets unkept, than a little brother. One day when I walked over to the "shooting range" I heard my fate under discussion. In my jealousy of being deprived of having or using the gun, I had ratted on my brother and his friend. Or so the crime thesis went.

I hadn't—but dead birds do indeed talk. I was to be punished by the Sundance kids.

Little did I know, my alleged tattling punishment was to be that I would be crowned the next great target. Instead of when the hard-ass cowboy in old westerns would say to the tenderfoot, "Dance, or I'll blow yer head off!" I was told to run.

It didn't take two seconds for me to learn a law of physics: you can't outrun a BB. Two of the little buggers homed in on my butt, and no buts about it, they stung like someone had inserted a hot pin into my rear end. It stung enough to bring tears to my eyes—a lot of tears.

So that's part one. It ends with me being shot and ridiculed, shown no mercy, and left to cry.

Part two is a story of revenge born of unintended consequences.

There was a Baptist minister who lived around the corner but whose backyard was adjacent to ours. His name was Rev. Chadwise but of course we called him "Mister."

On Sunday mornings, he would open his kitchen window, prop the radio on the sill, and blast church services in the hopes that we Jews would learn something about the future of our fate, if we didn't get with the program, literally and figuratively.

He was a mean son-of-a-gun who had a real shotgun and who would terrorize anyone caught cutting through his weed-choked backyard. And God help you if you picked up a fallen peach from his always pregnant peach tree that stood tall in his field of weeds. If you stood in his backyard, you looked across ours, and beyond ours, you looked across into George's. The geography is important.

One late afternoon, my friend Sandy and I filched the BB gun from George's garage. We set up targets on the chain-link fence—no boxes, just targets. We would now have the fun.

We spent what seemed like hours "thitting" away. In retrospect, we did remember hearing a tinkling sound off in the distance, but we were having too much fun to pay much attention—until we went to collect the targets. Remember the geography. As we unhooked the targets, we were looking from George's backyard, across mine, and right at the Rev's garage.

"Oh no, Joe, say it ain't so!" All the preacher's garage windows were gone. Suddenly, we knew what that tinkling sound was.

Our stomachs dropped, and mouths became instantly dry. We replaced the gun, and with quaking knees, made a clean getaway— at least until about 9 p.m. when there came a rap-rap-rapping at our front door.

It was the preacher and from his mouth poured the proverbial hellfire and brimstone. Justice was demanded and justice was received. My mother dragged my brother front and center and said, "Did you do this?"

"No!" he yelled.

Crack went the sound of my mother's hand hitting my brother's face." Don't you lie to me, Jeffrey Gralnick! (In moments of ire why do parent's think their children have to be reminded of their last names?) Did you do it?"

"No," repeated my brother. Crack!

And so it went until my brother was beaten, my mother's hand hurt, and the pastor was sated. I lay in bed, under the covers, guilty but realizing nothing tastes so good as revenge served warm.

I must tell you, on that night long ago, my sore rear end somehow felt better, and I fell asleep smiling.

"I have been down and out, living in Brooklyn, no money even for a subway, no food whatsoever. Like, I remember just sitting in my room all day—even my television wasn't working!"

– Viola Davis
Award Winning Star of
Stage and Screen

The "Waldorf Courtians" and others mixed in, Bill's Bar Mitzvah party
Union Temple, Brooklyn.

Games People Played

"All you needed was a Spauldeen."

In a comment to a friend, my wife described my sports viewing habits this way: "If it has a ball and the ball moves, he'll watch it."

Not quite.

But close enough.

No wonder though, considering most all the games I grew up with involved a ball. Beyond the obvious—baseball, basketball, football—there was:

- Box ball
- Penny ball
- Fluke ball
- Stoop ball
- Punch ball
- Stickball

There was one that didn't have a ball at all; we'll get to it later.

In my neighborhood, one was never at a loss for something to do so long as someone had the ubiquitous, round, pink ball known in some parts of Brooklyn as a "pinkie" and in my neighborhood as a Spauldeen. Except for stickball, it was all you needed for that whole column of games above.

Box ball was like tennis with no court, no racquet, and no tennis ball. Other than that, they were exactly alike . . . Three "boxes"—translated that's three sections of cement sidewalk—were marked off. One kid stood on the line of one; the other faced him on the other side. Using a hand, one volleyed and served, sliced and dropped—endlessly. The only catch was that each return had to bounce somewhere in the middle box.

Penny ball was low-end gambling. In this game, the battle took place using two boxes. A penny, dime, or quarter was placed on the center line and one had to hit it with the ball. It could be a cruel game. Hitting the coin wasn't enough. Unless it made some perceptible movement, it didn't count as having been hit even if it looked like you'd hit the coin dead center. Hence you could hit the coin and lose your money. Easy? Try it.

Back to three boxes (you can see how we were all math geniuses by the end of elementary school). Fluke ball was micro-baseball. One "pitched" by tossing the ball into the center box. One batted by smashing the ball with an open hand, but back through the center box where it had to be fielded by the other guy. Each bounce before capture represented a base. If it got past the fielder after it bounced in the center box, it was a home run. Winners had to have good hands and good reflexes.

Another reason it wasn't a one-pitch game was the amazing things one could do with a Spauldeen, if one's fingers were strong enough. "Pitching" was a real art. One could create fastballs, a "drop and stop," a curve/screwball/knuckleball. Like any good baseball pitcher, one always tossed with the same motion. Each of us had two or three pitches that were our aces in the hole. Their "action" all depended on how hard you squeezed the ball and where. These factors put different kinds of "English" (why English and not German or Senegalese, I don't know) on the ball. I've seen fastballs jump forward at twice the speed with which they first hit the ground. I've seen balls with so much reverse spin on them virtually stop in midair.

The batter positioned himself on the balls of his feet and tried to guess what was coming. It was possible to make someone look really foolish when the right pitch and wrong guess coincided. Foolish to the extent of totally wiffing on a pitch. Foolish to the extent of swinging so hard one could end up on the cement.

Truth be told, these were the minor league games. The majors began with stoop ball. A stoop is the staircase—usually cement or brick—the walkway to the small landing to one's front door. If one faced the stoop, Spauldeen in hand, and threw it at the steps, it would fly off into the "field" (better known as the street) where the opposing team (better known as the other guy) would try to catch it. Hits were catalogued by bounces. The ball had to pass the sidewalk, after that, one bounce was a single, two a double, three a triple. An uncaught fly ball over the fielder's head was a home run.

In retrospect, two things stand out. First, is the precision it took to get the desired results. Depending on where the ball hit the stoop created the results, often frustratingly poor. It wasn't strength; it was a combination of physics and geometry. Throwing the ball full force often produced puny results. If you hit the middle of a step the ball would bounce off the one below. That was a strike or an out depending on the rules you were playing. The stoop was an unforgiving help-mate. Do it right, it did wonders for you; wrong and you were out.

Key to the strategy was when to go for the "pointer." The pointer was where the vertical bricks met the horizontal ones creating a horizontal edge across the stoop. There was no point at all, but then again, I don't ever remember anyone asking, "Hey, why's it called a pointer and not an edger?" Hit the edge just right the ball would travel amazing distances; a sure spot onto the edge and a home run was virtually guaranteed, short of a Willie Mays fielding play. The brilliant players could cross their bodies with their pitch, hitting the pointer on the other side of their body, thus making the ball fly off into right field instead of center or left. It was foolproof—so long as you remembered to duck! Nothing made you look more like an idiot than to stand there and get hit in the face from the results of your own strategy.

How could a parent complain? Geometry, physics, and chess. Doesn't seem like a waste of time to me . . . . And yet they did. Mostly from the foul balls that went backwards into the door instead forward into the street. Some of those doors were glass storm doors, and some of those foul balls shattered them. Maybe, after all, they did have a case . . . .

Another math teaser was punch ball. Depending on the ages, there were usually two players but sometimes three. One marked off two "sewers" (spelt sewers but pronounced sue-wahs) or three on the street.

Why punch ball was called punch ball was a no-brainer. One punched the ball instead of slapping it or hitting it. No math involved in this one.

There were two standard ways of "hitting." One served the ball up high like in a tennis serve, and punched it overhand on its way down, or bounced it on the cement and hit it side arm on its way up. Each had its rationale. If you were strong and long armed, overhand was your choice. The ball went far—except when it didn't. Miss it and you looked like an oaf. Miss your angle and you were an easy out.

Us side-handers had much more versatility to overcome a lack of hi-test behind the hit. The ball could be more easily placed, hit "where they ain't," or lined solidly over the infielder's head (when three were playing). Yet, we were rarely big hit threats and if we fell behind, we side-armers, we usually stayed behind.

Punch ball was often played with bases, maybe a chalk mark or stone mark on the curbs, and a sewer as second base. This then required running. And if you got a hit, then what? There weren't other team members. The runners after the first batter became imaginary and moved—or not—according to what you did as the next batter. Confused? Simple. Two real players; the rest was imagination. The rules were pretty standard. There was rarely any bloodletting during a game, unless of course one tripped chasing a ball or running the bases. Cement is not a forgiving surface.

The granddaddy of these games was stickball. That's why it got its own chapter.

But what of the no-ball game? I don't remember what it was called. I do remember how it was played. Remember those baseball cards I stole from the Russian? Well, we, on occasion, bought some as well. Our collections grew. Some cards were rarer than others. We knew Topps put in a lot of cards of newer or so-so players and fewer cards of the greats. This game was a variation of marbles. By gambling on your skill, you could win the other guy's cards, which sometimes contained ones you really wanted for your collection.

All one needed for this game was a wall and some cards. There were two variations. One was the match game. You'd hold a card between your four fingers on one edge and thumb on the other. The arm would go back. On the forward motion you'd let go. We believed there was a strategy to this, that letting the card go at a certain point on the swing forward would produce a landing that was face up or down. Garbage. Anyway, the point was, the second player had to match the first, front facing up or back facing up. If he did, he got the cards; if he didn't, he didn't get the cards.

The second variation was the exciting one. You needed a wall for this one. You'd hold the card on its tip between thumb and forefinger, and, kneeling about twenty feet from the wall, you'd flip it. The object was to skim it low enough that it skimmed the ground but didn't hit it, yet not high enough that it would pick up a draft and flip over before it got to the wall. If you had the right touch, the card either hit the wall softly enough to stop, not bounce off, and come to a rest touching it. Rarely could players produce leaners. These cards got to the wall and a few inches before contact tipped up and came to rest leaning against the wall. Leaners were awesome. If it were a toucher, in order to win, the next guy either had also to produce a toucher; that was a tie. To win he had to knock over the leaner or produce his own, again for a tie.

Mindless? These games produced the heat of a Harlem dice game. It was that heat that etched them into the memory bank.

"*I am not Jewish and I am not from Brooklyn, but the tales in this book make me think that as youngsters, regardless of race, creed, or color, we were all the same.*"

– A.J. Catanese, Ph.D., FAICP
President Emeritus, Florida
Atlantic University and Florida
Institute of Technology

The Fire

"The building sounded like it was in pain."

Why do little children have such amazing memories?

The likely reason is that there's not very much otherwise clogging up those developing brains. Any schedule-like thing is taken care of by parents, leaving the primary memory concern the location of a favorite toy.

When a child, I saw some things that are as fresh in my memory as if each happened yesterday. In pondering them, one tops the charts: the fire.

But I get ahead of myself.

Researchers have confirmed that young children can, and do, remember, i.e., I told you I remember with clarity the day our German shepherd, Salty, was taken because of my mother's allergies. She became a guide dog—Salty, that is—not Mildred, my mother.

I remember hugging that big, soft, and hairy neck. My parents later pooh-poohed: "You were too young. You're remembering what you heard us talk about."

Wrong, say current researchers, discovering evidence that demonstrates that children can have very early memories, especially of dramatic or traumatic events; for me, Salty's departure was both.

I remember the first time I saw the connections sparking on the wires when I rode on a trolley car in Brooklyn. That, and when coupled with the trolley bells, was a clearly memorable event—so much so for apparently many people that the bells became the subject—as mentioned—of a popular song: *"Clang, clang, clang went the trolley . . ."*

And it was in this neighborhood some years later where burned the fire.

It was a bitter cold and snowy winter's day during Christmas break. The streets were slick, and the sky was a forbidding, dark gray. Dusk approached. The sounds of sirens could be heard from blocks away—and when those sounds got louder and louder that meant the suspected fire was closer and closer.

Curious, we drifted out of our houses on this nasty, Saturday afternoon. Now we could not only smell the smoke, we could see it. It was rising into the sky, way higher than the housetops, visible from far and wide. We pinpointed the fire. With that realization, all of us took off at a run. It was on Avenue H, only three blocks away.

The fire scene rivaled anything ever seen on TV. Huge, black waves of smoke poured from every orifice in the building. People were hanging out of windows. Bricks had fallen out of this eight-story apartment house and smoke was actually coming out of what here-to-fore had been—well, a solid brick wall.

And the roof. "OMG!" as it would be texted today.

Pillars of fire seemed to be standing on top of the building. As it burned, the building was like a Rice Krispies box that had been part of a Japanese horror movie. There was snapping and crackling and popping. The building sounded like it was in pain.

Men in large, rubber jackets and swept-back, black hats had put up a line to keep all the freezing gawkers at a safe distance. Alarm after alarm was called in, until the fire became the storied five-alarmer.

Yes, it was awe-inspiring to see the ladders go up on the walls and firemen bring people down to safety. Yes, it was breathtaking to see circular nets held out for people to jump into.

That's worth saying again—circular nets held out for people to jump into.

Yes, it was frightening to see and hear the windows shatter from heat so intense it could be felt hundreds of yards away. But the most distinct memory is about the fighting of the fire itself.

The hoses poured water onto and into the building. As soon as the liquid hit the building, it turned to ice. The building was soon decorated with two- and three-story long icicles. To this day how that happened in a blazing fire I don't know—but there it was ice:

- On the walls.
- On the cars that hadn't been moved.
- And on the trees along the sidewalk.
- Ice floes had formed on the street a half inch thick or thicker.

As we watched, those patterns changed constantly because more and more water shot out of the hoses onto the building and in turn changed the flows. The street itself became a skating rink. Fire truck tires were encased in ice. The firemen were slipping, sliding, and cursing while lugging hoses, or racing with entry-creating-hatchets from one place to another.

Fires don't just end. Like in a fireplace, they sort of die out. Eventually, the flames became smaller followed by less intense heat, and the fire finally was under control.

At that point, we realized how unspeakably cold we were—unspeakably because our faces were numb, and we couldn't speak. It was like trying to talk after the dentist had shot you up with Novocain. So we went home.

Once a normal corner in a normal neighborhood, the next morning the corner of Avenue H and Rugby Road looked like a war zone. And there stood the old apartment building broken, battered, and charred, with big, black scars of soot reaching eerily in random directions. But for a few men to fight possible flare-ups, most all the firefighters were gone. Left behind was dirty, black ice that had gobbled unto itself pieces of the building, pieces of people's clothing, a child's toy.

That was sixty years ago, give or take. Tell me again children don't remember.

*You've heard of the Three Musketeers. Here are the five Gralnicks—
Al, Pauline, Frieda, Abe, and Irving.*

The Dogs, and Duck, of My Life

***"It didn't seem to know which direction it
wanted to go, so it went in all of them."***

It took years for the curse of the famous allergist to be broken. Years went by after Salty left and another dog came into my life.

I'm not sure why anyone wants a dachshund, until you own one. So why, after a decade-plus, we bought a black and tan dachshund I'm not sure. I named him Wolf. I am also not sure why anyone names a dog, Wolf, that isn't more than five inches off the ground, but I did. Wolf was a wonderful dog who came to a horrid end.

Some say dachshunds are stubborn. They are; they're German. They are bred to hunt badgers, ferocious animals that live in burrows. That is why they are only five inches off the ground. You've got to have grit and determination to go into a dark, close place and with no room to spare, fight with an animal that has longer teeth and longer claws than you do. Oh yes, it's a fight to the death.

A dachshund is one tough cookie. But you'd never know it looking at it as a pup. They are adorable, playful, spunky. With head cocked and ears hanging, they look like you could throw a hat on them and they'd be the mascot of the "Lil Rascals." They are also smart and affectionate and love to be where the action is. A dachshund is a great dog for a young boy. I adored Wolf and he adored me. He was a male with moxie and topped out at the top of weight the American Kennel Club said he should—thirty pounds. He was one solid wiener.

One weekend we went up to my Uncle Al's. He lived in Portchester, New York. A famous psychiatrist, he had established a hospital that became a teaching hospital for the treatment of schizophrenics. Unfortunately, in those days the treatment of that illness was roughly akin to what produced "Frankenstein"—electro-shock. The hospital was high on a hill at the back end of over 240 acres of land. My brother, not too fondly, called my uncle "The Baron of High Point."

The hospital had its own farm. It grew a lot of its own vegetables, even raised its own pigs and cows. The grounds were a wonderful place for a boy and his dog, so I begged my parents to let us take Wolf. We arrived Friday night and all was well. On Saturday, I mostly did the "boy and his dog" routine; it was just like out of a book. Wolf ran all over hell and begone, often out of sight but always to return when called.

By dinnertime, Wolf and I were pooped. About nine o'clock something went terribly wrong. Wolf, as if he suddenly understood his name, began to howl. It was an awful sound, a sound of mourning like he knew something bad was wrong. Then he began to run around the house madly, in the true sense of the word. His eyes were burning. Foam flew from his jaws enveloping his lips and splashing onto his face and body. He was snarling and gnashing his teeth. It was horrifying. I was frightened to the core; my heart was breaking for my dog. My father and uncle got a blanket, cornered him, and trapped him. They left me behind and ran to the vet. The next morning Wolf was dead.

The story was that a disgruntled employee had poisoned him. Who knows? All I knew was that he truly was poisoned by someone or something, and I had witnessed the incomparable pain caused by death through poisoning. It was a sad ride home.

Well, it is said that when you fall off a horse you need to get back up and get on again. We needed to get another dog, and we did. Having had a wonderful one, we wanted another dachshund. My mother heard that they came in miniature and that's what she wanted. I must confess. A miniature anything is not a boy's dog.

A miniature dachshund certainly is not. This one was red and a runt. For Wolf's close to thirty pounds, this dog, whose name is gone from my memory bank, weighed maybe twelve. It was also a candidate for my uncle's hospital. Because the specter of the allergist hung over our house, no dogs were allowed upstairs in the sleeping quarters. We had a pantry in the back of the kitchen that had about a 3'x5' space under it, perfect for dogs, which are by genetics cave dwellers. This dog, however, unlike his ancestors who craved chasing things into dark tunnels, was afraid of the dark. She also was afraid of most everything else. When startled she would shriek like a banshee. This often happened in the middle of the night, to the dismay of my father, who was usually out of the house and off to work by 7:30 a.m.

We consulted the vet who advised that the dog was a hysteric. This was long before most of the meds for anxiety so common today had been developed. His advice? Do what you would do when a person gets hysterical. Slap them across the face. Well, that didn't sit well with me. I wanted to comfort the dog and for a while that was my job. I'd get out of bed, go downstairs, and calm the dog. Most oftentimes it worked but took all night. Some nights were two and three trippers. My father was at his wit's end. It was slapping time. The next night when the shrieking started, he marched downstairs, me in tow, took the dog by the scruff of the neck, and swung back his arm. Unfortunately, he needed about four feet of space in that three-foot kitchen cave. He split his knuckle on his right hand, hitting it on the lip of the shelf, a very bad thing to happen to a dentist.

The following Sunday there was an ad in the Times. "Free to a good home."

The story, though, has a happy ending—bizarre, but happy. We interviewed each prospective buyer patiently, honestly explaining that this dog would either have to be slapped silly or basically carried around for life. We had no takers, until a Zsa Zsa Gabor look-alike showed up. Some really wild Hungarian with papers to prove it, she was heir to long defunct royalty back in Hungarian history, took one look at this cute nutcase and fell in love. For several years, she stayed in touch with us. She and the dog were in Seventh Heaven. She never put the dog down and the dog never uttered a peep. Love knows no bounds. It is said, God provides someone (or something) for everyone.

And then came Champ. He was a Boston terrier with a face only a boy and orthodontist could love. He had an undershot jaw, so his bottom teeth stuck out. That must have created more room for his brain because he was the smartest dog I've ever owned. Boston's are mistakenly called by some Boston Bulldogs because of their bulldog-like faces, but they are terriers for sure.

Known for their wide grins and jaunty demeanors, Bostons, like most terriers, are fun to have around. Terriers are known to be quick-witted, a little A.D.D., but smart. Champ was a spectacular learner. I could take him down to the end of the block, walk the 110 yards to the other end, tell him to stay, and he wouldn't budge until called. He sat, he lay down, he rolled over, he fetched, he gave his paw. He took no time to become house trained and would explode rather than have an accident. He would even go from a sitting position, to sitting up. He then would let me balance a dog biscuit atop his nose and would hold the pose until I said, "OK!" whence he would flip it up in the air and happily catch his prize.

He was always up for playtime but was very intuitive when it came to the moods of a teen. He just knew when just "being there" was all that was required so that was what he did. Sometime when I'd be sitting on the floor pensively, he would put his front paws on my knee, lean up, and splash my face with his impossibly broad tongue.

Champ became sort of a neighborhood legend, and me along with him. A neighbor who had television connections suggested I try him out for the obedience trials during the American Kennel Club Dog Show Week at Madison Square Garden. Unless my father was to put braces on him for a few years, a best in breed, no less show, was never going to be his, but he did seem to be able to learn anything, and quickly. I don't know what happened to that idea. One thing did come of it and that's the next story.

THE WAR of the ITCHY BALLS

A story of a little old lady and a young, strong dog.

It's the story of Mrs. Cameron and Shadow. She lived around the corner on Wellington Court in a big, old house with a large wrap-around porch. One day, while I visited a friend who lived across the street from her, her door flew open and across the porch lurched Mrs. Cameron being dragged by a black tornado, far her superior in strength and desire. How she got down the stairs to the sidewalk was worthy of watching a circus act. Of course, I had to investigate.

I knew her casually and helped her carry groceries on occasion. She had no husband but wore a ring, so I assumed she was a widow. Even at my age, I knew those were questions little boys, at twelve or thirteen, didn't ask. I knew also she was older than most everyone else, looking back maybe now I'd guess late sixties, early seventies. She was sweet, quiet, reserved, and frail. Whatever possessed her to get a black, Labrador retriever is unfathomable. A dog, yes. She decided she was lonely and wanted companionship. But this one? A dog that, when mature, weighs in at, as much, if not more, than she—a dog who had read into its genes that fun is charging through marshlands, in forty degree weather to pull dead birds out of the water when her bathtub was the closest thing to a body of water this dog would ever see? A dog whose muscles verily rippled under its shiny, black skin?

Bad idea.

The puppy was a "whirling dervish." Its eyes seem to go in different directions. Its tongue flung out of its mouth this way and that. Its ears flapped liked Dumbo's, not yet having had a chance at four months old to grow into them. It didn't know which direction it wanted to go, so it seemed to go in all of them at once. It didn't know who it wanted to greet first, so it greeted everyone. Attached to this tornado was the little, old lady, hangin' on for dear life.

Several weeks later, I was walking along Rugby Road to her street, actually hoping to meet them again, when around the corner came the dog looking like the lead dog of a team of sled racers at the Iditarod Dog Sled Race. Behind her, whipping around the corner house hedges, into view came the sled in the person of Mrs. Cameron, the little, old lady, still hanging on for dear life.

I grabbed the pup and said to the musher, "You know you really need to get a choke collar for this maniac and register the two of you for some training classes, otherwise one day you're going to open the front door, and before you know it you are going to be out of Brooklyn and into Queens—or New Jersey!"

She said to me, "I've noticed you and your dog and how well-behaved he is. How about if I pay you to train him. I'll give you some money and you go buy what you need. Take as much time as you want. I just can't handle him." Truer words were never spoken. Stressing under my twenty-five cents a week allowance, the thought of actually making ten dollars a week brought on euphoria, yet I managed to be honest and say, "I have to tell you that usually a dog listens to whomever (back then I probably said whoever) trains it. Unless you work with us, you may get a dog back that listens to me and not you."

She replied, "Oh, I just can't. Do the best you can," to which I replied, "Okay, but in between sessions you have to practice what I've done with the dog that week." She agreed.

Until I owned a Great Dane, later into my youth, I had never encountered as strong an animal as this. Sleek, black, and rippling with muscles, had it been a human it could have been on body building posters standing next to Charles Atlas, who would be saying, "I can make you look like me and your dog look like mine." I was sure that by the time I taught the dog to heel, my left arm would be three feet longer than my right. If I didn't see something worthy of chasing before the dog did, and that could be anything from a squirrel to a leaf skipping across our path in the wind, the jolt on the leash and consequently to my shoulder only proved how durable young bodies are.

Slowly but surely, I penetrated this creature's skull, a skull I knew was cement-block hard because several times in his enthusiasm to express affection, he caught me unawares and almost knocked me stupid hitting my jaw with his head while jumping up to lick my face and connecting with my chin. He had the power of a heavyweight prize fighter's upper cut. Shadow would sit on command. Lord help anyone behind him because his wagging tail would have cut them down like a scythe. Heeling was a constant war, but I got him so he didn't pull, and though his head should have been at my hip, I settled for his shoulder being at my hip and his head leading the way. He would lie down fairly easily, sprawling out like a black blanket on the sidewalk. Getting up without acting like he had a train to catch was another story. Like GE, progress was our most important product. Two steps forward, one back, but forward none the less.

It took about six months, as I recall, to get this freight train of a dog under a semblance of control. After school, I would mount the steps of the house, knock on the door, and be greeted by thundering paws and the *basso profundo* of this dog's barking. His mistress watched with glee and a sparkle in her eye as off we went. If nothing else, she was being relieved of her afternoon pull from her pet. He was never going to be turned into a "Champ," but he seemed to get the idea that he needed to civilize a bit.

I gave Mistress fair warning that we were coming to an end of training and that she would have to go out with us several times. She would have to take the leash to begin transferring the training authority from me to her. I wouldn't say it was a grand success, but it seemed like we were better off than when we began. I turned the dog over to her, she gave me a nice gift, and we went on about our separate lives.

I hadn't been back to Wellington Court for a while, and one day decided to drop in on that same friend, the one across the street from the black tornado. We were outside talking when I heard that familiar *basso profundo* bark; the door flung open, across the porch and down the stairs came the dog, followed by the woman. Attached by the leash, they hit the sidewalk at a canter. She spied me, waved with one hand sort of like a cowboy waving his hat from the back of a bucking bronco, and disappeared down the street with the words, "Heel! Heel!" trailing far behind the dog. It seemed like they were on their way to New Jersey. I later heard she had died. Happily, it had nothing to do with the dog.

Next came "Earthquake" nee *Terremoto* ("earthquake" in Spanish). I was off to college, my parents were off to Newkirk Avenue from Waldorf Court, downsizing from the house to an apartment, and Champ was off to my cousin's manse with three children, an eighteen-room house on Long Island Sound, and a love for dogs. Champ lived another two years until Father Time caught up with him and took him away. It wasn't until my junior year of college, having moved out of the dormitory before the next dog showed up.

I remember how we named her, just not how we got her. My roommate from the dorm and two other guys decided to rent a walk-up apartment diagonally across the street from where the soon to be famous Watergate Office and Apartment Building had risen from the ground. Our little apartment, above an architect's office, was notable for having a red door, which it still has (I saw it just a few months ago from this writing whilst on a ride out of Rock Creek Park, Washington, DC, with my daughter and grandchildren.)

The apartment was also notable for how part of it was furnished. Across the street was a Howard Johnson's Motel. One of my roommate's uncles was a congressman from Texas. He therefore had a rather causal attitude about getting in trouble in DC. One night, he rented a room at the "Ho-Jo Mo-Lo" as we called it, and did so of course with a fake license and ID. At about three a.m., with another friend, he slipped a chair, a desk, and most everything else that wasn't nailed down and would fit through a window or be carried out the back door, across the street, and up the stairs. By morning, we had a lot of cheap orange pieces of furniture.

For the life of me, I can't remember how we came across this three-month-old, tan Great Dane. I think it was from a litter that was born to someone that one of our fraternity (AEPi) brothers knew. Anyway, one day we had her. Great Dane puppies grow so fast you can almost watch them do it. And they can be, like most puppies, fairly exuberant. It wasn't long before we realized that this pup had a unique way of saying, "Let's play!" She'd be prone on the floor and begin slapping her forepaws on the floor creating a rumbling like an earthquake and also creating rumblings from our landlords, the architects.

My principle roommate had been raised much of his life in Venezuela. His dad was an executive with Mobil Oil. He spoke Spanish and named the dog *Terremoto* (earthquake) as soon as he heard the first rumblings of the call to play. We nicknamed her Teri and now we were four college students and one Great Dane.

I have this thing with dogs and little kids. If I got along as well with adults as I did with them, I could probably run for office. I don't, so I didn't (well, I almost did but that's for another book). It didn't take long for Teri and me to be attached to the hip. The apartment was about five blocks from the center of campus, which was also where the fraternity house was. Teri was a happy, friendly, smart dog that was a chick magnet, so I didn't at all mind being in her company. She chose my bed to sleep in (sleeping in a twin bed with a dog that tops out at 130 pounds doesn't make for a great night's sleep), but it paid off the night she saved my life.

My klepto roommate was not much of a student, but he made up for that lack with his abilities to drink and smoke. As you might imagine, male college students, responsible for themselves, aren't the neatest group of humans you'll meet, especially when you throw a big dog into the mix. Since we were in a walk-up, it doesn't take much imagination to realize that there was a staircase that ran from the front door up to the apartment. The bottom of the staircase was where the garbage bags and newspapers went, until someone decided to take them outside to the garbage can. The architects had their own entrance, so they knew not the possible infestations that could abound just the other side of the wall.

It didn't take but a few months before we laid the law down to the Texas flash, whom we, surprise of surprises, called "Tex," about being the only chimney amongst us. He had to put out his cigarettes at the curb. He could smoke in his room but with the door closed and window open. One night, drunk as a lord, his

213

neon sign that said, "No Smoking," went on a bit late. He didn't remember until he was through the door, so he rubbed the butt against his shoe and dropped it on the floor. Or it would have been the floor were it not for the pile of newspapers and garbage between it and the linoleum. Enter Teri—begin the "boy and his dog" music and add a scene from the Keystone Cops except with the DC fire department.

It was a night not too different than any other. Teri and I were wrestling around for territorial rights as to who slept on the wall side of the mattress. The one of us who didn't get that side often ended up on the floor at least once before dawn. The door was closed. Suddenly Teri began barking and pawing at me and then the door. While not normal, since she usually went through the night without needing a walk, I figured she had to go out. As consciousness seeped into my brain and I awakened, I smelled smoke. I opened the door, which faced the staircase, to a cloud of thick, acrid smoke through which I could see orange flames licking at the bottom of the stairs. I closed the door and did what one sees done in every movie that has a fire. I opened the window and yelled, "FIRE!! FIRE!!"

The only phone was in the living room. There were flames between me and it. And glory be, someone heard me, and I heard sirens.

Now for the comedy.

In my neighborhood, there was a cement factory, now long gone. Much of the content was made from crushed shells dredged up from the Potomac and the Atlantic. You could smell it in the dead of winter. Imagine what it smelled like in the heat of the DC summer. It also was in a spot that was causing greater traffic difficulty from the burgeoning Watergate complex and the ever-expanding Georgetown section of DC.

Someone got the bright idea that a new exit-ramp was needed. Mind you this was before DC was self-governing, so Congress, which had a DC governance committee, made the decisions. This was not one of its better ones. To make a long story short (as my wise-guy son would say, "Too late!"), this large, curved ramp took shape outside my window. Know that I was never a good geometry student, but even I could see that this ramp was coming down at an angle that just wasn't going to connect with the roadway. It reminded me of an old beach joke:

A man was drowning offshore. He was pulled to safety where the lifeguards began to work on him, furiously pumping his chest at a feverish pace with strength and determination. They're pumping and pumping and not getting any results. A passerby looks in on the scene and says to the lifeguard, "I'm an engineer and I can tell you unless you pull his ass out of the water, you can pump all you want, and you won't get the water out of him!"

Ba da boom . . . The end of the ramp story is that it was built right into the ground nowhere near the connecting ramp on sort of the path a small plane would take as it turned down towards the runway but forgot to stop turning. So, there we all were. The fire department, apparently without the latest map, on one side of the ramp, and I with my head out the window yelling, "Over Here!"

Over here was actually over there and ne'r the twin could meet. The smoke was getting thicker and the dog's barking louder. In a flash, no pun intended, two of the firemen made their way through the debris, knocked down the chain link fence, kicked in the door, and put out the fire. Without too much overstatement, Teri was the hero of the night.

The fire was the last straw, again, no pun intended . . . for our landlord. It didn't take too much more imagination to see a scenario where all their work went up in flames. Our lease was not renewed and now we had a problem. Teri, who was almost full grown, was harder to get an apartment for than we college students. She stayed at the fraternity house for a bit until the summer, then she also went to the estate on Long Island where Champ had gone. She happily walked the children to the bus every day and barked at the neighbor, tennis star Ile Nastase, who hated her and she him. Another unhappy ending. Someone didn't stop for the school bus loading. Luckily, they didn't hit my cousins. They did wipe out Teri.

For a while thereafter, I was dog less . . . but not duck less. In a fit of insanity, I acquired Quacks, a white, Pekin duck that lived in my basement, in Johnstown, Pa.

For those of you who are Marx Brothers movie buffs, you'll remember Chico trying to pronounce the word, "viaduct" from their classic hit *Cocoanuts,* set in Florida at a resort. The twisted dialogue is a forerunner to Abbott and Costello's, *Who's on First?* The viaduct is part of a description of a property Groucho is trying to sell Chico. From Chico's mouth it keeps coming out "Why a duck?" while Groucho kept trying to answer the question. Well, you should be asking right about now, after all these dog stories, "Why a duck?"

I don't know. Well, I do. It represents the power of beauty, not the duck's, but my girlfriend's. We had friends who raised ducks and said they made great pets and insanely good "watch dogs." Maybe that's the answer to why a duck? Now I'm sure these duck qualities are correct, but I'm sure they assume that one has a farm, or at least a big back yard. I had neither. Besides, if I put the duck outside it wouldn't last a night before a fox ate it.

"Your basement!" exclaimed beauty about the beast. "You've got a huge basement." That was true. I was living in a solid, little house out at the edge of the Johnstown, Pa. suburbs on the inauspiciously named "Coon Ridge Road." Honest to Pete. One day we filled the basement with straw and a tub of water and put this adorable duckling into it.

Now let me tell you about ducks:
- They don't stay ducklings for long.
- They are very unhappy without large bodies of water.
- They eat insane amounts of food.
- They poop insane amounts of digested stuff from the insane amounts of food.
- They are never quiet.
- They are very nasty.
- They don't quack when the doorbell rings, although they do bite.

Near as I can tell, they have no redeeming qualities, unless browned with orange sauce. I needed a farm and fast. After six months of sleeplessness, being attacked and pecked at, I found some fellow "down the road a piece" who did have a farm. Shortly thereafter, he had a farm and a white, Pekin duck.

I have owned more dogs; I have never owned another duck.

The immortal #42, Jackie Robinson; below "The Duke" gets his home run welcome from "Campy" #39.

The World Series

"I remember after one game, throwing up for hours."

There is nothing like it, walking through the tunnel that ends with a panoramic view of a major league baseball field, before anyone has taken the field of play. The white chalk lines against the red/brown dirt contrasting against the green grass (or so it was before Astroturf). Everything else—the blue seats and the blue, steel girders that held the place together were also "Dodger Blue." It was Ebbet's Field, home of the storied Brooklyn Dodgers and was to me, breathtaking. It's a first-time sight that a little boy has forever etched in his memory.

I don't know why we never went to many games as a family. Everyone was a Dodgers fan, even my mother. Ebbet's Field was an easy subway ride away but a less easy drive because of parking, but no major, big deal. And Ebbet's was a wonderful place, mostly, to watch a ball game. It was small, only holding about 32,000 people when packed. Except for a minor engineering flaw that put a few seats behind steel pillars, every seat was a good one. I don't know how people managed it, but in those days, baseball was a day game and there were always thousands of people in the stands, so most any game, any day, was a noisy and exciting event, and a lot of office workers in Brooklyn were not at work.

There was something else about Ebbet's Field. It had the worst food imaginable. I remember after one game, throwing up for hours. Maybe that's why we didn't go more often. Getting the food, however, was fun. Old time hawkers sold things and the most fun thing to buy were the peanuts, or anything that came in a bag because the venders threw the purchase to you, perfect strikes, on a line, no matter where in the row you sat.

The peanuts, I believe, were stored in salt mines for specified periods of time so that when you ate them the lining of your mouth shriveled up. That, of course, was by design, so you needed a drink, Coke or a beer—the Coke watered down from melted ice—the beer, a brand no longer found easily, Schaefer Beer. Really bad stuff. But the Steven's hot dogs were the killers, maybe literally. Ever see a grey hot dog? The vendors carried boxes the size of 50-gallon fish tanks filled with warm water in which the hot dogs swam. He stabbed you a dog from the water, plopped it in a bun. The relish, for those who did that to a hot dog, had both a color (bright green) and a taste (awful) that should have been outlawed. The sauerkraut was great. What one did to a hot dog, or what it had in it, to make it grey was a mystery for the health department or maybe the emergency room.

But you didn't go for the food, you went for a team that was known, only partly in affection, as "Dem Bums" from their ability to snatch defeat from the jaws of victory.

They had great, colorful, mostly flawed ballplayers. And, of course, Jackie Robinson. They had pitched, bitter rivalries, especially against the New York Giants, the Philadelphia Phillies, and the St. Louis Cardinals. It was a different game then. Players wore spikes and slid high. You were either in the National League or the American League. No divisions, so pretty much a fan knew at least something about every player in the league in which his team played. Oh yes, and mostly nothing about the other. The games were played for keeps. Runners would slice you up; pitchers would throw the ball at you.

There were very few trades. Pitchers in both leagues hit, some very well, and they threw nine innings of baseball if they had "their stuff." No pitch counts, you threw until you were being slaughtered, or until your arm was going to fall off. They threw spitballs and most pitchers had no qualms about knocking someone's head off if they deserved it—sometimes even if they didn't. It was not yet the era of the helmet. Of the several, notorious, chin throwers was Sal "The Barber" Maglie of the hated Giants. He painted a bulls-eye on every batter's chin. If the batter didn't move fast enough or moved in the wrong direction, he woke up the next morning with a fearsome headache.

The other major difference was the baseball players themselves. No matter their talent, they were laborers. They made no more than carpenters or plumbers or such, little enough that they all had off-season jobs. You could buy a car or insurance or men's clothing from your favorite ball player, if you knew where they worked.

Another major difference was that they signed autographs. And I collected them. There were two ways to get them; each was as exciting in a different way as the other. I would get a copy of *Sport Magazine*—the *People Magazine* of sports. It often featured full-page color photos of ball players. I would write a letter to the player, enclose the picture, and a stamped self-addressed envelope, address it to the player at his ballpark—and wait. Some never came back. But fairly often, there would arrive an envelope addressed to me in my own hand. The excitement was palpable as I tore it open. Sometimes, it was just a signature. Sometimes, a player would write a note and sign it. Once, when Montreal had come into the league, one ball player was kind enough to put the extra postage on the envelope because he had signed and mailed it when playing in Canada.

The other way was to chase down the players after a game. Everyone knew the locker room door opened right onto the sidewalk. The players parked in the same parking lots everyone else did and had pretty much the same kind of cars. Some stopped as they exited. That was no fun. It was chasing a guy down the sidewalk right up to the car that was the real challenge.

All that changed with the multi-million contract. Now, most players' cars are worth more than most fans make, and they are in protected lots. Get too close and someone would have to bail you out of jail, that is, if the ball player didn't poke you. Security would have you on the cement in a moment. Now, players exiting the stadium do so through tunnels leading to fenced-off areas where their bus or own cars were parked. Very safe. Very sanitary. And all that is assuming they hadn't signed a contract with some company that prohibited them from giving out their autographs for free.

Harumph!

The Dodgers were perennial winners of the pennant, and losers of the Series to the Yankees, except the year of that awful "shot heard round the world" when Ralph Branca gave up the home run to the Giants' Bobby Thompson. It took the pennant from my beloved Bums in a playoff game on the last day of the season. Sudden death was never so sudden.

I'd always wanted to go to a World Series game; who didn't? Even in the 1950s, seats were not cheap. In yesterday's dollars, a 1953 World Series ticket would have cost ninety bucks. It never even became part of a discussion, so I never thought it would ever happen. Until along came Uncle Ben, he of the black, medical bag and after-hours visits.

This was not the Uncle Ben of rice fame, but my uncle, married to my father's oldest sister. Trained as an ophthalmologist, he had a little, black bag and served also as the family doctor. He was as sweet a man you'd ever want to meet and had a feather-fingers touch. He and Aunt Frieda were the annual hosts of the family's overcrowded, raucous, Passover *seder,* and during the days when dimes and quarters were the normal prizes for things, at Uncle Ben's when you found the *afikomen* after *seder* you got a dollar bill—and so did everyone else who went searching for it.

One day the phone rang. My mom handed it to me, and said, "It's Uncle Ben for you." I couldn't imagine what he wanted, or why any adult would be calling me at all, except maybe Aunt Pauline. Adults rarely called children in those days. I took the phone, and he said, "How'd you like to go to a World Series game tomorrow?" I gagged. "You'd have to miss school. Ask your mother." There was a strong chance she would say no, so my heart was in my mouth. She hesitated, not for drama, but because school came first. But Uncle Ben had star power. "Yes, you may go," she said. No sleep for me that night.

I have no memory of how I got to the game. Did he pick me up? Did my mother drive me to his apartment and he drove? Maybe a magic carpet plopped us down in an amazing crowd all surging towards the World Series bedecked Ebbet's Field. The Dodgers were up two games to one with home field advantage. If we won this game—I couldn't even get the thought out.

Now, I must say that, at other times when I'd gone to ball games, I always sat on the first base side near as possible to the dugout. Good box seats. So, when we got into the stadium and kept walking, and walking and walking, I kept wondering and wondering and wondering. Finally came the sign that indicated we were in the right section. We walked through the ramp way and my magnificent view was not of the infield with its brown dirt and white baselines, it was of centerfield's expanse of green grass. Uncle Ben had brought binoculars, and though I never uttered a word, I was crestfallen—and I'm sure he knew it.

But there is something to be said for those seats. In a small park, they gave a commanding view of the field, and we were after all in the third row looking right down the necks of the outfielders. It was an exciting game, exciting because we were winning by two or three runs. A victory would mean a real shot at winning our first World Series. Another shot took care of that.

With two on, the already legendary Mickey Mantle stepped to the plate. After a few pitches, he hit one on a line drive right over my head, giving the lead, and eventually the game, to the Yankees, who as always, went on to win the Series. We went from winning to losing in about three seconds. Mickey Mantle was a young kid from Oklahoma who loved life and loved baseball and was very good at doing both. There were others on the Yankees one could hate for ruining my one and only (to this day) World Series game, but he was not one of them. He was too good and too nice.

So, home we went, bummed out, Uncle Ben trying to paint a black picture with light colors, and me not even being able to have a villain I could blame for beating us. It was one of those "Careful for what you wish for . . ." moments. My dream came true but ended in a nightmare.

Every kid who gets to see a Series game should see his heroes win. Problem is, sometimes they don't.

"I rooted for the Dodgers when they were in Brooklyn."

– Kareem Abdul-Jabbar

Losing Your Marbles

"In every neighborhood there was a marble king."

It was clearly a replay of David vs. Goliath but let me escort you to the stage and take you back even to the production notes that set the stage.

On my dead-end street, Waldorf Court, Flatbush, Brooklyn, each house had a front yard, a backyard, and at least one tree that grew in Brooklyn. Between the house and the street were two things: the sidewalk, used as previously described, for a lot more than walking; and a rectangle of space roughly the length of the houses' front yards. These held the aforementioned tree and grass. That is except for a house across the street.

That house didn't look like most all the other Victorian style homes. It had an enclosed, square, wood, front room added to it. And it had no grass in that space that had no name. Instead of grass it had dirt—dry, dusty, fine silt dirt. Mud when it was wet but when dry, it made for a perfect place to shoot marbles. Marbles?

Here is a game that has gone the way of many that take time, strategy, and patience to play. The game pieces were, well, everyone's marbles. Back in the day, kids collected marbles. They were so popular you could buy them at the candy store—that ubiquitous neighborhood institution that sold a zillion more things than candy. They came in plastic packs and cost about a quarter. These round pieces of glass came in solid colors, clear, and swirling patterns. Like baseball cards, they were usually not bought for quantity, but for the hopes of finding the unusual, the odd, or the rare. Most prized were cat's eyes but more than those were ones that had a thin line that ran straight through the middle. They had a name—like many things it is long gone from the memory bank.

The game itself was a ground-level cross between shuffleboard, poker, and pool. The table was this dry, silt-covered rectangle. Instead of six pockets there was one "pot," a concave space at one end of the field. The balls were the marbles. Replacing the cues or sticks—a thumb and forefinger. The object? Hitting the opponents' marbles on the way to sinking one's own into the pot. At the end, it was winner take all, a game of strategy to place your marble where it couldn't be hit, but in a place where it might be more likely to be used to hit the other. The winner "took the pot." That meant winning all the marbles from the other guy—and for some reason it was always a guy. The girls, even then, weren't often about to kneel down in the dust and then compound the idiocy by putting their hands into it.

And that you had to do.

To "flick" a marble, one balanced it on the first knuckle of the forefinger and propelled it with a—yes—flick of the thumb. The rest of the fingers had to be held tight and parallel, seated flat, resting on the field. If they were not, you were cheating and could forfeit the match. Depending on the play, one "cunny-thumbed it" (hit it gently) or one "let-it-rip" (propelled it far across the field of play). On a good day, one left a game of marbles excreting dust from one's sneakers, pant cuffs, knees if wearing shorts, hands, and forearms. Add hair if it was windy. Conjure up Pigpen from *Peanuts*.

"This," you say, "makes no sense." I've just told you that two kids are inhaling dust into everything that will hold it to shoot little round glass balls with their fingers at other little glass balls for the prize of taking home more little glass balls than they started with. And you expect it to make sense? Come now.

In every neighborhood, there was a marble king, a champ who most always won and whose collection of marbles was so large that on non-competition days others went to his house to ogle them. Marbles, again like baseball cards, were traded both for uniqueness and for advantage. Some marbles made better shooters than others.

"Nonsense," you say?

"See previous paragraph," I retort.

In my neighborhood, it was King George. King George had a five-gallon tin trashcan brimming with marbles. He also had large, strong fingers. When he deigned to play, which wasn't often, he was near invincible.

Until he wasn't.

The set was the OK Corral of marbles. King George had called for a round-robin winner-take-all. Near the end of the afternoon, he had taken everyone's—all but mine. How he did this was what made him fearsome.

You see there was no rulebook definition of what constituted a marble. If it was round and glass, it was a marble, even if you took it off the top of a light fixture and it was half again as big as a golf ball. With his strong hands and thick fingers, he truly rolled over the competition. Finesse was not an issue. All one's marble had to do was make a loud enough click to be heard and the clicked marble was yours. With "Big Bertha" all he needed to do was come close. Goliath rolled on.

I, however, had other ideas. The "no definition" cut both ways. I had found a blue marble about the size of a pea, nicknamed of course "Pee-Wee" after the Brooklyn Dodger shortstop of the same nickname. In order to hit it, one had to have a direct hit. Also, it was so small that unless a marble did roll right over it, one would never hear a click. David had arrived; he (it?) would rise to the challenge.

I no longer recall how many marbles were put in the center for the break. The King took at least half of them on the first roll. I had a harder time because unless well "thumbed" Pee-Wee would get lost in the dust, stopped by a ripple in the dirt. Flicked too hard, it would take off, flying over the very marbles it was to hit. By and by though, two were left in the dust ready for battle.

For a while, it was a dust-up. King George kept missing my Pee-Wee and in returning fire, my Pee-Wee kept drawing more dust than marble. Then it happened. The King had a near miss leaving me with a "can't miss." David again triumphs!

This silly but true story, dear reader, had a "be careful what you wish for" ending. King George was deposed. "The King is dead!

Long live the King." I assumed that throne. That match, however, effectively ended the "Waldorf Court Marble 500." No one else had any marbles, and for reasons of age or just plain moving on, no one was going to hit the candy store for a new store of glass globes. I now had five plus gallons of marbles in a canister I could barely lift.

But lift it I did. Carry it triumphantly across the street, (or as triumphant as one can look trying not to get a hernia) I did. Schlep it up the seven steps of the house, I managed. I had my treasure but I couldn't get it through the front door, so I used my knee to support it from underneath, and my arms to keep it from tipping left or right (imagine trying to round up a thousand or more marbles each looking to up-end some poor, unsuspecting neighbor trudging home from work), and poked the doorbell with my nose.

To the rescue came my mother who looked at me, looked at my stash, and said, "What the hell do you think you are going to do with those?"

You know—I didn't know. I had no answer.

For all I know, they are still in the attic of #12, sold some forty-five years ago, where I deposited them, just barely avoiding an early heart-attack getting them up the three flights of stairs. Or maybe their weight caused them to drop through the attic floor into the bedroom below.

Hopefully someone is enjoying them.

"I grew up in Marcy Projects in Brooklyn, and my mom and pop had an extensive record collection, so Michael Jackson and Stevie Wonder and all of those sounds and souls of Motown filled the house."

– Jay-Z, Rapper,
Music Producer,
Entrepreneur

Itchy Balls, yellow with tinges of black.
They only looked harmless.

The War of the Itchy Balls

"I hear youse guys are looking for a little rumble."

There are many riffs on the old, Arabian proverb that "a man is known by the reputation of his enemies." At age twelve, I was to learn that maybe one should work one's way up to big enemies, not start with them.

It all started with a newcomer to the neighborhood. How he found us, I do not know. His name was Steven. He had a penchant for acting like a tough guy. So this story starts with a newcomer and ends with what could have been a gang fight but for the fact that you need two gangs to make a fight.

Now you might think a gang fight somewhat perilous, being done on a dead-end street and all, but it takes into account that like guerrillas in warfare, we knew all the trails and outs: who left their basements unlocked, which backyards had the lowest fences, what you could hide in, on, or under. This becomes important as the storms of war approached.

So Stevie, who it turned out went to the same synagogue we did for *bar mitzvah* lessons, though he was just across the dividing line from our high school district for Midwood and would go to the hated Erasmus Hall High, became a junior high school fixture around the block. He referred to us as "his guys." That too should be tucked away for the run up to war; oftentimes, it is the seemingly innocuous phrase or deed that can turn something nasty into something ugly. The Archduke of Ferdinand knew something about that stuff. It seemed that when not hanging with "his guys,"

Steven was causing trouble with someone else's guys. These guys were Irish, older, came from the other side of the ethnic divide—Coney Island Avenue—and all seemed to be named Frankie. It was, however, the last name of "those guys'" leader that struck fear into one's heart.

Slaughter.

Known to the local constabulary as the "Slaughter Gang," these young thugs (sorry to you PCers who are erasing that word from white vocabulary usage) had been in and out of juvie, one at least had done real time, and were really strangers to us. Not only did they live on the other side of the divide where none of us went without being in a car or on foot and being with a parent, they attended Catholic school, and principally were the problem of the priests. Why then did they cross the divide? I thought you'd never ask. Steven lived pretty much on the corner where the two neighborhoods came together—or separated.

He often made forays into forbidden territory. One excellent reason was the Irish Deli that made its own potato chips. To die for, they were, figuratively, and at least in our minds, literally. While there, he'd bump up against the locals to make a statement. He might have been a stranger in a strange land, but it would be his choice when to be there and when not. One day, the heat of the potato chip maker, I guess, caused a spark; heated disputations began over territorial lines. Like many negotiations begun under adverse circumstances, these broke down. There was no chivalrous glove slap to the face with secretaries making a time and place for a duel to resolve their animosities. There were a lot of threats and a lot of "oh yeahs?" Finally, one of the Frankies said, "Let's settle this. I got my guys, you get your guys . . . ."

Steven chose our block because he knew that's where the store of itchy balls was. A three o'clock rumble was set. If you can't already envision how ridiculous this was, wait. It gets more so, truth being stranger than fiction.

Playing Dwight David Eisenhower, Steve had a strategy which he breathlessly explained as he raced onto the block raving about the appointed appointment. He would place "his guys" in strategic places. Armed with piles of Mother Nature's golf balls, we would allow the enemy to filter past the mouth of the street and then we'd surround them pelting them into submission with our rich store of itchy balls and then use our knowledge of the escape routes to run for our lives. Fortunately, it was Eisenhower who planned D-Day, not Steven.

Three o'clock came and so did they. The Slaughter Gang was a real gang. They came swinging bicycle chains; swishing stolen, broken-off car antennae, this being before satellite radios did away with the need for them; a pair or two of brass knuckles; and they all wore black leather vests with metal studs over their white tee-shirts with rolled up sleeves holding packages of—well you get the idea. And there were a lot of them. One was the size of an NFL defensive tackle. Faced with this oozing mass of terror, it was probably the first time many of us, all seven or eight of us, had ever uttered, "Holy shit!" And I think we did it in unison.

The moose of a guy grabbed my next-door neighbor. Moose had Sandy by the shoulders and said something like, "We heard youse guys were lookin' for a little rumble." The only sound Sandy made didn't come from his mouth, but from his pants, or so it seemed. "Cut and Run" was redefined at that moment. With nary an itchy ball being fired, we turned for the exits. Except there were none. Like a cloud, these goons had everything covered. "No place to run, no place to hide."

So you ask, "You lived to tell the story, how did the war end? Was an armistice signed? Did you lose the rights to your street having to play ever after in serfdom under the weighty thumb of the Slaughter Gang?"

Nah. Mom saved the day.

Timing is everything. It was time for me to practice the accordion (see, isn't this getting more ridiculous? Wait . . . the show's not over yet) and I was late. My mother, who believed that five minutes early was being on-time, came to look for me. She opened the front door, stepped out onto the stoop, and saw this Cecile B. De Mille scene.

(If you're younger than fifty, goggle'im.) My mother, who had a bit of the sailor in her, didn't use the "HS" words, but she did launch an F-bomb. It was part of a series of verbal cluster-bombs that, to this day, amaze in my memory. It went sort of like this—but probably faster than you can read it—and a lot louder.

"What the F are you doing here? Who are you little (she'd obviously had not spied Moose) bastards, and what are you doing on our block?!? You better get the F outta here or I'll call the F'ing cops . . . ." And thus began a riff that just trilled off her tongue.

"Forget the cops. I'll call the F'ing Navy" (then I guess she realized we were landlocked between Rugby Road and the railroad tracks and followed up with . . . "Forget the Navy. I'll call the F'ing Army!!" Then, I guess she remembered we lived in the flight path of Floyd Bennett Air Force Base because the sights and sounds of streaking F-86 Saber Jets and B-47 bombers were etched into the balloon above the head of what had become a cartoon character. Enter the Air Force, each plane carrying a load of F-bombs.

Then came the *pièce de résistance*.

"Goddammit! Get your asses out of here or I'll call the Goddammed MARINES!!!"

All this with her cigarette hanging from her mouth. What was so amazing was that this riff was from a woman born in New Brunswick, New Jersey—college educated, married to a dentist, and fancied herself a bit of a fashion plate. Where the potty mouth came from, I knew not.

Well, "Cut and Run" was again re-defined. They took one look at this foaming fury spewing poison from her mouth, with smoke coming from her nostrils and probably her ears and thought she might actually come down off the stoop after them.

They just evaporated.

Gone.

Never seen again.

She had affected a permanent armistice. Peace reigned. You go, Mom!

*"Brooklyn's good. Brooklyn's funky.
Brooklyn's happening."*

– Waris Dirie
Somali Super Model,
Special Ambassador, UN,
Leader in the Fight Against
Genital Mutation

*"I'm from Brooklyn. In Brooklyn,
if you say, 'I'm dangerous', you'd
better be dangerous."*

– Larry King

Blizzards Make (Cold) Heroes

"Like Nanook of the North, We Fought the Elements."

I was very, very frustrated. I finally gave up. Delta Airlines was busy. Period. Couldn't get through. Continental Airlines' message cheerily said, "Your call will be answered in . . ." And then came the not so cheery electronic voice that said 112 minutes. Still though, I relaxed. After all, I was here and the blizzard was there.

Our daughter had called from Washington DC. Twelve inches were on the ground with maybe another twelve coming. Friends from Baltimore reported that this one would go into the Maryland record books. My brother was the only bright spot. He had the good luck to be in Barbados!

Then I got an email from someone else in DC with whom I was trying to make plans. He and his wife were snowed in. I smiled. Not for his misfortune, mind you, but for the blizzard of memories that hit me.

The first was a DC memory. I have experienced two blizzards in DC. It was my first winter in college. The inauguration of John F. Kennedy was at hand. The streets had to be clear. In those days, the nation's capital didn't have its own snow removal equipment. When the city became paralyzed by weather, which didn't happen often but also didn't take much snow to clog things up, government had two choices. Shut down the city or call out the army. Given the up and coming events, they called the army. It was quite a sight to see huge army transport trucks affixed with snowplows coming across Memorial Bridge behind the Lincoln Memorial from Ft. Myer in Virginia. These noisy, lumbering mechanized pachyderms were a DC version of the cavalry coming to the rescue, albeit slowly.

Then there was the blizzard that brought the smile. I replied to the email that the writer had it backwards; one was supposed to get stuck in Florida and not be able to get back up north, not the other way around. It happened to me. The next year, I took the train to Florida during a break to see a friend. While I was there, a freak snowstorm hit much of the Deep South. I got snowed into Florida. Would that I had that kind of luck with any one of the zillions of lotto tickets I've bought.

But the most memorable was the blizzard of the heroes. It must have been '57 or thereabouts. New York had a doozy of a blizzard. I want to say seventeen inches. At that time, my grandfather lived on W. 17th in Manhattan. He called my mom and said the furnace died in his building and he was freezing. He was old and ill; it was a crisis.

There was no way a car would make it through the streets, and even if it did, the prospect of driving over the Brooklyn Bridge in such conditions was less than attractive. My brother and I came up with a rescue plan.

We would take the electric heater from our house by subway to save Grandpa. Mind you, the heater was the size of a small suitcase. Downsizing hadn't gone much beyond radios in those days. We trudged six blocks to the subway, this seventeen-year-old and twelve-year-old. It was freezing, and the going was tough. We realized that this hero stuff wasn't as easy as it seemed.

Things became further complicated when we arrived at the subway station and were told that because of the storm the trains were running only as far as the tip of Manhattan Island. The train would get us over the bridge, or I guess maybe under the tunnel, and then we were on our own. I'll never forget coming out of the dark, dank, dirty subway station and seeing the expanse of white far and wide. Like Nanook of the North we fought the elements, glad probably for the first times in our lives for the unsightly, nerdy black rubber galoshes with the metal hinge snaps that complained when you closed them. While snowshoes would have served us better, these were far better than nothing.

Well, we got there, and it certainly was cold in Grandpa's apartment although we had to thaw out from the trek before we were warm enough to feel the cold. Grandpa was many things, but a conversationalist wasn't one of them. Nor was he much of a host. He probably offered us coffee or scotch or something. So, after thawing out and depositing the heater, off we went into a white, clean, and quiet New York. Even at that age, we realized how rarely those three descriptors could be used at the same time for the Big Apple.

By the time we got home, we were thoroughly exhausted. Mom had better stuff waiting to warm us, but to this minute I can warm myself with the smile on Grandpa's face and the sense that it's good to be a hero. Then my brother went off to college. He left behind the snow shovel. Snow became a pain in the back, so here I am in Florida.

"Have you ever seen a more beautiful face?"

The Connecticut Collie

*"Kids my age grew up with two dogs,
whether they owned any or not."*

Older brothers have a special place in the hearts and minds of a younger brother. I worshipped mine, even though on certain days I wished I could have killed him—or at least gotten him in trouble. Twice though, things happened to him that made my heart sink. One, a burst appendix in the middle of the night, and several days in the hospital. I got through. The other, was a serious complication leading to what was in the '50s a serious operation. I might not have made it through without the Collie from Connecticut.

This is how it went, with a sidebar about a closet.

First my brother. He had some kind of head operation, sinus, adenoid . . . I really don't know. What I do know was that infection set in, they were worried about it, he was in the hospital for weeks, I was only allowed to see him once, and he looked awful. When he was released from the hospital, we were advised to take several weeks for him to recuperate.

It was decided that we would go to the Connecticut shore to a grand, old inn my aunt from Connecticut had recommended. The sea air would have a healing effect. The problem was that it was late fall, very blustery and cold. The other problem was that we were almost the only guests and were the only guests with children. Other than the pinball games that I played mercilessly for free, I had no one to play with, and nothing much to do except worry about my brother.

That's where the collie comes in.

Kids my age were raised with two dogs whether they owned any or not. One was the great German shepherd police dog, Rin

Tin Tin. The other, of course, was Lassie. If baseball, apple pie, and Chevrolet were the ringtones of Americana in the '50s so was the call, "Lassie! Come home!" followed by this magnificent creature coursing across the land, hair to die for sweeping back from its sculptured head. I had always wanted a collie. To this day, I don't think there is a dog as magnificent as a well-groomed collie, and there lay the problem—hair—lots of it. I was restricted because of old-fashioned allergy assumptions about longhaired dogs. Or so I was told. Could also have been that my mother didn't want all the hair being shed in the house.

Shy, nervous, anticipatory, I tumbled out of the family Buick in front of this desolate, stone inn. Morose would be a good word to describe my feelings until he appeared. It was as if I had become Bobby and yelled, "Lassie! Come home!" First, I heard the telltale Woof! Woof! And then bounding across the landscape came this vision of hair and happiness come to investigate the newcomers. The dog must have had a name, but it's gone. What I remembered was its instant adoption of me, its sense that here was a little boy who needed a pal, and for however long we stayed there, except for nights, he would be it.

On days the weather permitted, we walked the beach together. On days it didn't, he padded alongside me wherever I went and plopped down by my side when I'd gotten there. He was quick to lick my face or hand, quicker with a tail wag, and could always find a ball or a stick that he would chase endlessly and return so long as I was up for it. We had long talks where I poured out my heart and soul, and he listened patiently, tail slowly wagging to let me know that he was taking it all in—unlike adults who either pretended they were listening or had no time to.

In today's parlance, we were BFF's.

I mentioned that we were inseparable except at night when he went back to his family. We had rented a cottage down the boardwalk. At 9 p.m., I would be tucked into bed and my parents would walk up the boardwalk to join the other adults for games of cards. I was always told, "Now there's nothing to worry about, we're just down the boardwalk in the main house." It didn't take long after the lights went out for the wind to start the cottage creaking, and for the sound of the waves hitting the breakers to fill the bedroom with moonbeams making shadows I mostly didn't want to see.

One day, the teenage weekend help at the inn decided they would take in a Sunday movie. I think they felt badly for me, so they offered to take me along. I jumped at the offer. Collie and pinball games or not, I was a bit stir crazy. After some hesitation, my mother relented and off I went on this adventure. Unfortunately, we were in as it was said, "a one-horse town." Aside from one horse, it only had one movie house. What was showing was an action film about Genghis Khan and his Mongol hoards. Not exactly nine-year-old fare. But I was fine—until that night. When Mr. Kahn came to visit.

At 9 p.m., we went through the nightly good byes, and I huddled in my bed hoping sleep would win out over moonbeams and crashing waves. It did. On reflection, I know I was asleep and dreaming. But that night, I swore that the door of my bedroom closet opened and out stepped Genghis Khan in full regalia. He sported a metal hat with a point on its top, a beard on his face, an animal fur across his chest, and carried a large shield with a point in the middle. Before he had time to say one word—he might have been there to protect me or keep me company—I assumed he was there to murder me. I let out what Grandma called a *gashrei*, which is Yiddish for a scream that is such a scream its character is sold short by the word scream.

At the same time, I threw off the covers, leaped out of bed, shot out the door, and ran down the boardwalk in my pajamas—still screaming. I burst into the card room, "It's Genghis Khan. He's in my closet!!

And so ended the evening's card game—and trips to the movies for the rest of the stay.

My brother recovered and came the day we piled into the Buick and headed home. To this moment, I can see my friend wagging his tail and watching quizzically as I disappeared down the road leaving him to a lonely winter on the shore and leaving me with an indelible memory of the right dog, in the right place, at the right time.

"Everyone should walk across the Brooklyn Bridge. I did it three days in a row because it was one of the most exhilarating experiences I've ever had. The view is breathtaking."

– Seann William Scott
Actor, Writer, Comedian

Section Five

Mercury and Apollo Astronauts.

Adolescence Introduction

"Normal adolescents are abnormal."

How do you write an introduction to a period of life to which whole libraries have been devoted? In a part of life not covered in this epistle, I ran the largest multi-modality drug treatment program in the State of Connecticut. Multi-modality? We treated lots of different people who were screwed up in lots of different ways. We were known for an in-patient residential treatment center. Most of the patients who were court referred, were adolescents. Thus, we had a psychiatrist on staff who specialized in that field of treatment. Listen to this *bon mot* from him: "Normal adolescents are abnormal." Think about that a bit. Mull it over. If you've finished parenting adolescents, you should feel lucky. If you haven't, it should scare the crap out of you.

The problem is chemical but except in extreme cases it isn't drugs. It's good ole fashioned hormones. Estrogen makes girls girls. Testosterone makes boys boys. Unfortunately, at a given age, no one from the government knocks on your door, hands you a glass, clearly labeled, and says have the appropriate child drink this within twenty-four hours. That done, the process of being an adolescent is over. While I will rankle the conservative, anti-government folks among you, I've had adolescents and had a lot of experience with others' adolescents. Giving out the scientifically, exactly proportioned glass of hormones isn't such a bad idea, especially compared to how it really happens.

How it really happens is chaotic and therefore often produces chaos. Sometimes it's a drip-drip-drip of hormones into the system and while periods of weirdness can result you can measure the period like you measure rapids. This way it's between a one and a three. Sometimes, however, something happens at 2 p.m. or 2 a.m.; a hormone-dump takes place in the body. An hour later, you have no idea who the person is that is living with you in your house. It certainly isn't the same person who was there an hour before.

Finally, there's the drip-dump-drip-dump cycle.

This is the worst. Each time you think you have a handle on what's going on you realize how wrong you are.

I was pretty much a case of the drips. None-the-less, the stories reflect normal abnormality both in school and during the summer, to include many years at summer camp. You're about to divide with me the two major sections of adolescent life: High School and Summer Camp.

"I grew up in Brooklyn, N.Y. For part of my life, I was living in Detroit, and I remember a friend of mine commenting she could always tell when I had been speaking to my mother because my New York accent had come back."

– Deborah Tannen
Academic, Professor
of Linguistics at
Georgetown, University

Grandpa Willie, Great Tanta Dora, Great Uncle Pacey.

The Teenage Years

"Portnoy's Complaint? "Read it?"
"I'm living it!"

Take a breath, go to the bathroom, this section is longer than most. So too seemed being a teenager.

Aside from school, the life of an average teenager revolves around girls and pizza.

In my family, grades were gods, but in my head, girls were goddesses. Then came *Portnoy's Complaint.* And while it has been said that "all mothers are Jewish mothers," the Jewish mothers of America were Ground Zero for the book. My mother, who was always trying to have Kennedy-esque discussions at dinner, was one of the book's first readers in our neighborhood. She started—and ended—one dinner discussion thusly: "Have either of you read this *Portnoy's Complaint* thing?"

My brother piped up instantaneously, "Read it—I'm living it!"

I burst out laughing, thinking of my own special sweat sock hidden away upstairs. My mother turned crimson. She stood bolt upright, began erupting, and dinner was over. Only my father, seemingly oblivious to the torrents of emotion raining down around him, continued eating. He hadn't read the book.

And so, the stories that follow are not all about girls, but they are mostly about girls. Some involve pizza. Some involve other things. But most involve girls and the grand ability of this author to find himself in situations mostly beyond belief at least at the time. There were normal dates gone abnormal. There were possibilities of "assignments" in the French sense that totally went over my head. There were situations of pathos stemming from attempts at sex that were pathetic. All in all, they add up to a mostly miserable few years, the height of which began at fifteen and ended at seventeen.

I should add they only ended at seventeen because that's where the book ends. If you want Abnormality Redux you'll pick up my next opus. It will start right where this volume ends. It is tentatively titled, *I Slept with George Washington* and is about the college years.

So lean back and be prepared to be drawn through my neuroses into your own. I don't think you'll need a therapist on speed-dial, but you should feel that were speed dial available in those days, I should have had one set up and ready to go.

"Most people associate Wu Tang with Staten Island or Shaolin, but actually, I'm a native of Brooklyn. I was born in Crown Heights, raised in Bedford Stuyvesant, Brownsville, and Bushwick."

– Gza, Musician

"I am neither from Brooklyn nor am I Jew. In fact, I am Irish through and through and yet I found Bill's stories to be my stories, Bill's growing up pains to be my growing up pains. No matter where you're from and who you are, you will find this the kind of book we all need every-so-often—light and enjoyable with a bunch of laughs.

"As a life-long journalist, I have seen what Walter Cronkite meant when he said, "Bad news is good news." If you want to push aside the bad news, dive into Bill Gralnick's latest book. You'll smile your way to the end."

— Tim Malloy, assistant director of the Quinnipiac University Poll, has extensive political and wartime reporting experience. He provides analysis of national polls and polls in California, Pennsylvania, Colorado and Georgia. A 33-year veteran of television news and a seasoned political reporter, Malloy has won ten Emmy Awards for documentary work and war coverage. He coauthored a New York Times best selling nonfiction book with James Patterson in 2016. Malloy has a BA in English from Hamilton College.

Getting Ready for College

"The only thing standing in my way were the College Boards."

For about eighteen months, mid-fifteen to seventeen years of age, I was a very unhappy puppy. My older brother—rock, and at times savior, as well as gleeful tormentor—had left the house. I don't recall if it was the army first and then college or vice versa. What was important was that I felt like a quarterback whose line decided to leave the field right after the ball was snapped. My mother was getting sicker and sicker from alcoholism and drugs—drugs that theoretically were to deal with what made her drink, but in fact enhanced the impact of that drinking.

Lacking her favorite target, she had only me at whom to direct her ire. My father became more and more withdrawn from the troubles in the house. Two of my close friends had transferred to Adelphi Academy and I saw them less frequently. The girls I pined over wanted to be friends. The girls I wanted to be friends with pined over me. I had a wonderful internship with a veterinarian who thought I was such a natural he was going to support my entry into Cornell, then vet school, and bring me into his practice—until I had an overwhelming allergy attack to cats. How many of you can say you lost a career at sixteen?

It was all very confusing and, frankly, for me, school was my best friend. It was someplace to go where I was appreciated and did well. Even though I got cut from the basketball team, didn't make the baseball team, and got my nose broken on the first game of the soccer season, I was still co-captain of the rifle team, had my own gun, and was universally liked by my teachers. I was running an "A minus" average; prospects for college looked good.

Only standing between me and the fulfilling of promise were the dreaded college boards. I took the PSAT's. While I didn't do terribly, they showed I was not good at standardized testing. Of course, I was enrolled in a prep course. Came the fatal day, I was assigned to a high school far from my own. I felt nervous and isolated. My results showed it. In fact, they showed that maybe I shouldn't go to college at all. In math, my weakest subject, I got a 408 out of I forget what, 800, I think. In English, my best subject I barely broke 500. The saving grace was that in those days there were afternoon "achievement" tests in which you could choose to be tested in two (?) maybe three subjects. While I didn't knock anyone's socks off with the scores, my answers to questions based on fact not theory were more promising, high 500s and 600s. To say the results didn't exactly change the mood in the household would be an understatement . . . way under.

Then something really confusing happened. I had also taken the New York State Scholarship exam and damned if I didn't do so well that I won one. I could go tuition-free to any school anywhere in the state.

Sometimes when a hole is dug in one's life it gets filled. Feeling shovel-less facing my holes without my brother, God sent me someone with a shovel. Dr. Lindsey Perkins was a neighbor, a minister, and a professor at Brooklyn College. He stopped me one day to ask how things were going with college. It was like lancing a boil. My parents had offered me a deal. If I went to Brooklyn College, literally across the street from my high school, I could live at home and have a car, so long of course, as my grades held up. I knew living at home was a bad idea. Dr. Perkins agreed, but for a much wiser reason.

"Son," he said in his mild southern drawl, "half of what you learn in college you learn outside of the classroom. If you go to Brooklyn you get a good education, but you'll be going with the same kids you went to high school with even if they have different names." I knew what he meant. Brooklyn College would become sort of

AP high school. Once I got to college, The George Washington University in Washington, DC, and realized his wisdom had saved my life, I considered constructing an altar to him in my dorm room. Best of all, years later, I was able to thank him.

Back at 12 Waldorf Court, I began the filling out of applications. I wanted to go to Michigan, a revered cousin was a graduate. Michigan loved Midwood students and took a lot of them. But as luck would have it, the class before mine sent a record number of kids to Michigan. This time Michigan had chosen poorly. Several of the students got involved in a cheating scandal, and my year's class was blackballed. They would take no one.

Then I lost my seat at Rutgers University to a football player. My mother was a graduate and her aunt a huge donor. But as a state school, they took an absolute number of out-of-state kids and they needed an all-star, right guard more than a skinny, Jewish kid from Brooklyn.

For reasons that make no sense to this day, I applied to Harvard. They didn't laugh, nor did they accept me. I still have the rejection letter.

In the middle of this assault on my self-worth, my mother sat me down for a talk. It was at the zenith of what the Irish called "the troubles" between us. She was trying to make a peace overture; I was having none of it.

Her peace overture?

A simple question: "Where would you really like to go to school?"

My response? "The University of Hawaii."

Her response? "We could afford to send you, but we couldn't afford to bring you home (a joke)."

My response? "It's a deal!" In a nanosecond, I was on the floor. She had slapped me so hard across the face that it literally knocked me out of my chair. So much for peace.

The father of our country, or the university established in his name, came to the rescue. They were interested in me, but because of my board scores they would require an interview. Dr. Perkins urged me to go for it and prepped me. It was the dead of winter, so cold that the inside of the Greyhound Bus was cold. I was wearing a gray, wool suit, so heavy it probably weighed as much as I did. I got to school and was ushered into a room and offered a wooden chair in which to sit, a chair whose open slatted back pushed up against a steam radiator pumping out steam like John Henry was shoveling coal into the locomotive's furnace.

As the introductions began, I felt a bead of sweat form just below my collar and slowly, ever so slowly, roll down my neck, fixing itself in the track of my spine, and then wandering down to my belt. Came another, then more, until I could feel my undershirt sticking to my back, and then my shirt, where it met an impenetrable wall of wool, stuck too. It was miserably uncomfortable. I don't think, put under hypnosis I could recall who interviewed me, what they asked, or what I answered. I left beyond depressed. Yet somehow, I was still in God's circle of protected children because two weeks later I got "the letter." I was in!

Life would begin again—along with another book.

"Gleason used to rack balls for me when he was a kid in Brooklyn and in Long Island."

– Minnesota Fats
Legendary Pool Player

"I remember when I was 5 living on Pulaski Street in Brooklyn, the hallway of our building had a brass banister and a great sound, a great echo system. I used to sing in the hallway."

- Barbra Streisand

High School
The Annex

*"The girls were so salacious we dreamed
about them—it was safer."*

High School was a period of disappointments. Every class was called "a period;" at times, I thought with an English period, and a social studies period, I should have had disappointment period. The disappointment started actually before school did. Like today, school construction was not keeping up with population growth, and while Midwood at that time was only about fifteen years old and still looked great, its walls and halls were bursting, so the decision was made to re-model and re-open an old high school and call it The Annex. This was where the freshman class would attend—my freshman class. It not only wasn't next door to the school I had excitedly looked forward to entering, but in the opposite direction and a longer, dicier walk along Ocean Parkway instead of through the bucolic neighborhoods of the Midwood section of Brooklyn.

The annex looked exactly like what it was. An old building. It was dark outside, small inside, and offered immediately the sense of what it must have looked like before remodeling. Nor were the teachers any happier to be out of the glamour of the newer Midwood and into exile of the Annex on 18th and Ditmas Avenue. Some of the desks had etching that harkened back to the First World War, if not the Civil War. And things like gang fights between girls took place outside the front door with regularity, things that would never happen at the real Midwood.

This is worthy of mention. We had some "gun molls" in school— girls who wore explosion red lipstick, very short skirts, nail polish, hearts or rings around their necks, and chains around their wrists. Frankly, they were salacious looking, so salacious that we'd dream about them. They chewed gum, cursed, and were not to be looked at, no less touched. Dreaming was the safest option.

One day, precisely as school let out, a city bus pulled up and out poured a group of girls who, to the untrained eye, looked exactly like the girls just described. They, of course, didn't; they belonged to a different gang. Probably had different chains or the like for a distinctive note. In either case, what happened next was something out of a movie. These bus girls attacked the annex girls and there was this free-for-all scrum of screaming, scratching, kicking, punching, blouse-ripping with button-popping, chain-swinging fight that took over the sidewalk. Sirens sounded while the fighters became surrounded by boys and girls three and four deep, also screaming and yelling for blood, whose it didn't seem to matter. I might add, most of the boys had good old-fashioned boners. But within minutes, the sirens in the fight were set upon by a phalanx of siren-screaming cars and cops. The fun was done. It was over as fast as it began. It turned out to be just another day at The Annex where America's best and brightest were learning the ropes.

In a big school, there are a lot of teachers. I was finished with the Ms. McNultys and Mr. Proshans of PS 217. But I was blindsided by the coming of Eli Zutler.

*"I didn't have any sophistication.
I didn't really have any great taste or
anything like that. I was just a kid from
Brooklyn. But what I learnt is the why,
the how. The work ethic."*

– Jimmy Lovine

The interesting thing in the Cohen's garage, a 1905 Willy's Overland. Photograph courtesy of George Marks Photography.

The Tale of Eli Zutler

"A cell phone was still the pay phone found in jail."

I don't remember the subject, but I remember Mr. Zutler. He was hard to forget. He had no neck. Well, he must have, but maybe it stopped growing before it grew through his shoulders. His head seemed to balance atop his shoulder blades and it never turned. His whole body turned. He was short and stocky. He gave the appearance of a robot and he had a weird voice that went with his robot-like features. Now I'm sure there is a sad story behind it all, but they don't call sophomores sophomoric without reason. Mr. Z was just funny looking and why never entered in the equation in a teenager's mind.

In those days, before horrible things happened in school and school hardening was part of education talk, classrooms, at least at Midwood, had lockers in the back of every room. Every class that wasn't a lab was a homeroom where each of us started our day before we were dispersed to the far ends of the school. Coats, rubbers (oh you dirty minded people! Those things some called galoshes/rain gear were called rubbers in Brooklyn. Why? Because they were made out of rubber would be my guess), books, transistor radios, (no cell phones. A cell phone was still the pay phone found in a jail), and so on. This is not inserted for the sake of understanding school architecture; it is relevant to "The Tale of Eli Zutler."

Our teaching robot had an odd manner about him. While some teachers were aces at learning names, and others always had their "Delaney Books" (roll books) within eyesight, Mr. Zutler couldn't be bothered with all that. When he wanted a student to do something, his robotic body would slowly turn as if on wheels, towards a student. You could almost hear the whirring of the gears and the clanking of his parts. With biceps adhered to his chest wall, his forearm would rise to a 45-degree angle, his forefinger would shoot out, and he'd announce, "This student here (or that student there . . . followed by a command) will read paragraph four (or will take the hall pass and get more chalk or will stop talking in class)."

I now refer you to a chapter in which we mentioned the vaccinations. Well, we hadn't been inoculated against laughing fits, but mostly it was kept to quiet giggles and snorts because Mr. Zutler was a lot scarier person than Mr. Proshan. This was good for me because there was a time in my life that lasted until I got old enough to think in which I might have a stroke or a heart attack if something really, really struck me funny. I laughed so hard and long and loud that I thought, literally, I might die laughing. I turned colors. I couldn't breathe. I'd fall out of chairs laughing. I did not want this to happen in Robotics. But it almost did.

It was a day no different than any other day. Mr. Z was Mr. Z except that day the 'Fickle Finger of Fate' pointed at me. "This student here—stand up and . . ."

I could feel it coming, little vibrations building in my tummy. By the time they got to my chest, they were unstoppable. Then suddenly they burst out of my mouth and into his face.

"This student here—you will stop that laughing instantly."

Not only didn't I, I couldn't. Another student caught it.

"That student there, you will be quiet!"

Then a third and a fourth. Mr. Zutler became exasperated at the impotence of his forefinger. He got so mad that he pointed at one student and shouted, "THAT STUDENT THERE. STOP THIS IMMEDIATELY OR I'LL PUT YOUR HEAD IN THE LOCKER!" He was referring of course to the book lockers on the back wall of class.

That was it; the dam gave way.

Flash to the visual image, as did I. Classmate with head in locker, rear end facing out. I was standing, remember? Well, not after that. I literally fell on the floor in a paroxysm of laughter. My seat was in the first row, fourth seat, about three or four feet diagonally from the open classroom door. Like a soldier under fire, I crawled on the floor, howling with laughter, tears spotting the floor, until I breached the doorstep. I was several feet into the hall, and noticed I was looking at a pair of shoes. Wearing them was the Assistant Principal.

He had a question. "What's so funny, if I may ask, Mr. Gralnick?"

I stopped laughing.

I did get to explain. To (jail), the principal's office went I, no passing Go, no collecting $200. How I survived that class for the remainder of the year, I do not know, but I am proud to say, "That student there" got his "A", but has never since been able to look at a toy robot without a little vibration beginning in his tummy.

"Snazzy cover. And appropriate. As a longtime believer that everyone should write a memoir, I'm delighted to report that Bill Gralnick fulfills the mandate with gusto. It's lively, personal and savvy, filled with characters that will either make you gasp with recognition (between laughs), or inspire you to celebrate the cast of your own life. Or both. Read it. Then write."

— Lynn Sherr, former ABC
News Correspondent; author;
memoirist.

Physics

"I hope you're not as dumb as he was!"

Never did I do so poorly in a subject in which I learned so much. That's about all I can say when it comes to physics.

Except this.

I walked into class to be greeted by a silent, male teacher of no particular physical distinction except, I believe, a mustache, itself of no particular distinction. The teacher, Mr. Doskow, waved his newest wave of students to their seats. He then began his ritual.

He looked at his class list and called out a name. If that was your name, you'd raise your hand. He'd then make some notations on your Delaney Card as he asked a question or two. Since the list was alphabetical, it took a bit of time before he got to me.

"Gralnick!"

I raised my hand.

And then in a lower voice he mused: "Gralnick . . . Gralnick. Gralnick. Didn't I have a Gralnick a few years ago?"

I replied. "Yes sir, my brother, Jeff."

The next thing out of his mouth was not a question. It was either a statement or a plea. "God, I hope you're not as dumb as he was."

Unfortunately for both me and Mr. Doskow—I was.

But I still remember why water boils. And I know why it boils faster if you put a top on it.

That's at least something? Isn't it?

"Midwood—then and now one of the city's finest high schools."

OMG! Dead?

**"He didn't want teaching to be a struggle nor
did he want learning to be one either."**

It wasn't because he was a male. Midwood had plenty of male teachers. It was because he looked and acted like the leader he was: a former combat infantry man in the not so long ago Korean War, or "Conflict" as it was called.

When you walked into his class, it was quiet, and it stayed that way. The subject was social studies and he went at it like it was a mission, not a job. If something was important, he'd accentuate it by punching the blackboard with a strike hard enough for the students to think Ouch! and the blackboard crevices to explode chalk dust. Several of his fingers went in different directions. It made one think that maybe at some time, somewhere, he did a lot of hitting of things that weren't chalk boards.

He was one of those teachers you learned from because you knew he wanted you to learn from him. He didn't want teaching to be a struggle, nor did he want learning to be either. Prompt could have been his middle name. He was never late for anything and he expected that from his students. Be in your seats, books open, mouths closed before the bell rang, and all would be well. When it wasn't well, he would look at you with a murderous, silent gaze. Better it was to be prompt and silent.

He was never late for class, as I said, except one day when he didn't show up at all. He hadn't seemed sick or particularly different in any way the day before. When he didn't show up the second day, we really wondered; rumors abounded. By the end of the day we were told: The Conflict's end left him a wounded and somewhat broken man. Most of his scars were on the inside. Now we call it

PTSD. We were told he fought to get well, but suffered intensely, sometimes not sleeping for nights on end.

The night before he broke his attendance streak, he committed suicide. No note, no nothing. Rope around his neck tied to something on the ceiling.

I guess it was true. Who would lie about something like that? I wish I could remember is name. He deserves that.

"It would take me three or four lifetimes to do everything I want. I'm a Brooklyn boy who learned to hustle, and I have to do something every day or I get the guilties."

– Wolfman Jack
Famous DJ

"Bill Gralnick's colorful memories of growing up in Brooklyn are likely to make any reader wish they, too, had spent their childhood in the wonderful neighborhoods of Brooklyn. The author's vivid stories of the Brooklyn Dodgers and Ebbets Field rang true with me. As a kid, I had the good fortune to spend summers in and around the Dodgers clubhouse and among the great Brooklyn ballplayers of the '50s—Gil Hodges, Carl Erskine, Jackie Robinson, Duke Snider, Pee Wee Reese, and Newk and Campy. There was no place like Brooklyn. Bill Gralnick tells us why."

– Peter Bavasi, former Toronto Blue Jays and Cleveland Indians president, San Diego Padres general manager, and son of legendary Brooklyn Dodgers general manager Buzzie Bavasi

The Star

" . . . he was 'the piano man.'"

Some kids just have the right stuff. Bob Shatz was one of those—born cool. He wasn't tall, dark, and handsome. In fact, he was shorter than I, stockier than I, and at times a little goofy looking, but he had everything I wish I had, starting with jars full of *chutzpah.*

Bob lived about eight blocks out of the neighborhood off Avenue J. He showed up one day with my next-door neighbor, the Garden's older boy, who had been taken out of public school and put into Adelphi Academy. Adelphi wasn't a top tier private school. It was rumored to be for middling students whose parents had money. The school had the reputation of having the contacts to get kids into better colleges than they might have gotten into from public school.

Bob was not a close friend of my friend, but he had heard that we all had basketball hoops in our backyards and there was always a game. In some places in Brooklyn, it was a craps game or card game. For us, it was basketball. Soon, Bob had become a fixture.

It turned out that, for his size and shape, he was a helluva ball player. One of the advantages of going to a small school is you made teams that in public school you wouldn't because of the competition. He made his, and I got cut from mine. And when you played competitive ball and practiced five days a week, you got even better than you started out being. I was jealous.

He was also a helluva piano player, an early Billy Joel—The Piano Man. At a party, he was a magnet. I learned quickly that almost everyone we knew had a piano—and no one had my instrument, an accordion. Bob would walk in, sit down at the piano, begin playing boogie-woogie, and he instantly owned the place, and all the girls in it.

Bob would do anything for a laugh. For a time, in Cracker Jack boxes the prizes were these little things that looked like mini mustaches. You put them between your lips and blew and you could play "music." Blown the right way, they sounded exactly like a squeaking mouse. One day, on a lark, we jumped on the subway—to me, the subway was a conveyance to somewhere; to Bob it was a prop—and began squeaking. The reaction was amazing. Women's bodies began to contort along with their faces. Feet were picked up off the floor and, of course, we played it to the hilt by pretending we heard it too. We'd begin mouse hunts in the immediate vicinity of our seats. This became the new "thing" and Bob dragged me off to the subway frequently. Even on a double date, dressed respectably—the mouse show would begin.

Would I ever do that by myself? No way.

But it was with girls that he shone—if you believed him. He had a "little, black book." It was kept in alphabetical order and had notations by the names of who would do oral sex and who would not. He took me up to his apartment one day while his parents, who owned a family business, were at work, pulled open a drawer next to their queen size bed, and displayed a bowl of prophylactics. "They have no idea how many there are in there, so I dip in every so often."

My parents slept in separate beds. There were dental journals in the drawer on the nightstand between them. I'd checked.

It wasn't until sixteen that I finally bought a "bag" of my own to put in my wallet. I knew if I'd gone into Cockeye's to buy one, he'd be on the phone to my mother before I hit the street—or so I thought. I had joined a high school fraternity, and everyone carried one. So, I went to a pharmacy outside the neighborhood.

By the time I got to use it, it was bone dry . . . .

In fact, it had been in my wallet for so long it had left a circular impression on the leather. The first time I actually tried to use it . . . well, that's a whole story in and of itself.

Bob told stories about dates he'd walked out on because the girl balked at his plans for the night. One classic was of this adorable girl, whom I knew. She looked as pure as the driven snow. They were at dinner at a deli (Junior's), and he said, "My parents are out for the night. How 'bout a blow job?" Her response? Not "How dare you?" but "You said we could go to the movies this time. I want to go to the movies." He got up, said he was going to the bathroom, and walked out the back door. He told me, "Boy was she angry the next day."

Nothing like that ever happened to me.

Bob was a year older than we were. I think he got left behind in kindergarten. So, he was the first with a driver's license. His parent's car was a convertible. Bob was a radio button pusher. He'd put the top down, crank up the radio, and punch the channel buttons, until he found the right song. When it was over, push again he would until he found the next right song. More annoying yet was not being able to find the song he felt like listening to. Pieces of songs would fly out of the radio, into your ears, and be gone in a second. Four or five bars—poke the button. Next station, four or five bars—push the button. This went on until he got the four or five bars he wanted. Often, we'd howl in protest because some one of us would want to listen to one of the songs he had just crushed into radio space. No matter. He was master of the radio.

"Cruising Around" was his middle name. Then one day, he came with news. He knew where there was a brothel. Well, he didn't exactly know . . . but he was pretty sure he knew. It was over off 7th Avenue near Eastern Parkway he thought.

So, we made a date and one late afternoon on a Saturday we set out, top down, radio blaring bits and snatches of songs. Bob was playing professor. This is what to say when we got there. This is what would happen when they let us in. He had robbed his parent's personal store and had a rubber for each of us. Mind you, I was still at the stage of sex education where I was arguing with my fraternity brothers, if, during the sex act you were looking at the ceiling or the mattress. To think it could be either was not yet in my picture dictionary.

To say I was anxious doesn't come close to covering the actuality of it. How about jumpy as a cat in the face of a pack of stray dogs?

We got to the area. It was street after street lined with two- and three-story brownstone houses, each and every one of which looked the same. He said he only had part of the address, but we were instructed to look for a small, red, light bulb that would be visible through the curtains on the first floor. As the sun set, we began our quest. Up one street, down another. Four guys peering at curtains in a car going four miles an hour. Every time Bob was "sure this is it," he'd double park and run up to the door for a closer look, sometimes even knocking. His anticipation, along with other parts, would rise while my stomach would sink. "Bob, what if when you double park a cop comes along? What are we going to tell him?" My real question was, "When they call my mother from the precinct, what am I going to tell her?"

He'd laugh and we'd move on.

Never having failed at finding something has ever brought me such relief.

When we quit, up went the radio's volume, out went our chests. I had a story to tell and got into no trouble for having it.

At sixteen, that was a good night out.

"There's a certain type of character that you can't help but come in contact with growing up and living in Brooklyn and Long Island. A certain mixture of moxie, heart, and a wise guy sense of humor."

– Steve Buscemi
Actor, Movie Producer

The East River Bridge, 1883

The First Time

*" . . . the hootin' and hollerin' of the football
team on the other side of the door."*

Honesty and expectation, mine and yours, demands this chapter be part of the teenage years.

I could tell you her long, sad, at-times-tragic story—molestation, borderline poverty, a woman's body in childhood, and finally rape—and that it would take you only up to the junior year of high school.

I could tell you how she had no girlfriends and how she ended up becoming "the mascot" of the football team.

I could tell you that somehow, one day she chose me as her "only true" friend and that is how I learned everything written above.

Then there was the end of season football party at someone's apartment to which she invited me, how drunk she got, how she took me into a bedroom, pushed the bed against the door, and told me she wanted to thank me for being such a good friend.

I could tell you about the guilt and anxiety and the hootin' and hollerin' from the team on the other side of the door.

I wouldn't even leave out the graphic details of the fumblings and foreplay—and that dried out condom, and its impression in the leather of my wallet—if I were going to tell you this story. But I'm not.

I'm only going to tell you that it was the night I learned you don't unroll a prophylactic before you use it.

As Dickens points out in *Great Expectations*, great expectations can end up not so great.

My Fair Lady

"She was to be my fair lady."

My brother always took "big brother" as a job description, stood as a last line of defense between my adolescent years and my mother's alcoholism. Once he left the house, we actually grew closer. I was often his confidant, as he was mine. Rarely though did he ask me for favors.

This time he did.

He called me up Saturday morning, breathless, and said, "I need a favor. Tonight, I need you to be eighteen."

I was sixteen. I asked, "How do I do that?"

He advised, "Put on a suit and tie. I'll pick you up. Follow my lead. You're now a freshman at Brooklyn College."

Intriguing.

As we headed into the city, I got "the rest of the story," as Paul Harvey would say. Jeff had a date with someone he really liked. As the Space Correspondent, he became tight with the Apollo and Mercury crews. He and Alan Shepard, the first American in space, hit it off. Shepherd was America's Hero.

He was in New York and had been given four, third row, center seats to Broadway's hottest show, *My Fair Lady*. He couldn't go; did Jeff want the tickets? Ordinarily, he would have picked two friends or colleagues from CBS, but no one was available on such short notice, and the day of the show his girlfriend called and said her best friend had unexpectedly shown up, and unless Jeff could get her a blind date, she'd have to pass on the evening. Oh, and did I mention her friend was runner up in the Miss Virginia/Miss America pageant? She was to be my fair lady.

That's how and why I became eighteen. She was twenty-two, but eighteen seemed close enough for what was going on.

Commander Shepard had thrown in dinner at some fancy place where we arranged to meet the girls. Sixteen, fancy, and beauty pageant contestant—it was going to be a night for multiple packs of Tums. Introductions were made, dinner was delicious, and frankly, I wasn't bowled over by her looks. She was, however, sweet and had a very, very Virginia accent that I could have listened to all night but didn't have time. It was time to go.

And time for disaster to strike.

Ever the gentlemen, I bounced from my chair to lead her to the door, which was one of those circular, round-robin glass 'thingees.' Not wanting to crowd her or have to think of another two and a half seconds of conversation, I made sure she had a compartment to herself. I ushered her in, gave her wing of the door a push. Around she went to the sidewalk.

Now it was my turn. In I go. No Sir Galahad to swing the door for me, I pushed the pane of glass in front of me and started the door in motion going around to the right. Watching my date standing patiently on the sidewalk but noticing it had started to drizzle, I tried to hasten the ride. I had the umbrella. I felt some urgency to reach her and her hair, whose coif wouldn't stand much in the way of New York City rain.

As soon as I saw daylight, I exited—or tried. The next thing I heard was a sound that might have come from Gerald McBoing-Boing, a cartoon character I loved who could only talk in Boings. The sound? BOING! The next thing I noticed was that the door was vibrating, or was it my head? I grabbed for the handlebar that was on the door. It kept my buckling knees from dumping me onto the floor and then my getting smacked in the back by the patrons following behind. Finally, I stumbled out, wobbling towards my date who had, of course, a panoramic view of the goings-on.

"Are you alright, HUHNEE?" she drawled.

"I think so." I touched my forehead to find what the throbbing was. The throbbing was a knot already the size of a golf ball, red as the sunset, turning black, blue, and yellow, and growing like it had been planted by "Jack" of Beanstalk fame.

"Ouch!" I said as she tenderly touched it.

I looked back to see how that had happened and noticed that the architect decided it would look sharp if the building intersected the cylinder at both sides. Thus, you saw the sidewalk before you actually got to it. Seeing the sidewalk, I made my premature exit. I'm sure someone else had done that before me, but I didn't feel so sure of it at that moment.

By this time, my brother and his date had hit the sidewalk and caught up to us. He had seen what happened, took one look at my forehead, and said what sounded like, "Hopeless . . ."

The play, by the way, was great. The next day's headache wasn't. Never did hear from almost Miss Virginia again.

"I love Brooklyn; it's a part of who you are."

– Paul Dano
American Actor,
Singer, Screenwriter,
Producer, and
Musician

Section Six

Camp Samoset, Lake Winnipesaukee, Laconia, NH
where my baseball career ended.

"It's Summer Time, Summer Time" Introduction

" . . . heat hot enough to melt the brain, long days that seemed endless . . ."

This electric prose comes from a song all of you over sixty-five remember, and many of you who are younger, but "oldies" fans have heard numerous times. Those times are usually during the summer.

I have chosen to focus on summertime not as a youngster but as an adolescent. Why? Because up until that time, summer was ghastly boring. If it was ghastly boring to live, imagine what it would be like to read about. I mean we'd played in sprinklers and I stepped barefoot on a bumblebee that took great umbrage at the act and stung me on the bottom of my foot.

That kind of stuff. You can thank me later.

But summers as an adolescent, now that's the good stuff, remembering the good psychiatrist's nostrum that, "Normal adolescents are abnormal." It would be well to remember the hormone issue as well. Time . . . lots of it, heat hot enough to melt the brain, long days that seemed endless, nights that were never long enough—add hormones and you get the summertime section of this *corpus delicti*.

"Hi folks. Remember me? 'not nearly am I as cute as I look."

Too Young for Grossingers

"Human or Frogs, women are all alike . . ."

The Catskills

Ever sit in a car climbing a steep incline behind a fully loaded log truck, a set of chains the only thing keeping forty or fifty feet of mostly whole trees from smashing through your car's windshield? Such was a common predicament on the trip up Route 17 to the Catskill Mountains. The sight of the freshly sawn logs was so riveting it all but removed the ability to look at the also breathtaking scenery. Before the camp years, our family, sometimes my uncle's family, and the family of close friends, would rent cabins at a rustic resort called the "N".

Absenting the truck, at a certain point one could look up at the mountains and know we were fairly close to our destination because we could see a big "N" carved into the mountain's forestry. Not such a quick study then, it took me years to figure out why it was called the "N". The family owned property belonged to the Swedish Nichol's family. Genius was I.

The "N" was the antithesis of the world famous Grossingers, a town or two over. No entertainers, no straight-from-Brooklyn-Jewish waiters, no dozens and dozens of activities to which the assembled were herded by social directors. There was a main house and dining room, with a screened front porch that faced the lake. Adirondack chairs dotted the lawn. There was a tennis court. Nature provided the rest.

The "N" was not so much a resort as it was a place to go and relax, meaning for kids you either made your own fun or were bored stiff. One of our friends, whose daughter Amy, on whom I had a killer crush at all of seven years of age, was a school principal and very good about spending time with us. He taught me to swim in the big lake the property abutted. We'd take long educational hikes along shale-covered paths where we'd find salamanders galore, some of which I'd take home to put in a terrarium made with the moss I'd pick up as well. Every so often, a garter snake slithered by. Once or twice I caught one and got to feel its strange dry but oily skin. Also, with enough time and patience, if one skittered a walking stick or one's toe through the shale, one would see a glint of red. The walls of soft, easily breakable shale held billions of garnets. They were mined throughout the area. Some finds were worthy of being taken home to the jeweler, polished and set.

Sometimes we'd go rowing or canoeing. Fun was looking for bullfrogs while sliding through the endless fields of lily pads that hugged the shoreline. At night, they could be heard burping to each other, male enticing female, female signaling she either was or wasn't impressed. Females are females, I guess, frog or human—all play hard to get. If one were stealthy enough, one could sidle right up alongside one of these bright green and black owners of the pads. Some could weigh two or three pounds. That's a lot of frog. They sat quietly but warily upon a pad that could be a foot or more in width, in a field so thick that one couldn't see the water below. It was like the water was wallpapered with lily pads. Eyes darting around, the frog would, on occasion, audition right before your eyes like from *National Geographic* as its tongue exploded out of its mouth to pull in a fly or moth that had ventured too closely in range of that sticky weapon.

Polio

Three stories from the "N" have embedded themselves in my mind: the polio epidemic, the day the Nichol's family cat decided to show its undying love for my mother, who hated it, and the day my uncle probably saved my life.

One summer, the scourge of polio, as yet undefeated by Dr. Jonas Salk's miracle research and vaccine, hit New York with a vengeance. Since it was assumed that the close quarters of city living, both work and residential, spread the virus like, well, a virus, people fled to the countryside. Fortunately, each year we left the "N" we made the next year's reservations, so we had, as they said, "where to go." And we went.

I was sort of a sickly kid. Well, not sickly, but I had allergies, and when I got sick, I usually got very sick. I never had a cold that didn't have a cough that didn't become bronchitis. Ahhhh, to feel again the fiery warmth generated from that clear medicinal brew, terpin hydrate with codeine, burn its way into my chest and slowly lift my body to the Heavens. (I believe that's now called a drug addiction high.) Every head cold would turn into a sinus infection and I'd have to go to a doctor with a machine that looked like it came out of *A Clockwork Orange*. It had suction tubes that were literally eased up into the sinus cavities and sucked out the infected mucous. The worst part of the deal was, the machine was clear glass. If one ever wondered what the inside of an infected sinus held, including its color scheme, well, there was your answer lookin' you in the eye. Yuk! Anyway, whisking me off to the mountains seemed the more than appropriate thing to do.

Of course, I got sick, very sick, so sick that my neck muscles were sore, and it was difficult to turn my head. Now it could have been many things, including having swung a bat so hard at a pitch that I strained my neck. But the high fever ruled that out. The fear in my parents was palpable. They took me to "Ole Doc Smith" or whomever was the local doctor who'd been there since leeches from the lake—and there were plenty, and big ones—were used for healing. He probably also subbed as the local vet when things got slow. Or maybe it was the other way around.

I remember comparing his office to our family doctor's. Let's just say it was dark and sort of basic. He took my temperature, poked prodded, twisted turned, helped me off the examining table and sent me to the waiting room. Through the cracked-open door, I could hear words that sounded like what you heard when the needle skipped across a scratched record. Fever . . . muscle weakness . . . diminished mobility . . . polio.

My parents exited the doctor's office looking like death warmed over. It was a silent drive back to the "N". I was put to bed while my father the "DDS" and my uncle the "MD" huddled. The next day, we drove into the infected cesspool of hell, New York, to see our doctor. I had a sinus infection, big time. All the symptoms matched what would be the early onset of the polio virus, except I didn't have it. I hope the horses got better care. By the way, my father called the ole, country Doc and ripped him a new one.

The Cat

Then there was the cat. My mother hated cats. This cat was determined to prove to my mother that she was wrong, that, as a cat he deserved her love. In the country still in the '50s, if one had a dog or multiple dogs, they served a purpose, and it wasn't to sit on your lap while you listened to the radio. Protection, hunting, guarding the livestock, that's what they did. The dog earned its keep. Same for cats. They were there to keep the mice and rats out of the grain, out of the house, out of the barn. In getting a cat, people asked if it, or its parents, was a good mouser. Did it just chase, or did it catch and kill? Catch and kill was what you wanted.

This tabby found my mother's feet no matter where she put them. He'd rub against her ankles in the dining room and again in the card room. After she went for a swim, he would find her and endeavor to run that prickly cat tongue over her feet to help her dry off. Each of these acts of loving kindness was rebuffed, sometimes with loud vocalizations including "not for prime time" language, others with kicking feet also accompanied by loud vocalizations that included "not for prime time" language. There is nothing as tragic as unrequited love, even for a cat. Each time it was rebuffed it would slink off thinking, thinking. What can I give my love to prove my love? What will make her see me as worthy of her attention and affection? Surely there must be an answer, he must have thought.

Now, unlike a human, a cat can't just amble into a jewelry store and ask for some knock-her-eyes-out stone or even share his blues with a barkeep and seek advice. No, the cat is restricted to the world he knows. He has only his instincts to fall back on and one day it hit him. He would share his prize possession.

Every afternoon after a hard dawn of doing nothing and expending great energy chewing her lunch, Mom would go out on the expansive green lawn, possess an Adirondack chair, and take a nap.

One afternoon, our lovelorn feline, had his plan come into sharp focus. While his love slept, he went hunting, successfully, I might add. Across the lawn he pranced, mouse hanging from his mouth by the nape of its neck. My brother and I had a bird's eye view of what was unfolding because we had been hunting ourselves and caught about a three-pound bull frog that we planned to plop in mom's lap and then run for our lives.

What we deduced was about to happen was far better. Cyrano the Cat noiselessly padded across the lawn and effortlessly leaped up on the broad, flat arm of the Adirondack chair, mouse in mouth. It seemed that just as the mouse left his mouth and was dropping towards her lap, Mother opened her eyes—wide.

They say on certain days, when the weather conditions are just right, you can hear a scream cross the lake and echo through the mountains. With the ensuing scream, Mildred the Mad had permanently etched herself into the natural landscape. I'll bet the scream still reverberates.

The cat? Who knows . . .?

Snakes

There were other things beside frogs, and lizards, and gemstones hidden in the rocks of the mountains. One of them rattled and hissed. The area had Copperheads and Water Moccasins, both deadly. A Water Moccasin is an evil looking creature, dark and ominous made all the more frightening because you could be out fishing and see them swim towards the sound and scent wafting across their territory. Legend? Truth? Don't know, but that story about a Water Moccasin that wrapped itself around a fisherman's oar and wriggled his way into the boat where in a fight for his life the fisherman had to beat it to death with the other oar, kept me awake at night. Like I said, legend? Truth? Don't know. Scary, I do!

Not that a Copperhead was a beauty, but in a sense, especially compared to the Water Moccasin, it was. Bronze, a skin that glinted in the sun, a hard, triangular, prehistoric looking head. Mind you, while pretty, it was also pretty damned dangerous and prone to being quite nasty.

To get to the lake one had to follow this winding, tricky path littered with large rocks, pieces of downed trees, and a man-enhanced natural pathway of crushed, rotted, pine bark and needles. It was idyllic in its own way, and at times gave off a smell that was as sweet as nature's own essence. One day, hustling down the path to meet my uncle at the lake for a promised fishing trip for trout, bass, pike, and pickerel, I noticed a glint to my left. I stopped and looked hard into the rocks, and there it was—a very real, very live, and very unfriendly Copperhead.

As it curled itself tightly, never taking its beady, black eyes off me, its tail rose off the ground. I learned why they are called rattlesnakes. I also froze. Fixed to the ground, not a muscle worked. And I hadn't even been bitten yet! Fortunately, I wasn't with the country doc or for sure he would have, again, diagnosed me with polio.

Who knows how long we—the snake and I—were fixed in our places in this epic stare-down? Then all of a sudden, I was pushed to the side. I heard this crash, and it was over. My uncle had come to the rescue. He had wondered what was taking me so long and came to look. Figuring out what was going on, he picked up this very large stone, and like Hercules, lifted it with two hands up over his head, and brought it down on the snake. My hero.

We did go fishing. And we did catch fish. And we didn't have a snake wind itself around an oar and attack us in the boat. A good day after all.

"I am happy everywhere except in places where I see glitz and rich farts. I am happiest in Brooklyn, where the concentration of rich farts is minimal."

– Nassim Nicholas Taleb
Lebanese American Author,
Writer, Statistician

The View: Coney Island's Ferris Wheel, Parachute Jump and the Atlantic Ocean.

The Role of the Radio

"Ahhhh-bay! Ahhhhhh-bay!"

You haven't listened to rock and roll on the radio until you've listened to it coming from one million individual speakers at the same time. Such was the way it was at Coney Island Beach any sunny summer's day where one of the news spots was not just the body count in Korea, but the "body count" at the beach.

On a nice, beach day, a million people was the expected number. On holidays, it could be a million two or three (as in hundred thousand) or more. Coney Island/Brighton Beach was implicitly understood when someone in the neighborhood said, "Let's go to the beach today." It was also understood this meant boarding a packed, un-air-conditioned subway car, being bathed with sweat by the time you arrived because you were already wearing your bathing suit under your clothes. You then walked several blocks to the beach listening to the noise level rise higher and higher the closer you got, threading one's way on the scorching hot sand, until one was able to find enough vacant sand for one more blanket. Within minutes, one's sweaty body was coated with sand either from a puff of wind, if there was any that day, or more likely someone's screaming kids chasing one another around and kicking sand all over the place. This was called fun. Notice the lack of an exclamation point. But it was what you did.

No matter how many times I went to the beach, when I mounted the boardwalk to look out at an expanse filled with bodies that stretched to the edge of the ocean, an expanse that moved up and back with the tide, the sheer magnitude of the crowd took my breath away. To the left and right were the sights and sounds of Coney Island Amusement Park: the screams from the Cyclone as it rumbled and rattled across its wooden slates at close to sixty miles an hour, the hoots and hollers from the fun house and side shows, and of course the indefinable, but always delicious smells of Nathan's, the most famous hotdog emporium in the world.

Two things stood out on the beach itself. The first was the girls who dressed for the beach in ways none of the parents I knew would let their daughters dress for a bath, no less a public beach. The bikini was in vogue, but there were also some one-pieces that did a good job of reducing the need for much imagination. The other thing that stood out was the guys who sold ice cream and soda out of white, metal insulated boxes hanging from a strap over their shoulders. Normally they were dressed in white and they were sweating like pigs as they trucked what must have been at least fifty pounds of items and the dry ice to keep them cold. It was a sight that said, "Pay attention in school. This is not how you want to make your living!"

Except if it was early summer, and the water was chilly, running into the waves was like diving head first into a saltwater bathtub. There were some differences. Since your skin temperature had risen to about oven temperature, the eighty-five-degree water still could be a shock when you hit it. You could hear the same sizzle as when you took the frying pan off the stove and ran it under the faucet. Or so it seemed. You also knew to swim as far from families with babies as possible because you would be swimming in water unlikely to pass any sanitation department test. Again, this was called fun.

Older kids with their significant others who were good swimmers would push out pass the crowds and tread water beyond the break of the waves putting on often eye-popping shows for us pre- or early-teens. And I don't mean with their swimming prowess. This was truly fun.

So was making out on the sandy blanket, covered with sand, in the broiling sun, and the ritual of helping your date put suntan lotion on both of you. Those tough enough, and I mean tough, to find a spot under the boardwalk were treated to cool, damp sand as their playground. They didn't know, or maybe didn't care about the occasional liquid that sluiced through the very old, very warped wooden slats. The possibilities were many. Coke? Water? Pee? (And not necessarily from a baby.) What the hell. They were busy, and that's what the ocean was for anyway, God's public bathtub.

But let's us not forget the battery driven entertainment. It was the age of the transistor radio and the "boom box." AM radio was king. The Top Ten on the charts was the hourly fare. And depending on the time, the DJ was Cousin Brucie or Alan Freed of blessed memory. The Bruce Morrow Show began with some desiccated voice calling out his name as if from a tenement window: "COUSIN BRUUUUUUUUcie, COUSIN BRUUUUUUUUUUUcie." And remember you were hearing this from a million radios, give or take a few, propped up on piles of sand that had hundreds of yards of depth and went for a mile or more in length. With each succeeding section of the beach's sound being passed off to the next, it produced almost a vibrato in the air, but a nanosecond slower than the previous one. And all the listeners were Cousin Brucie's cousins so up and down the beach one heard him answer not quite in synch, with his signature opening of, "Hey Cousins . . ." This too was fun.

The rival stations, principally WMCA at the beginning of the dial and WINS in the middle of it, each had their rival deejays. Along with Alan Freed and Bruce Morrow were Murray the K and Herb Oscar Anderson. Each put on Rock N Roll shows at the theaters around the city. Some were so successful, like Murray the K's that they had major impacts on neighborhood economies and crime stats, especially shoplifting.

Murray the K had a direct impact on my father's dental practice. The shows were booked at the Brooklyn Fox Theatre, above which was the office building in which my father practiced. For an 8 p.m. show, lines could start forming in the late morning, and by mid-afternoon wrap once or twice around the block. My dad's patients became less and less patient with the crowds on the subway, the impossibility of finding parking places, and the anxiety of having to cut through this mass of teenage humanity (giving many the benefit of the doubt) to get to the safety of the lobby.

All of this worked out to my mother's benefit. My father "moved on up to the big time," moving his office to Madison Avenue in Manhattan. Now her husband was not only a professional man, but a Madison Avenue dentist. Hoo-ha!

There were other impacts. Murray the K's show was on at night. It was called *Murray the K and The Swingin' Soiree*. One segment was "The Submarine Races." He would coo, "You're never too old to watch the submarine races." It even had a chant: "Ahhh-bay! Ahhhh-bay!" Who knows why? Not me. But it was fun.

The so-called races featured soft, romantic rock and roll. Freed became famous for several reasons. One was babies born nine months after his shows. Another was tickets given by law enforcement to illegally parked teenagers who were where they shouldn't be, at hours they shouldn't have been there, doing things that they shouldn't have been doing. He was a brilliant show business legend who called himself, "The Fifth Beatle." He was also famous for having had six wives, one of which he was married to for three months! And murders. Yes, murders. Some of the early Son of Sam shooting victims were teenagers parked in cars listening to Murray the K's submarine races.

For those unfamiliar with that period in New York, there was a lunatic skulking around the five boroughs shooting people mostly at night, mostly necking in their cars. He was David Berkowitz, self-named "Son of Sam." Sam was a demon—so-called in his head—who, when Berkowitz was drunk, abused him. Also called the ".44 Caliber Killer" for the very powerful pistol he used; his first attempt at murder was with a knife and failed. His exploits became known around the world as he eluded what was then the largest manhunt in New York City history. His notoriety caused the State Legislature to pass the "Son of Sam" Law that prevented prisoners from reaping financial benefit from their crimes. You couldn't murder people, then write a book or do interviews, and make money just because you killed people. Berkowitz is so famous that he can easily be researched. Suffice it to say, he was a real "looney-tune" who scared the crap out of the city.

THE WAR of the ITCHY BALLS

There was another dark side to rock and roll that we slowly became more aware of as we got older. It was the days of "pay for play," the so-called Payola Scandals. Deejays got famous for more than their ability to attract radio audiences, and therefore advertising revenue. The gold standard in the industry was for a record to "go gold," or sell a million copies. An artist or group couldn't do that, or even get on the air, without a deejay taking a shine to him/her/them. Since there were many more artists making many more records than there were major market deejays, it became a common practice for the deejays to be paid to play records. It wasn't just playing them, it was when during the show it was played (the time when Neilson rated the highest audience slot), and how many times during the peak listening hours it was played. It was almost counterintuitive. You'd think that if a kid could hear a record four or five times a day, especially if he was station-jumping, it wouldn't be necessary to buy the record. You'd be wrong.

The two most famous names attached to the scandals were Alan Freed, who is credited with inventing the term "rock and roll". He was fired from WABC for being an uncooperative witness in the Congressional hearings into the practice, and more recently deceased Dick Clark. Clark was able to sidestep the scandal by selling his small stake in a station that was targeted in the practice and then reinventing himself into the entertainment mogul he became.

In an "Only in America" story, Clark was labeled a genius when a new group, Danny and the Juniors asked him to listen to a song they called, "Do the Bop." Always in a hurry, Clark heard out the two some-odd minutes, said, "Change the title to, "At the Hop" and zipped away. The song and the group zoomed to the top of the charts and Dick Clark was now the guru of rock and roll success.

The other side of it was the part of being socially desirable, especially for boys. You wanted to be the kid with the best collection of 45s, a box filled with records that went gold. That got you invited to all the best parties. And you didn't care if the reason was your records; what mattered was the invite. You controlled things then.

If you left, so did the records, and so ended the party. If a deejay played a song to the point that it was forever fixed in your memory, that spurred you to buy the record. That phenomenon kept the cash flowing, started the aforementioned Congressional hearings, and sent a few folks to jail. It was a sad and sobering time for the fan base and the pain lasted until we outgrew high school, went to college, and found other avenues than the transistor radio to make the party lists.

"You go to Brooklyn, everybody's got a beard and plaid shirt. They may be able to tell each other apart, but they all look alike to me."

– Don Lemon
CNN Anchor

"I felt unhappy and trapped. If I left baseball, where could I go, what could I do to earn enough money to help my mother and to marry Rachel? The solution to my problem was only days away in the hands of a tough, shrewd, courageous man called Branch Rickey, the president of the Brooklyn Dodgers."

– Jackie Robinson
Brooklyn Dodgers

Labor Day Memories

"The smoke from the 'bar-b-cues' would waft across the beach either blinding or choking everyone."

I flipped on the Labor Day edition of what has universally become known as "The Golden Oldies," the wonderful music of the '50s and '60s. The music is timeless. The harmonies of the oldies era brought back a flood of Labor Day memories. Many were associated with Coney Island. Not these.

In Brooklyn, Labor Day was when hormones drove teens like lemmings to the beach at Coney. They infiltrated, overran, and in some cases ran over, the rest of lower middle class and working-class Brooklynites. Just as we all awaited the tally of the Jerry Lewis telethon, everyone waited for the "official count" of how many people were on the beach. Usually there were more than a million!

Normally, we did Labor Day as a family. We either drove at a snail's pace to the Five Towns on Long Island to our cabana at the Silverpoint Beach Club. Cabana? An 8'x10' room with running water and a toilet, no air conditioning, that allowed you to change out of the sweat-soaked clothing from the drive and put on cooler, but soon to be sweat-soaked, beach clothes.

We'd put beach chairs on the wooden walkway that connected all the cabanas in one's row and emptied out on the beach where the sand was usually hot enough to burn the skin right off the bottom of your feet. That's why people always ran into the ocean—otherwise it was like walking on hot coals.

We shared the cabana with three other families so there was never any room to move in it. One man I remember clearly because of his job. He was a matchbook salesman to bars and restaurants. I couldn't imagine how one made a living doing that, or why one would want to. He also was the hairiest creature I had ever seen that wasn't in a zoo.

As the sun began to set, out would come the barbecues and the smell of charred hot dogs, hamburgers, or flank steaks would waft across the area, either blinding everyone or half choking them to death. This mixed with everyone's cigarette or cigar smoke. With the setting sun came a stiff breeze off the Atlantic sure to blow sand on your food.

Night would fall. What would pass for a cool breeze would kick up. Then we'd shut up the cabana, drag everything to the car, sit on seats as hot as the sand, and crawl home in the traffic. The car was hot enough to poach fish. Sounds like fun, no? No.

"Even after Jim Crow was supposed to not be a part of the South anymore, there were still ways in which you couldn't get away from it. And I think once I got to Brooklyn, there was this freedom we had."

– Jacqueline Woodson
American Writer of
books for children
and adolescents

No explanation needed.

Sharon—A Command Performance

*"He wasn't wearing a gun because he
was a cop . . . he was a killer."*

Some dates with girls hold a place of their own. This is one of those stories. It includes, the mafia, jailbait, and stupidity drawn of naiveté. The jailbait that my brother picked up at Coney Island—who looked seventeen but was thirteen—he decided would earn my spurs. Yee-Haw!

Not even close.

He had prepared me for our joint venture to the beach. "How are we going to find one girl amidst a million people?" I asked, with a hopeful twinge of defeat in my voice.

He responded, "First of all, she's always in the same spot and secondly—you'll know." Gulp.

She was in "her spot." And yes, I knew. How to describe what I saw? A reddish-blonde haired girl sitting on a blanket. One leg was outstretched, the other bent at the knee. Her arms were up behind her head as she slowly, very slowly stroked her long hair up on top of her head. To do this, she had to arch her back in an incredible curve, not incredible because of the arch, incredible because of what the arch did for her chest. A pin-up girl poster. That's what I was looking at! This girl was for me? I thought I would die—of a heart attack.

My brother said, "I told you. Now go talk to her."

Go talk to her was more of a command than a suggestion, and it came with a shove. I could embarrass myself in front of my brother or embarrass myself in front of this goddess. It was a hard shove and physics solved the dilemma. There I was, at her blanket. She knew I needed help, so she opened with, "You're the brother, aren't you?"

"Yeehss," I stammered.

"Hi, my name is Sharon. Pull up some blanket and sit down."

Also, more of a command than suggestion. She was not sitting on a beach blanket the kind that are traditionally the size of small bed sheets. She was sitting on a towel and sitting next to her was really being next to her, close enough so that the sweat pouring out of every pore of my body mixed with the suntan lotion, the application of which was the close of her show, she smoothed it all over her body.

What transpired was idiot talk. She wasn't the going-in-the-water type. My mouth was so dry I needed the ocean to swallow and just as I figured all was lost, and said, "I guess I better be going." She said, "Aren't you going to ask me out?"

Damn! Almost forgot that part.

So I did. "How about Saturday night?" The next question I should have been shot for: "You like to bowl?"

"Sure, why not?" she responded.

I had a week to prepare for the disaster that was going to occur but let me tell you why I should have been shot.

I had no car. I had no idea how to get to where she lived. Nor did I have any idea where there was a bowling alley in her neighborhood. I had set myself up for failure and boy did I ever succeed.

Back in the day, local directions were gotten using the telephone books and telephones. I looked up "Bowling Alleys" in the *Yellow Pages*, a book as big as the white pages, to find none near where she lived. I picked what seemed to be the closest and called for directions. We would have to take a city bus. How cool is that? Not. The only good news was the bus stopped in front of her apartment building, and in front of the alley. Cab you say? Parents offered nothing towards this outing; I would be lucky to have the money I needed for the bus rides and the bowling.

Then I got directions from my brother as we both prepared for our Saturday night dates. I said, "Should I kiss her goodnight?"

His flat, scornful response? "No *schmuck*, shake hands." I got the point.

Aside from getting slightly motion sick on the bus, the trip to her apartment building was uneventful. That is where "uneventful" left the stage. I knocked on the door. Her mother answered, and I was greeted like she had never seen a clean-cut, freshly scrubbed kid come to pick up her daughter. It was an effusive greeting, a little overwhelming actually. She took my hand and said, "Come. Let's see if Sharon is ready."

Again, a command, not a suggestion.

I thought there would ring out from her mouth in her oh-so-Brooklyn accent a call like, "Sharon? Bill's here. You ready?" and a response would return through the bedroom door. Not quite.

She pulled me across the apartment to Sharon's bedroom, knocked once, and in the same motion flung open the door. Sitting in front of a dressing table mirror was Sharon in a state I'd call definitely not ready. While her back was to me, the mirror gave a full-frontal view of pulchritude in bra and panties. With no particular alacrity did she pull up her dress, sitting on her lap, to cover herself. She smiled and cooed, "Hi! Be ready in a few. Mom, close the door."

Speechless, that was me.

A few minutes of small talk later, she made her entrance. She was wearing a herringbone jumper that some artist had painted on her between the time her mother and I exited the room and she made her entrance. This dress had straps that went over both shoulders, each with a black button that buttoned right on top of her nipple, like a pasty on a stripper, except she was wearing a blouse underneath. One of these pesky buttons kept unbuttoning during the evening. It was all very disconcerting.

As we left the apartment and waited for the elevator, I said," You look great, but are you sure you can bowl in that outfit?"

"We'll see, won't we?" she said in what was the first time I had ever heard sexy in a voice.

Came the bus and the next event, getting up the stairs. Initially, there were two people struck into stone by what they were seeing. One was me, behind her. The other was the bus driver, who had a front row seat in front of her. It was something to watch. I was so transfixed and so zeroed in on being a gentleman that I walked her to an open seat with every pair of eyes, male and female rider, fixed on her, that I forgot to pay.

This booming voice rang out, "Hey, kid. This ain't free. You plannin' to pay?" So, I got her settled, and in a very unsettled state, walked back to the front to face this very large, unhappy human being who thought he was dealing with a wise guy rather than a kid who was in way over his head.

To compound things, being a subway rider, I had no idea what the bus cost, so I handed him a bill. He snapped, "Change only. Goes in the hopper." The hopper was about a two-foot high, glass container that had indented slots onto which you threw your money. The machine separated nickels, dimes, and quarters while making these very mechanical noises. I asked how much, reached into my pocket, and threw in the exact change. Remember, I said it counted nickels, dimes, and quarters? You didn't read pennies and pennies were all I had to make up the fare. He was not a happy man but had to drive his bus. "Go sit down!" Another command.

But he wasn't done with me. He must have been watching me in his mirror because as I got to where I had seated Sharon, holding the metal hand holders attached to the aisle side of each seat to steady myself on the rocking bus making its way down Nostrand Avenue, he hit the brakes—hard. He hit them just as I released one seat handle and was reaching for the next. I was catapulted forward into that handle, which was at crotch height. To say I oozed into the seat next to Sharon breathless and sporting a color on my face not found in the large size Crayola box wouldn't be exaggerating much.

Not much transpired on the bus because I was looking out the window hawk-like for our stop. You had to see it before you got to it, reach up, and pull the bell cord or the driver would pass it. For sure, this driver would be making no exceptions for me. I spied. I pulled. He stopped. This time we exited the bus from the rear, giving those paying passengers the show they had missed on our entrance.

And there it was in all its neon glory, the bowling alley. We walked to the desk to pay for games to be played, and over to the other side of the desk to get our bowling shoes. Each attendant gave Sharon a very quizzical look, sort of an unsaid, "You know we don't have changing lockers here."

We soldiered on.

I went first, managed to knock down a bunch of pins, and impressed her with a spare. I helped her choose a ball. She bent to pick it up and pop! went the button. One strap now waved to and fro across her chest. She took the ball, did her run up, and threw it into the gutter. "Maybe you better help me on the next one."

I'll save you the reading—just imagine sex between animals. While it probably didn't happen, at the moment I approached her from behind, the lights in the place went up, the sounds of balls-hitting-walnut wood ceased, pins stopped dropping, and the setting machines stopped setting. Everyone and everything looked at us.

I think we got through three games and two Cokes before calling it a night.

I was terribly preoccupied on the return trip, so preoccupied that having seen the opening of her act, having watched her make her body do things almost unnatural as she tried to bowl, and seen her get on the bus, it wasn't the finale that was too distracting. I had "the kiss" on my mind.

Apparently, so did she.

I had it all worked out. We'd take the elevator to the fifth floor. At the fourth floor, I would turn, embrace, and kiss her. This unfortunately was not her plan, which was to hightail it off the elevator, cut left, fly down the hall, and kiss me good night in front of her door.

Being nervous, my timing was a bit off. As the doors opened at floor number five, I turned to embrace a girl who had flown by me and was on her way to her apartment. I was astounded. I was now in hot pursuit, but the doors, beginning to close, hit me like two linebackers, one from each side. When the rubber protrusions on the doors are hit, the doors jerk to a stop, so the passenger isn't squashed. As loud as in Dolby Stereo came a sound. It was ka-chunk, ka-chunk, kachunk! as the doors tried their best to shut. Finally, I untangled myself from these willful monsters. I raced after Sharon who was already in position in front of the door, eyes closed, lips pointed upward. As I closed my eyes, reached for her waist and puckered my lips—the apartment door opened.

No longer was I greeted by the effusive Mama Bear. There stood Poppa Bear. He was wearing a shirt and slacks. Under the arm he used to open the door, hanging below his armpit, was a .38 caliber pistol. Teenagers know these things. In one smooth motion, he snatched his daughter and thanked me for what he was sure was a lovely evening and shut the door. Just before the door closed, out slipped the words "Call me."

So I did, and here is the postscript.

Sharon invited me over one afternoon to hang out with her friends. I met her on the corner wearing my standard chinos, sneakers, and tee-shirt, what you wore just in case a basketball game broke out in front of you somewhere, sometime. Sharon, dressed as only Sharon could, was surrounded by motorcycles that in turn were surrounded by, to borrow a word from my mom, hoodlums. Suddenly I understood Mama Bear's effusive welcome to me at the door on our date.

I learned two things as I gingerly interacted with the players on the set. One was that a very standoffish guy who looked like carpenter nails were his afternoon snack had a crush on Sharon, and it would be better for my health if I didn't develop one too.

The second thing I learned was that Poppa Bear wasn't wearing a gun because he was a cop. He was a killer, a captain in the mafia.

I saw Sharon once more at the beach, but the thrill had been replaced by fear and but for a few phone calls more, dim the lights, the party was over.

But the worst of the worst?

Sunday morning, I had to explain to my inquisitive brother, act by act, the play that was our date. He listened impassively, turned away, muttering, "Hopeless . . ."

"Va Va Va Voom!"

Coney Island in White

"It was a dead body . . . it had no head."

Every winter, one finds in the New York papers a picture of a large group of lunatics. It is taken in mid-winter when it is freezing. They are in bathing suits plunging into the mind-numbingly cold Atlantic Ocean at Coney Island Beach. Meet the Polar Bear Club of Brooklyn, New York. Those who take the plunge and haven't dropped dead from a heart attack because of the shock to their systems, repair to Nathan's to warm up and, of course, have a hot dog. I wish I had the phonetic skill to write dog the way it is said in Brooklyn. You'll have to take it on faith; it doesn't sound like the furry thing that may be at your feet while you're reading this.

I give you this little preface so that when I tell you about a winter adventure in Coney Island, you'll know that other lunatics went to Coney Island in the winter besides me. My friend, Neil, lived around the corner from me on Rugby Road. It was a short walk, crossing Glenwood Road. His house was neat looking, stone and wood, a "cottagey" look one didn't see a lot of in Brooklyn. It must have been a house built well after mine. Now I have a friend who went to Coney Island in the winter as well as the rest of the year.

Neil's household was quite different than mine as well. His family kept kosher. One day, I walked into the kitchen and saw that Mrs. Goldman had put a fork into a flowerpot. It was sticking up out of the dirt, handle in the air, like a stainless-steel flower that hadn't yet bloomed. Jews who keep kosher have different utensils and dishware for meat products and milk products. If you mess up, which one of Neil's three older brothers had recently done, the misused item was to be buried for a length of time in the ground to be purified. This little trick being used by Mrs. Goldman, one of many the Orthodox use to simplify life, was making sure to heed the law and also making sure you could find your fork or spoon again. Also, in winter, which it was, you didn't have to dig at the frozen ground to either bury it or find it.

Unlike my mother, who went bat-shit when she discovered my one copy of *Playboy* magazine, which Neil incidentally had given me, Neil's mother seemed unfazed by the collection of Playboys in her home amassed by four boys and their father. There were literally pounds and pounds of them, piled up in the rooms of the different boys, and some downstairs as well. The house was always in an uproar, but in a good-natured way. I enjoyed going over there.

The Goldmans had moved into the area after we did. I met Neil walking to school the first day of high school. He was a different kind of friend than my others, being devoid of both athletic talent and interest. He had a great sense of humor but could rankle me, like the time we were walking to school, and I stepped on a twenty-dollar bill that I did not see. He picked it up and wouldn't go halfzies with me. Not funny. Grrrrrrrrrr!

Anyway, his dad was also different from the dads of my other friends in that he was a manufacturer, not a professional man. I mean, he was professional at manufacturing . . . well, anyway you get the point, not a doctor, lawyer, accountant, or such. He owned his own knitting factory and had his own clothing label. Don't ask me; I don't remember. The factory was in Coney Island, sitting on an inlet that ran into the ocean. His goods were not only delivered by truck but by boat. Because of the location of the factory it was an easy target for thieves on the weekends. It was off the sightline from the street, and most of the cops were deployed at the amusement park.

On the weekends, he liked to drop in just to make sure all was well. He did this year around. It was but a few blocks walk from the factory to Nathan's. Mr. G. liked company. He and Neil had this winter routine. They'd check the factory, take a brisk walk on the boardwalk, sometimes play some games because Coney Island was always open for business and then have lunch at Nathan's. Once we had become friends, I was an occasional addition to the party.

One winter's day we entered the dark, dank, and dingy factory. It took only moments to feel the chill. The lights were off and the machines, which when running produced a lot of heat on their own, were silent. The boss did his tour around and when he got to the back he said, "Oh no! Not again!" We raced to his side to find him looking out the window into the water. "We'd best go outside and have a better look before I call the police."

Suddenly this became the stuff of real adventure.

My bones got a lot colder and they were pretty damned cold to begin with. We stepped out the back door onto the dock and huddled around Mr. Goldman who was looking—no foolin'—at a body. It didn't take Joe Friday to figure out it was a dead body.

Why? It didn't have a head.

Apparently more than Mr. G's customers used the inlet. It was an every-so-often drop-off for the unfortunates who crossed wires with the real Tony Sopranos.

My appetite waned as we contemplated lunch and I contemplated the headless floater, but it was one of those happenings one doesn't forget. It's one of the reasons I only eat kosher hotdogs, no matter where I am . . .

Jeff and Walter Cronkite/Vietnam
Being asked to go abroad and produce a
show for Walter Cronkite was like being asked
by General Eisenhower to produce a battle
plan for the invasion of Normandy. Such was
the reputation of both men in their fields.

Celebrity: The Great Naming Debate

". . . and Gralnick was not one of those names."

My father was a mild-mannered man. That's why that night at dinner was such a shock. But I get ahead of myself.

Gralnick actually means something. In fact, once after a speech I gave, an elderly gentleman came up to me, and said, "I'll bet you don't know what your name means." He lost.

In "old Russian," a Gralnick, sometimes pronounced Guralnik was an innkeeper or barkeep. It is centuries old and got attached to a clan of Jews, I suppose because of their profession, from the Minsk area of Russia.

Except for African Americans born with perceived "slave names" or many immigrants who changed their names to sound more American or made alterations in their full name to make them sound less old country: ie. Matchowsky to Match, most kids don't think much about their last names. It is what it is. That is until you became famous. Legendary comedian Jack Benny was born Benny Kubelsky. George Burns was Nathan Birnbaum. Eddie Cantor came to us as Eddie Itzkowitz. It was no different in the movies or television.

And if you were going to be an on-air personality in the news business after WWII, the same held. You needed a name that Americans could identify with—and pronounce. My brother, whose star had begun to rise quickly at CBS, and in the field in general, got the idea that Gralnick was not one of those names. So the scene is set.

Once my brother began covering stories, even pre-national news, dinner table topics changed. Not everything was my mother's idea of table talk but talk my brother did anyway. He had covered the crash of the Electra Jet on 7th Avenue in Brooklyn, including a story on the body of a boy, I believe named Stevie, whose body was found on the sidewalk. Just like combat soldiers, journalists who repeatedly cover grim stuff, develop thick skins and dark senses of humor. "Stevie" jokes went around from those who had covered that tragedy and we heard them at dinner—but only once.

Of great interest, because it was ongoing and therefore a current threat, was the mad-bomber, George Metesky, who planted in New York's subway cars what we now call IED's, often separating people's legs from their mangled bodies. More untold jokes.

Jeff had gone on recommendation of his boss at the International News Service to an opening on the *Douglas Edwards Show* and then soon after to the coveted Walter Cronkite show. In baseball terms, he had gone from the Pittsburgh Pirates to the New York Yankees. Yes, both were in the major leagues, but there were major differences between the two. He came home one night with an idea that must have been percolating for quite some time, but maybe not long enough. For someone trained to find the heart of a story, in analyzing this one, he missed the heart completely . . . because it wasn't in a news story.

A journalist knows there are at least two sides to every story. What side did he miss? The impact that this tidbit would have— that if he was going to wear the Yankee pinstripes of major league news broadcasting, Gralnick wasn't the name to have. Grant was the name he hit on as in Lou Grant of the *Mary Tyler Moore Show*.

He didn't know it, but we were about to have a dinner table explosion matched only later by the one after Philip Roth published, *Portnoy's Complaint*. This time, however, it would come from the other side of the table. The dinner table—actually a cherry wood antique from the late 1700s that I now possess—was a rectangle. My mom sat at the head of the table closest to the kitchen, a mystery since she rarely cooked dinner and more rarely served it. My dad did not sit next to her but sat at the other end of the table. My brother and I faced each other across the long sides of the table, probably so we weren't within touching distance of each other.

Soon it would begin and innocently enough.

"So," said my brother. "I've been thinking about changing my name."

Later, I learned there was a whole rationale that was to follow. Today, thinking back, it reminds me of the automobile commercial where the teenager comes into his parent's bedroom to tell them about a "minor fender-bender" and how he'd already contacted the agent and how smart his parents were to have accident forgiveness coverage. In the middle of this expostulation his mom says, "Four weeks without the car!"

It was a conversation stopper.

My brother never got past the first sentence. In fact, the first sentence was the only sentence. A bit later in his career, my brother was promoted to correspondent at what was then Cape Canaveral covering the lives and training of the early astronauts and of course the space shots. What happened after "my name" would prepare him well for that assignment. It was blast off in the dining room.

Something began to happen down at the end of the table. Around mild-mannered Abe, the ground began to tremble, the table began to shake. A deepening, almost deafening sound arose from under his chair and enveloped his 5'9" frame. Like the desert sky at sunset, his face turned red. Like the face of an astronaut dealing with incredible amounts of pressure on his body, his face contorted, changed shape. And all of this before he had said a word.

I was maybe fifteen. I looked at him and thought, Uh-oh. He's gonna drop dead right at the dinner table.

He didn't. But he came closer to becoming a murderer than a corpse. They don't make a type size big enough to capture what came out of his mouth. "WHAT DID YOU SAY? CHANGE YOUR NAME? GRANT? SO YOU CAN BE A GOY?" (Sorry folks, that means gentile, its biblical Hebrew, but in common use, it is not a nice term.) Most shocking, there was even a F-bomb somewhere in there.

What followed were his responses to the dissertation that never got out of my brother's mouth. It was stunning. It was like watching a tabby cat morph into a rabid tiger. I sat stock-still, nailed to my chair. Even my mother, who had been married to this man for several decades, was amazed at what she was watching and hearing. Unusual for her, she said not one word.

And my poor brother? He sat there mumbling, "But . . . but Dad, but, but Dad . . ." These were batted back like a pro tennis player leaping on a "meatball" coming right into his forearm swing. Bam!

Having finished his harangue on being Jewish, on Jews as a people, the name we Jews at the table carried, he stood up and threw his napkin—linen of course—onto the table, and I thought, I'm about to become an only child. But no, he wheeled around smartly, 180 degrees. It was about five paces to the staircase, which he mounted, and all this ended with the slam of the bedroom door that came down the stairs the same route he had taken up.

You can Google my brother, Jeff. He had a brilliant fifty-seven-year career as a journalist, producer, and executive—all as a Gralnick.

"I like L.A., but I'm definitely a Brooklyn girl; I'm a city girl. I need the cars honking. I need the bright lights. I need people yelling in the middle of the night screaming at each other. I need all of that."

– Justine Skye, Actress

"I was raised on the streets, in hot, steamy Brooklyn, with stifled air."

       – Barbra Streisand
       World Famous Singer, Actress
       Stage and Screen

From Plump Kid to Playboy Bunny

". . . my name changed from Bill to Cyrano."

We'll go without a name here because this person lives about ten miles from where I'm sitting and is very much alive. We met as freshmen in high school. She was sweet, round, vivacious, fun. I went away for the summer. When I returned, God had re-arranged all her roundness, smoothed, sanded, and sculpted her in magical ways. He had turned her from a blob into what looked to me like a *Playboy* bunny. She was still sweet, vivacious and fun, but she also had very long legs and was, to use the parlance of the day, stacked. She was personality-plus with a smile that could light up a city block at night.

I was smitten; she was not.

I had been invited to join a high school fraternity. One night she shattered me with the revelation that she had a massive crush on one of my fraternity brothers. How was she going to meet him? Suddenly my name changed from Bill to Cyrano. Under the guise of discussing this other guy, I invited her to the beach. She accepted and on the appointed day, after an insanely hot subway ride, we joined the masses on the sand. Lucky at all to find space, we spread out about halfway between the boardwalk and the water.

In all innocence, maybe, she asked me to help spread out the blanket. When she leaned over, I almost fell over. Then, of course, could I help her with the suntan lotion? Had I Cyrano's sword, I would have killed one of us with it, the psychic pain was so great. It wasn't long before we were both cooking at a temperature more suited to boiling lobster than relaxing people, so she decided she needed to cool off.

She arose to run into the water, and I had a moment of insanity. I also rose, chased her down the beach, and just before the water, I tackled her! Where's Freud when you need him?

She rolled over, and said, "I can't get up." I said, "That's not funny."

She wasn't being funny. She could neither get up, nor walk. She was a big girl, probably 5'6" or seven, and not feathery light. Now, dear friends, think of the aforementioned subway. What a ride home it was. She had her arm around my shoulder. We limped off the beach to the 'El', somehow managed to get up the flights of stairs, and soon entered the pressure cooker pot called a subway car. She leaned on me all the way home, which would have been wonderful if it had been about thirty degrees cooler. As it was, we were squishy with sweat. Frankly, I don't remember how I got her home, but I did.

I called that night. All seemed well and be still my heart, she was not only talking to me, but invited me over late the next day, Sunday afternoon.

When I went to visit . . . well, let me set the scene for you.

She lived in a two-story walk-up. It was a modest apartment. The front door opened into the living room across from which, against the far wall, was their couch. My heart raced me up the stairs I was so excited to see her. I knocked.

She yelled. "It's open, come in."

There across the room I was confronted with a foot attached to a very, very long leg, coming out of very, very short shorts, flanked by brand new crutches, and covered with the longest, whitest cast I'd ever seen. I had torn the ligaments in her knee. She would be crippled for the rest of the summer.

Then this scruffy guy, unshorn for Sunday, walked into the room. It was her father. I didn't know him but had heard stories. He was a candy storeowner in a pretty tough neighborhood and was rumored to be a pretty tough guy.

She introduced me. "Daddy I'd like you to meet my friend Bill. He was the one who did this to me."

He took my hand, looked me dead in the eye, and deadpanned, "Nice to meet you. Which wrist would you like broken first?"

I reflexively recoiled. He didn't let go. Fortunately, he was joking.

They made a lot of movies about summer and beaches. *Beach Blanket Bingo* comes to mind. Annette and Frankie, and Elvis got rich off them, as did Connie Francis singing the songs of summer romance. This story ended up on the cutting room floor.

But it did have a happy ending for someone else. I made the introduction. They've been married about forty years, grown children, and are happily retired. Probably why she lives nearby in Florida . . .

"Brooklyn is not the easiest place to grow up in, although I wouldn't change that experience for anything."

– Neil Diamond

Sacré Bleu!
Lucy in the Sky Smiling

"You'll pardon me but . . . my nuts were on fire!"

I didn't like the first summer camp I went to. I was not quite nine; I was put inexplicably in a bunk with both guys and girls, and my counselor was a girl. It was awkward. I hated it. The next year we did better, and that lasted until my fourteenth summer.

The beginning was inauspicious. I could get motion sick from turning around too fast. A multi-hour bus ride, winding roads with peaks and valleys, was not something I was looking forward to. My brother was given secret instructions—distract him. We counted cars, we counted types of cars, we counted cows, we counted kinds of cows, we talked baseball and the pennant chances of our Brooklyn Bums that summer, we counted again—birds, trees, red barns.

Then I threw up.

The rest of the summer wasn't as bad, but I wasn't sure I wanted to go back, so my parents, who I'm sure dreaded the idea of having to spend a full summer with me at home once they'd experienced a few summers of being kid-less, began exploring ideas.

The winner came from an unlikely source. There was a kid around the corner on Wellington Court who had absolutely nothing to do with us. He shunned sports, was a child prodigy in school, and by fourteen was being touted for his tooting. He played the flute. Read that again—in Brooklyn, he played the flute! Yet, what he was doing that summer was really, really unusual, something neither my parents nor I had ever heard of. He was taking an American Youth Hostel Bicycle Trip. They came over one night, sans flute, to tell us about it. We then invited an AYH representative to give us the spiel. Clearly, I did not want to go to Fluteland, or wherever Richie the flautist was going, but I did want to go somewhere.

French Quebec, Canada, was my choice. I was going into my junior year in high school, was a good French student, and on my way to becoming somewhat of a Franco-phile. I hadn't learned yet what the French thought of French-Canadians and their French, and that basically the French were right. And while I had begun to live on my bicycle at home when I had nothing else to do, I didn't know if I wanted to spend two, three, or four weeks on it. This trip was to a foreign corner of a not-so-foreign country and was only ten days long—long enough to fall madly in love, and while doing so have some really odd-ball experiences.

I was relieved to find out that the trip started by train. We were not riding to Canada on our bikes. Whew! We all (about a dozen of us, I guess 60/40 boys and girls) met at Penn Station, got introduced to one another, and boarded the train for the overnight trip to Canada. It didn't really dawn on me what a youth hostel trip was until I realized that there was no camp trunk to be packed, only a duffel bag, that we would be sitting up all night on the train, and that our first night's lodging would be in a barn *sans du l'eau chou et sans une salle de bain*. Impressed? No hot water, no shower, no toilet.

Of the first, there was none at all, of the second and third, they were outside. It was summer, so you'd think it wasn't so bad. Well, it wasn't, but summer at night in the Laurentian Mountains can be a bit nippy, but not nippy enough to kill off the thousands of bugs that were out there all waiting for some young flesh to present itself for cannibalism.

That should have portended the first great mishap of the trip. We were riding in file along a country road singing in French at the top of our lungs and waving to the natives who would look out from their windows or from their front porches at the young American idiots riding their bicycles through the middle of nowhere. Suddenly in mid-wave, I was hit with a pain that would have stopped me short if I hadn't been atop something with its own forward motion.

The pain was in my groin and in seconds it felt, you should excuse me, like my nuts were on fire. Holding the handlebar with my left hand, I began pounding my groin with my right. Oh yes, and I was screaming, really screaming, movie theatre horror-movie screaming. The bike wobbled and swerved, the saddlebags, one each hanging over the back wheel, shifted. I lost control and ended up a heap of bicycle, saddlebag, and boy, on one of the waver's lawns. I was still screaming like a banshee and still pounding my groin like I was tenderizing a piece of meat. The wavers rushed to my aid and my co-travelers circled back to see what was up. It certainly wasn't me that was up; I was writhing on the ground.

It seems I had interrupted a flight of pollinating honeybees while they were doing their thing. It was hot as blazes, so we were all wearing shorts. Mine were Bermuda's that pouched out in the breeze while riding. They acted like a scoop into which about a dozen bees flew, a dozen, instantly angry bees. It was dark, confining, and there were no flowers to be had. Not being able to de-flower me, they got so PO'd they bit. Suffice it to say the next few days of bicycle riding were very, very uncomfortable. Fade to black.

A few days later, we found ourselves lost. We were headed for a logging camp for overnighting and a traditional logger's breakfast, a feast I can taste as I write this. The centerpiece of it was a flapjack twice the size of a Frisbee that was floating in hot maple syrup.

Getting lost in a car is one thing, on a bike it is totally another. You can't refer to the map, turn around, and floor it to make up time. Our feet were the gas pedals and behind each of us was thirty pounds of saddlebag. Fortunately, we were found by a provincial policeman. He was "Paul-Bunyan-big" and didn't, or wouldn't, speak English—a not uncommon occurrence in Quebec Province.

Being the French speaker of the group, I was prodded forward to explain, as best I could, about our predicament. Added to it, I was having trouble understanding his directions in French. I am reminded of the famous French-speaking, New York Rangers, goalie "Gump" Worsley, born and raised in Quebec. Once he began making good money, he took his family to France for a vacation.

He chose a five-star restaurant, began ordering, and the waiter said, "Please sir, we all speak English here." Worsley's French was so Quebecois and idiomatic that the waiter assumed he was an American trying out his French. My French teacher was academy taught, as were we—the cop not so much.

He was growing frustrated and finally said to me, *Allez en arrière!*

Okay, I understood that. I just didn't know what it meant. He repeated it twice, then he grabbed me by the belt and collar and literally tossed me into the back of his cruiser. Now I knew that *allez en arrière* meant "get in the back!" He showed me the road where we had to turn, drove me back, and sped off late for dinner. I suppose because there was no chamber of commerce have-a-wonderful-time-keep-up-your-French-studies with his also absent *au revoir,* that he was unhappier about being late for dinner than he was happy about helping us.

The next French lesson I had came at the expense of my bladder. It was hot, still or again, and we were drinking copious amounts of water. Like what goes up must come down, what goes in must come out. I needed a bathroom and quickly. God provided a gas station and then proceeded to have a good laugh on me.

My two years of French had taught me that bathroom was *la salle de bain.* Literally, the room of the bath. In my house when one had to go, one said, "I have to go to the bathroom." It had nothing to do with the furnishing of the room just the act it was being used for. The gasoline attendant, however, was a bit of a stickler for his language. Squeezing my legs tightly, I strung together a really good sentence. *"J'ai besoin de la salle de bain."* Perfect. I need the bathroom.

His response was, *"Nous n'navons pas une salle de bain."*

We don't have a bathroom.

We all know that in every first world country, every gasoline station has a bathroom, so I tried again as he began to walk away. This time I said it a little louder and with some urgency. *"S'il vous plait. Où est la salle de bain?"*

He turned, looked at me and said, *"J'avais dit, nous n'avons pas une salle de bain."* As I said, we don't have a bathroom.

When he turned what he saw was a kid, in long pants, wearing a tee-shirt and sporting a white sailor's hat, whose legs looked like pretzel twists, and whose eyes had gone from hazel to yellow.

It was then he decided to give me a French lesson explaining that I had asked for a room that had a bathtub. That they didn't have. What I wanted was *une toilette*, which they did have. "*C'est la bas.*" It's over that way.

Hard way to learn a language, but effective it was.

Then there was the grand finale. It included death-defying stunts, breath-stealing speed, unbelievable close calls, and Jesus. We would finish our trip in Montreal. Coming out of the mountains, we entered the city from the top and stopped for a magnificent vista. Montreal means Mt. Royal in French, the mountain the city was built on. That would mean that "uptown" is really up and "downtown" is really down. Looking downward, in the distance, we could see our destination, a magnificent church called The Notre Dame Basilica. Our leader advised us all that parts of getting to downtown were pretty steep and to remember to obey the traffic rules, stopping at red lights and yielding to pedestrians in the cross walk. With that said, we pushed off, the survivors to gather again at the steps of the church for a tour.

The best laid plans . . .

All was well at the beginning. It usually is. It took a while to realize the impact of the thirty pounds of weight on the back of my bike heading downhill. I was picking up speed pretty quickly and beginning to pass cars. Every so often I'd hit my brakes without much effect. My heart was beating about as fast as my bike was going, which was, judging by the cars I was passing, faster than the speed limit of thirty-five mph; I could have gotten a speeding ticket.

Then I noticed a scene unfolding before me that looked like it could have been from a Bing Crosby movie. A nun was waiting in the crosswalk. She was in full habit. As the light changed, an officer in the Royal Canadian Air Force, also in full habit, stepped to her side, tucked his crop under his left armpit, took her elbow in his right hand, and stepped her out onto the street. They were right in my crosshairs.

My thumb leaned on the button to my bicycle's electric horn. *Bleet! Bleet! Bleeeeet!* I think he heard it because he looked my way. Being who he was, and what he was doing, I'm sure he expected me to stop, especially since they had the right of way. Suddenly divining that, I squeezed both handbrakes with all my might. The bike shuddered, began to slow, and then I heard a pop, more of a SPRONG! and a clatter.

The bike shot forward. Looking over my shoulder, I saw both my brake pads tumbling down the street behind me going one way, the metal braces that held them going another.

I was headed towards oblivion.

I now had no brakes, literally. I went through the nun's habit like a bull through a toreador's cape. I also avoided the swipe that came my way from the now untucked Colonel's baton. I was going even faster than the epithets I heard coming from him but couldn't make out. I looked forward and realized A) the church was a ways to go, B) depending on the intersection, either cars or people were in my way, and, C) I had to start weaving in and out of obstacles or someone, likely me, was going to get badly hurt. I became a rodeo barrel rider who had traded his horse for a bicycle.

Amazingly enough, I hit no one and no one hit me. However, in short order, it dawned on me that the end of my ride was looming. The church was famous for its steps, which were ascended on certain holy days by pilgrims making their way to the cross on their knees. Picture Rocky in Philadelphia heading up the City Hall steps on his knees instead of his feet. From the moment I saw the curb, to the moment I hit it was a flash, no longer than it took to write this sentence. And hit it I did. The sudden stopping force brought the back-end weight up and forward. The next thing I knew I was tumbling through the air and like an astronaut, I was separating from my capsule. People must have been watching this unfold because by the time I landed on the steps, they had gathered around and were babbling at me in French.

I was very groggy, half unconscious. I was lying feet pointed at the street, head pointed at the church. I slowly opened my eyes figuring I'd check that all my body parts were still attached and not spread across the steps for future pilgrims to trip over. Because my head was tilted back, when my eyes focused, they focused on a huge statue of Jesus. He seemed to be smiling and I thought I heard him say, "See. I don't let that happen to Christians. Can we talk?"

I was unbroken, literally, and in much better shape than my bike, the front wheel of which was smashed well beyond circular and probably beyond fixable, and the handlebars were so askew that if I did have two round wheels, I could only have ridden in a circle. And I felt in my bones, or the ones I could feel, that I was going to be black and blue, and very sore all over, for quite a while.

Standing above me, just to the side of my sightline to Jesus, was Lucy, framed by the sky. She was smiling. That's where the second part of this story beings.

Lucy was one of my fellow travelers. There were several notable things about her that, early on in the trip, had caught my eye: 1) She had tiny teeth, noticed because my dad was a dentist. 2) She had a block buster figure, noticed because I was a teenager. 3) She was very short, noticed because I had had my first major teen growth spurt and was close to six feet tall. She was also sweet, quiet, demur with a cool, light touch and older than I was. We had kissed once. I think the night of the bees. After this trip, she'd enter college while I'd finish high school. The trip was coming to an end. I got another kiss that night to soothe my weathered brow, and an even better one when we parted at the train. We had exchanged phone numbers and promises to stay in touch. We kept those promises, but I assumed since she lived in the suburbs, that the fantasy of the mountains would recede and be replaced with the reality of college applications and an overbearing mother.

Little did I know.

Spring rolled around. Lucy had joined a sorority and there was a big spring dance. The phone rang; it was she calling to invite me to be her date to the dance. I was stunned. It was one of those times when I was hit with diverging impressions. I saw myself as a kid, and here was someone else, a girl no less, who saw me a lot more grown-up than I saw myself.

I think Lucy lived in Scarsdale. She went to college somewhere up there. The plans were for me to take the train to her, and she would drive us to school. After the dance, a group of her friends and their dates would head to the city and stay at her aunt's apartment. My head was spinning, much as it was at Jesus' feet. In an equal fog, I accepted.

Then I told my mother.

The argument that ensued was epic. "College? Eighteen years old? Overnight? Apartment in Manhattan? Not happening!" There was screaming and yelling, and stormy exits followed by stormy re-entrances, more tears, supplications.

Somehow, I got through to her about growing up, letting go, and mortification. She assented. But there were conditions—always conditions. There would be no overnight at an apartment. I had to walk through the door at 12 Waldorf Court at the stroke of one a.m., which meant I had to leave Manhattan and get on the subway by midnight. My mother never realized, or so it seemed, that anything that could happen after midnight could happen before. But it didn't, and that was the last time I saw Lucy who shortly thereafter informed me what a wonderful time she had had with me, what a shame it was I couldn't have stayed (given the plunge in the dress's neckline she'd chosen for that night, I had a primordial sense of what a shame it really was), she'd met "the nicest guy recently," thanked me for a wonderful summer and wonderful night, and basically hoped I had a nice life. Oh . . . Jesus!

"I remember perfectly my first trip to New York, when I was on the bridge between Brooklyn and Manhattan, when I saw the skyscrapers. It was like an incredible dream."

– Diego Della Valle
Entrepreneur in Footwear,
Chairman internationally
known footwear
company Todd's

'53 hard top Chevy. The Barumshack nightmare 'obile.

A Brush with The Law

"It said, ONE WAY, and wasn't pointing the way I was going."

Aside from school, two things occupy the male teenager's mind. Girls and cars. This is about cars. Every teenage boy I knew had memorized the roster of his favorite teams, baseball, basketball, football, and probably hockey. He also knew the makes and models of every single car made in America that had four wheels. Some even knew motorcycles. A brief digression. In my crowd, we didn't know motorcycles because we weren't allowed to read the magazines that featured them. Why? Because of the stunningly sexy girls who appeared in them along with the motorcycles.

So, cars it was.

In the memory-reviving scene from the movie, *Avalon*, several characters are shown stealing out of synagogue during *Rosh Hashanah* services (the Jewish New Year part of Jewish High Holy Days) because that was the first day the new models were released. You might think knowing names, positions, and stats for every player on three of four professional teams is a feat, especially when most math is a challenge. It is, but cars were equally complex.

First of all, there were a lot of them: Ford, General Motors, Chrysler, American Motors, Studebaker. Then came the models of each make, for instance Oldsmobile by GM. But Oldsmobile or Buick or Pontiac had sub-genres with their own names. Some were convertibles. Each had its own horsepower numbers and, of course, most importantly, how fast it went from zero to sixty. To be able to spot a new car on the road was not enough. For bragging rights, you had to be the first to see it; that occasioned a lot of lying. Then you had to reel off the stats like they were as familiar as the names and ages of your siblings. Detroit ruled.

There was sort of a pecking order in car ownership. Successful businessmen—or those who had to look like successful businessmen—or just had the egos of successful businessmen, drove Cadillacs. Big ones. Seeing some of those models today, they look like aircraft carriers. The Smart Car is designed to fit in one half the normal parking place. One Cadillac Eldorado needed a space and a half. The Mini-Cooper is about a third the length of the mighty, iconic twin-finned Eldorado.

Professional men—doctors, dentists, not yet king of the hill lawyers, drove Buicks or Oldsmobiles. They were big—I mean business cars—without the ostentation of the Cadillac. That's where we fit in. Our first car was the Buick Road Master. It was a monster built of steel and chrome. It was solid as a Sherman tank, and drove like one. It weighed about 4,700 pounds. That would be north of two and a half tons! Nobody then thought about such things as miles per gallon. The Oldsmobile, especially the '88, gave you what you got in the Buick, but in a little more 'hip' package.

Cars did not become an issue in our household, until we went from one to two, and then to three driver's licenses. My mother decided she'd had it with staying home or walking to the store. She knew how to drive and usually had a car at her disposal because oft-times my dad took the subway to work. But it was a status thing for her to have her own car, especially since she hadn't yet snagged her desperately wanted mink coat. We got a red Nash Rambler. Nothing special in the stat's department, a car no teen would want to be seen dead in, until its parent company, American Motors, came up with the marketing idea to end all marketing ideas. You might not be able go from zero to sixty before lunch in a Rambler, but you could sleep in it. It came equipped with two metal braces that hooked onto the floor in the back of the car allowing the front seats to drop down into a double bed.

Now I don't know who besides homeless people would have any use for that and in the '50s homeless people slept on freight trains and in railway stations, not on the street. More cogently, most homeless people could not afford to own a BRAND NEW car, or they wouldn't be homeless. But with this little marketing gimmick, the Rambler went from the car no teen wanted to be seen dead in, to the car every teen was maniacally trying to figure out a train of logic that would get his parents to buy one. Somehow, it was the car my mother picked, probably because American Motors made the least expensive line of cars. The very first thing she did was take the braces out of the car and hide them, probably under her bed. Oh, you could still put the seats down, but unless one were a midget there would be no double bed canoodling because the top of the front seat fell right down onto the back floor. Nothing was impossible in a car, as many kids proved, but this was pretty close.

My seventeen, then eighteen-year-old brother got that car at night for dates. Not happily, but he got it. When he went off to the Army and then college the Rambler was history, replaced by a white Plymouth Valiant. It was about equal on the coolness scale to the Rambler. Its reach to being close to cool was that it was the first car to have pushbutton gearshifts instead of a stick on the floor or the steering wheel.

And this, dear reader, is where my troubles began. I went away to college at seventeen. One couldn't have a driver's license in New York State until age eighteen. Thus, when I would come home and be able to use the car, I had no idea of street names or directions because I never needed to. I either walked, or someone else drove. One vacation day, I was asked to drive something over to a friend of my parents. Remember, no Siri, no GPS, only maps and memory. I remembered that a certain street was two-way so I gave no thought to making my right turn, tooling on down to where I had to go. About halfway down the street, I noticed a police car, stopped and its driver looking right at me. As his lights went on, flashing red like a whorehouse on steroids, I noticed there was no longer a white dividing line on the street.

Out comes the cop; down goes my window. I am sweating and trembling.

First words through my window were, "Whatsa matter, didn't they teach you to read?" I hoarsely replied, "Read what, sir?"

He pointed to a sign that at that instant looked to be the size of a highway billboard. "That one!" he said.

It said, ONE WAY, and the arrow was not pointing in the direction I was going.

He didn't seem like the kind of guy who would appreciate my saying, "But officer, I'm only going one way," so I said nothing.

Next came the obligatory command: "License and registration."

Understand this is maybe the second time I've driven the car and the very, very first time I'd driven it in this part of Brooklyn, I almost dropped dead driving over the Brooklyn Bridge into Manhattan traffic. Not only did I not know what the registration was, I didn't know where it was. I fumbled around until it became obvious to the policeman that I was clueless.

He said, "Some people keep it in the glove compartment." I knew what that was, so I opened it.

It was in there, but so was a small depository of papers. There were ads for things to buy, ads for things already bought, receipts for both categories, there were booklets about the car, there were notes to self, and Lord knows what else. There was also a bunch of stuff that should have been in the garage but hadn't yet made it. So, what my hand came out with was a ream of paper none of which said, Registration. My hand was shaking so badly that pieces in the pile fluttered out onto the seat and the floor.

Patience was not a gene this cop had. He said, "Dig deeper." I did.

Now I have to tell you something about my father. He was not exactly cheap, but he was a product of the Great Depression. He always feared the dollar in his wallet might be the last one we had. As sole wage earner of a family of four with memories of what happened to his father and the family of six during those awful years, he tended to save a lot of stuff, stuff he didn't immediately need but could be used surely for something at some future time. Thus it wouldn't have to be bought. That is how I came to have the bottoms of a pair of drawstring, blue and white striped men's pajamas unfold from my hand as it finished its second dig. Mortified wouldn't cover it.

The cop said, "What the hell?"

And I didn't have an answer. That night I was told in all earnestness that they were there to clean the windshield. God was having a good time with me, but I decided the officer was reaching his explosion point. The next thing I pulled out was in fact the registration, but I didn't know it. He did and grouched, "Gimme that thing!" I did.

Wouldn't you think, after I explained my circumstances, and he told me that yes this once was a two-way street but it had just been changed to one-way, that a little sympathy was in order, that I might get a warning and a kindly, "We all have days like this, kid."

Don't waste the thought because I didn't. I got a ticket and an order. "Pull over there, park this thing, clean up this mess, and figure out where the hell you're going before you kill someone. And don't start the car again until you do!"

The story ends in New York City night court, but I'll spare you.

"In my experience, growing up in Brooklyn and all that, the real tough guys didn't act tough. They didn't talk tough. They were tough, you know? I think about these politicians who try to pose as tough guys—it makes me laugh."

– Pete Hamill
Columnist, Author

Section Seven

Irv, Abe and two schmeggies one of whom is wearing a shower cap to play tennis.

Summer Camp

*"It was Brigadoon **for the summer and the re-entry
into the real world was a bummer."***

Remember when summer was endless, especially when your family didn't find something to occupy you during it? Day after day of heat, humidity and playing in the water spray from garden sprinklers or open fire hydrants. Even if the family took a week or two in the mountains the summer seemed to go on and on until you almost couldn't wait for the start of school. Almost.

Then came for some of the lucky, summer camp. Not everyone loved it. I did. It was in the early years a wonderland of kids, activities, and adventures so totally different than home the memories, like being allowed to take home the Guinea Pig I cared for at the nature lodge, and to whom it turned out I was violently allergic stayed with you forever.

When you were older, an upper camper then CIT (Counselor in Training), Junior Counselor, and Counselor you were a leader. Little kids looked up to you. Your responsibility grew and with that responsibility came tips from grateful parents who were sure their child would be lost, kidnapped or eaten and when they saw them happy and whole on visiting day couldn't wait to part with some green in relief.

Camp also meant girls, girls with whom you could begin to "figure things out" without parents' questions. Camp was *Brigadoon* for the summer; the re-entry into the real world was always a bummer.

*"It's ironic that no matter where
I go, I meet people from Brooklyn.
I'm proud of that heritage.
It's where I'm from, who I am."*

– Howard Schultz
Founder of Starbucks

Camp Food

*"I let it melt into a cool mash, chewed the fruit,
and let it slide down my throat."*

As mentioned, my first summer camp experience wasn't a good one, starting from before I even got there.

Then, I was in a bunk with eight-year-olds; I was nine. Our bunk, heavens knows why, was on the girls' side of camp. To add insult to injury, we had a girl for a counselor. At nine, I was just old enough for that to be embarrassing.

Even though he didn't want to go, my brother was somehow convinced—brow-beaten? bribed?—to go with me, watch over me, make my summer go smoothly. My brother was always a very job-description kind of guy, very task oriented. He took big-brothering seriously, even when it was a pain. While at times, he exacted his revenge (read Red Ryder, Red Ryder), he both taught me and protected me. He was committed to making sure all would be well and looked after me assiduously. The fact that he was fourteen and my bunk was on the girl's side of the camp may have had something to do with it, but let's give him the benefit of the doubt.

People don't choose camps for the food. It falls somewhere between the army and the college cafeteria in both menu and taste. Enough years in camp, you learn that if you can't identify something that you either don't ask what it is, or you just don't eat it. Generically, the word meat meant mystery meat. It didn't matter what it looked like it might be, it probably wasn't, and didn't taste like it anyway.

I was a kid with a lot of food allergies. At that time of my life, instead of having a list on the refrigerator of foods I couldn't eat, we had a list of what I could eat. It was a lot shorter. This of course was shared with the camp and my counselor; my fork was watched like a hawk. Nothing went into my mouth that shouldn't. Every week I got allergy shots.

People who run camps know the food is lousy. Food is a big budget expense and experience has taught them that some kids will eat anything no matter what color it is, or how it smells, and some kids will find fault with rack of lamb or crown rib roast. They hire a "chef" and the chef is told to find a level for the food that is just above "you'll be closed down by the health department" to just below $1.99 per pound.

The director knows that there is also a rebellion point, and that it needs to be avoided. Sometimes there would be a barbecue. That way you could see what your food was before it showed up on the plate. Sometimes there would be fresh corn on the cob, something every kid not wearing braces loves, and is cheap. And sometimes there would be a special dessert. And that, dear reader, is where the problem started.

The chef made homemade ice cream; some of us even watched. It was banana-strawberry with real fresh bananas and real bright red strawberries. He even used cream. The problem was that I had allergies to both bananas and strawberries. My *mazel* (luck)! It was odd too because bananas are the go-to food for allergic babies. No one is allergic to bananas. Wrong!

This prize was served in large, cold, metal bowls from which the counselor doled out spoonsful. When I saw this treat brimming with berries and such, I was crestfallen. My counselor wouldn't let me have any. I was desperate. I needed my brother. His bunk was at the opposite side of the dining hall. I ran over to him and begged, really begged. Finally, instead of pulling a W.C. Fields and saying, "Go 'way kid, ya bother me!" he said, "You want it? Eat it. It ain't gonna kill ya! Let's see what happens."

I was ecstatic but there was still a problem—permission. I dragged him to my bunk's table, and he told the counselor, "It's okay. Give it to him, just not too much." There are few things in life that taste as good as really real ice cream. Even stuff like Ben and

Jerry's, that purports to be the real stuff, can't compete. I mean this stuff would provide forgiveness for multiple meals of mystery meat. On this steamy summer's night, I savored it, put it to my lips and let it slide into my mouth. I chewed the fruit. When reduced to a cool, creamy mash I let it slide down my throat. Ummmm good!

Then we saw what happens.

By the time we were released from the dining hall, I felt warmer than usual. And itchy. Kids looked at me funny. "Billy—you're turning red. You've got bumps on you."

Sure enough, I did. Giant hives. They were the size of silver dollars, very large and very red. Along with these decorations, I began to cough, and my chest felt funny.

My counselor grabbed me. "Right to the nurse! Did you eat anything you were allergic to?"

"Weeeell, sort of." Meanwhile I was swelling up like a beach ball with pin-cushion-sized hives all over my body. Out came the hypodermic, out came the epinephrine, in went the needle.

In minutes, I was well on my way back to normal but for hours I was twitchy as a Mexican Jumping Bean from the adrenalin.

And my brother? We decided this would be our secret for as long as we could keep it.

Summer of '42—to a pre-teen every older woman who looks like this . . .

Girls Redux

*"It started like a Hans Christian Anderson fairy tale
and ended like one from Brothers Grimm."*

So where do we start? We could start with the girl whose name I don't remember, but who was the first girl who invited me on a date. We were high school freshman; she was cute. She invited me to come over one day after school. She lived in an apartment house, which for our neighborhood meant she knew that my living in a private house meant that my family had more money than hers. I was a step up, a catch.

I was to come over and we were going to play games. Not the kind like, "I'm hiding in the biggest closet we have that has no lights so come find me" games. Chess, Checkers, Monopoly, Sorry. I don't remember which ones. I do remember this. I walked in and she said, "Hi, I hope you don't mind, but my mother's not home." I remember this too—my heart beginning to race.

True to her word, she pulled out some games and we chose one, sat on the carpet, she on one side of the board and me at the other. I remember something else. She was wearing a three-button, tight cotton pull-over, un-buttoned, and every time she leaned forward to move a piece on the board, she'd look up at me and the stretch of her neck made the buttons spread, revealing well . . . nirvana. And with that lean came a look that for a thirteen- or fourteen-year girl could be called pre-alluring. It took many moves on the board, many forward leans, many pre-alluring looks for me to realize that maybe playing this game was not the true purpose of my being invited over. By the time "I got it," her mother came home.

I was never invited over again.

Or maybe we should start with someone whose name I do remember, Robbie. Robbie was a show-stopper, the kind of kid you noticed coming at you on the sidewalk and that you turned around to look at as she passed. She was "the little redheaded girl" who lived in a house across the Marine Parkway Bridge in Belle Harbor. Her father was a successful manufacturer of a name brand dress shirt, and she had a very big brother who was very protective of her.

We met at an inter-camp summer dance. It was the perfect meet for me who danced like a spastic, as was the term in those days. As was the custom at such things, all the boys were on one side of the floor, the girls on the other. The middle of the floor was filled with music, not dancers.

Then I spied her.

Adorable doesn't cover it. However, the cover that made it perfect for me was the one covering her leg. She had broken it and was dressed in a half-leg length brilliant white, brand new cast, which accentuated her very red hair. Talking and joking I was good at, dancing not so much. This was a match made in heaven. We had one more social the second half of the summer. She was still encumbered, meaning I was still safe. I took her number and spent the rest of the summer dreaming about her.

I've had the experience that every female to whom I was attracted had something distinctive about her. Aside from Robbie's red hair, she had lips shaped like a bunny's and I wanted to kiss them—badly. How, thought I, am I going to impress this girl enough to get a kiss? I decided I would ride my bike to her house. Such a trip meant surviving the traffic on Flatbush Avenue, surviving the military as I passed Floyd Bennett Airfield, holding my breath as I traversed the imposing Marine Parkway Bridge (now Gil Hodges Memorial Bridge) and its metal-grated roadway, and then not dropping dead from heat exhaustion the last few miles to her home. I arrived, as my ever-helpful mother would have said, looking like something the cat dragged in.

There to meet, and test me, was Robbie's brother, Mickey, many inches taller than I, a tryout for his basketball team, and wanting to see if I was good enough for his baby sister by taking me out on the court—this after my schlep to Queens by bike. Sometimes, you know God loves you. This was one of them. Mickey was taller, but I was faster. I don't know who won, but he was impressed. I passed the test, and the rest of the day I spent with a redhead who by now had two functional legs.

I have no idea what we did, but her parents were lovely and invited me to dinner, yet I had that daunting ride home. It was well before cell phones, and I didn't want to do it at night, which was a good thing since I ended up having a flat tire on the bridge and having to fix it, traffic whizzing by in both directions. So as the sun lowered in the sky, it was time for goodbye. She walked me to the door, and she let me kiss her. Then I said something remarkably doofy (another term of the time). I said, "Once more with feeling!"

This time she kissed me back. My first real kiss. I didn't really need my bike to get home.

Yet into life rain must fall. Her parents decided she was too young, and probably too pretty, for being so young, to be dating. And that was that. Two kisses and a flat tire romance.

About the same time, I met Roberta. Word had flashed around school that in the gym that there was to be a girl's inter-school volleyball game. For all the wrong reasons, a bunch of us went to cheer on dear old Midwood's female athletes, but it was a girl from Madison High who caught my eye, and dammed if I know how or why, but after the game I went to talk to her. That type of aggressiveness was not me. Soon, it was apparent we had a lot in common. Both of us had fathers who were dentists. Both had older siblings, I a brother she a sister. We both lived in private houses, and we both had sharp wits and a gift for gab. I went to see a few more of her games as getting to her neighborhood was infinitely easier, safer, and faster than going to Far Rockaway. Oh yes, and one other thing. She had those same damn cute bunny lips. I was hooked.

So . . . there was this brief period of time when I was dating three girls simultaneously, all of whom had names that began with

"R", and all of which sounded very similar. I made some phone calls that took great concentration. This third "R" could be a book itself. It started like a Hans Christian Anderson fairytale and ended like one from the 'Grimm Brothers'. It would end in a lawsuit. Methinks we'll confine the story to the early years.

It was a camp romance. She was thirteen and called Cat's Eyes (not by me!). It was an apt name. She had these Siamese-cat-shaped eyes. They were green, a color from then on, I always associated with impending trouble. I was fifteen. Within weeks, the camp newspaper was wondering for all to read, "Does the boy from Brooklyn love Cat's Eyes?" We did everything together, even performed at the camp talent show as Bill Dana's Hispanic astronaut, Jose Jimenez, and his interviewer.

We found a very large, very low-hanging, pine branch, which covered a rocky ledge that overlooked the woods. We spent countless evening hours there, even missing curfew one night because an inquisitive animal with beady eyes, an abundance of black hair, and a bold white stripe down his back, became curious. She looked at me, I looked at her, we both looked at the skunk and without a word spoken we knew not to move. Eventually the skunk got bored and left, but we didn't know that. Then when we finally figured out that he had turned around to take his leave and his scent with him, we froze trying to figure how we'd explain this one to the head counselor. But his leave he did take and, in an instant, we took ours, none the worse for wear—or smell.

In a sense, summer camp—a good and enjoyable summer camp—is like *Brigadoon*. It is a world of its own with little or no intrusions. The campers were *Brigadoon's* townspeople and it was inevitable that things never thought possible came to be. And such was our breakup.

I don't think there will ever again be a generation of so many different types of teenagers molded by the same music. One of the big summer names was Del Shannon and one of his big hits was, "Hats Off to Larry." It so happened that in camp we had a Larry. Larry was a competitive swimmer, handsome, and really nice—damn him. He could also dance. I could swim, but we've established that I could not dance worth much at all. One weekly dance he had the audacity to ask Cat's Eyes before I did and she the audacity to accept.

We were done. I felt like I had been wounded by every part of an open Swiss Army knife. It turned out, after the longest week or two of my life, that my misery had its own attractiveness, and "R" and I were back under the pine tree. (Larry died a very untimely death; I think he was in his twenties. To this day when I hear Del Shannon moan, "Hats off to Larry" I still feel a flash of teenage angst in my bones.)

But it was the last summer together in camp before I went to college. It was my Summer of '42. It was the summer of improbabilities but let me preface it with some advice to parents and grandparents: teenage romance comes and goes. It's dramatic, draining, and unsettling to an entire household, even if the brokenhearted is a boy, and definitely if it's a girl. My advice, parents? Leave it alone. Unless you think the paramour is an axe murderer, like a virus, the love bug will die. But feed it with opposition, and it grows into a plague.

This is what my mother did. She never met my love through five years of dating, the last three which undoubtedly were fueled by her throwing kerosene at the fire instead of smothering it with affection and acceptance. Teenagers are always looking for a war; why give them one?

That summer the camp newspaper was running hot about the Sadie Hawkins dance and whom Cat's Eyes would ask to go. Early in the summer, I got very sick with a wicked sinus infection, an infection so bad the camp nurse had my mother come take me to the family doctor. I had been sick once before. The previous summer, a virus swept through camp and those of us who got it were quarantined. I was a CIT and one of my campers "slipt" up alongside the quarantine bunk and asked me in a whisper what was wrong. I, in a moment of insanity, decided to be funny and answered, "We all have hoof and mouth disease."

The next afternoon, quarantine or not, I was called to the director's cottage. He was not a happy man. A rapid-fire game of telephone produced a near riot started by parents calling to yank their kids out of camp. I had to confess to the crime and managed to get everything calmed down. Actually, I still think it was pretty funny.

But this time, I was really ill. High fever, and splitting headache when Mother's Ambulance Service came to the rescue. Had there been a betting pool, the odds would have been against my returning to camp because everyone knew about my mother—mostly from me. So there Cat's Eyes stood, on the hill, forlornly waving goodbye to me as our Buick trundled down the hill, headed for the "Big City," possibly never to return. For a week, my fate was unknown, but once cured, I had to go back to camp. I had a job after all. My mother called the director to tell him. Word spread like wildfire and as we pulled up the hill, there again was Cat's Eyes waiting like a faithful dog awaits its companion. I could smell the smoke. It wasn't from my mother's cigarette. It was from the grinding of her molars.

But this was all prelude. The drama was yet to come.

We had another week before the dance. Then came choosin' day. The girls dressed like characters from *Li'l Abner*. The boys lined up, a signal was given that released the girls who raced towards their chosen ones like baseball players trying to beat a throw to second. No one dared pick me. Cats not only have eyes, they have claws. The paper trumpeted that Cat's Eyes did choose the boy from Brooklyn. After the choosin' was done, the camp director, dressed like Marryin' Sam, performed a ceremony that ended with each couple getting a gold wedding ring. Made out of fabric, from a distance it looked real, and there lies the rest of the drama.

We were all hitched for the rest of the summer. Mind you, the counselor patrols were doubled and tripled after nightfall. No one was gonna' have the chance to misinterpret the bounds of hitched. The space between the two camps was the DMZ, and if caught in it, home the offender would go.

As a counselor, I, and my fellow counselors, had to stay an extra few days at the end of camp to pack the campers' trunks and get them ready for shipping. Cat's Eyes left me with a stern warning not to take off that ring because some of the female counselors were good-looking and not to be trusted.

We counselors set to our tasks until sundown. Then we drank and flirted, but I was true to the ring on my finger. At the appointed hour, my mother arrived to pick me up. I sullenly got into the car; it was part of a year, maybe eighteen months, of being sullen. Down the hill we went, passing the pine tree. I mumbled a don't forget us to the skunk and looked at camp for the last time, imprinting in my mind's eye its sign in faux Indian with the camp's name. Then I quietly disappeared into myself as my mom turned onto the highway. I was seated next to her in silence in the front passenger seat. That's important.

About fifteen minutes out, a chemical explosion took place in our car. Again, came the smoke. There was a deafening noise, piercing shrieks, flashes of light.

My mother had glanced over at me to see if I was getting ready to jump out of the car. She spied a glint of gold coming from the ring finger of my left hand that was about ten inches from her. (I told you they looked real.) The noise was deafening; my mother was hysteria in motion, about sixty-five mph in motion. It took a while before the torrent of fury slowed enough for me to be able to pick out words. Flashing before her eyes was that forlorn girl waving to us as we left camp.

That was followed by her seeing that same girl beaming as we returned.

I'm a parent and grandparent. Lord knows I know parents can do and think stupid things, but this hit the jackpot. Mark Twain once wrote of his father, how stupid he was when Twain was sixteen and how smart he had become by the time he became eighteen. I was sixteen.

Mommy Dearest thought we had eloped and that she was driving home her sixteen-year-old married son. I don't know who was more shocked, she or I. Now comes a final piece of advice, this time to teens: never, ever burst out laughing when one of your parents is hysterical with anger. It's not healthy.

So, of course, I had to take off the ring, but I disobeyed the order to destroy it. I kept it for over a year, slipping it on for each of our dates. I didn't part with it until our final parting which didn't involve a Swiss Army knife, but a spear through my heart.

Let's fast forward to orientation week at college. I went away with my best friend's hug and pledge in my ear, the kind of friend to whom you didn't have to talk because you knew what was going to be said, the kind of friend that could cause you to burst out laughing without uttering a word, that best friend promised me that he would protect Cat's Eyes from all comer's.

Alone and miserable the first week of school, one night I went to a local Italian joint and saw sitting there a young man I recognized from various places during orientation. He looked a little like Howdy Doody except without a wooden grin; he also looked semi-suicidal with misery. I sat down with him to learn he too had left his heart at home. As we bonded in our misery of faithfulness, call me a liar, but on the jukebox came Ray Charles crooning, "I Can't Stop Loving You." Truth.

The next week started pledge week. My new soul mate was not Jewish, but I was invited to the fraternity he ultimately pledged that was rumored not to accept Jews, Blacks and Catholics. That was not the stunner. The stunner was my seeing him in a lip-lock with a girl almost twice his size. So much for fidelity and soul mates. I would go it alone. Every day during my class break from noon to two, I wrote a letter to Cat's Eyes.

I was a profound lover of *Peanuts* and had a strong identification with Charlie Brown. That was the year that the "Little Red Headed Girl" entered his life. I felt his pain.

Often, I would cut comic strips from the paper and tape them to the back of the envelope. The mailman read them before Cat's Eyes, or the family for that matter, saw them. In fact, he gave her hell when she broke up with me because delivering mail without mine in it had gone back to being boring. Also true.

It came time for freshman dance. It would take place after spring break. Bolstered by the almost daily responses to my art majeure letters, I went home to ask CE to go with me. She had come down once already for my fraternity induction dance and while we weren't making the university newspaper, we were definitely an item—an item until the phone call.

There were no cell phones. Calls outside one's calling area were called long distance calls and they cost more, especially if they were long in duration as well as geography. When I got home, after the obligatory dinner with the family, I walked to the candy store, closed myself into a phone booth, and if such records were kept, probably came close to breaking Guinness for the longest pay phone call on record. So long was this call, measured in hours, that the operator, who every five minutes would cut in and say, "Deposit five cents to continue your call," didn't say that. What she said was this: "Sonny. I know you're talking to your girlfriend. I've never talked to anyone, including my husband, for anywhere near this long so Happy Birthday, Kid, the rest of this call is on me." Another gospel truth.

Here is where Hans Christian Anderson becomes *Brother's Grimm*. I had been told that my very best friend—you know the protector of my girlfriend, the one with whom I laughed when nothing was said, the one whose sentences I finished as he finished mine—that best friend? He had started out doing his job like a Pinkerton guard. But like many a novel or movie script, the more he played bodyguard the more he became ensnared in the web of deceit. At first, he took her to class dances and school events as a friend. Need I go on? Yes, because I have to explain why the phone call was so long after she told me she was breaking up with me for him.

I'd say a third, the first third of the call, was shock, despair, outrage. The second third, which was the oddest, was the both of us using memories for a hoped-for advantage. We relived the experiences we had had, she to salve my wounds—I was hoping she would realize she could never have the kind of relationship with him like she had with me.

The third third, the hardest, was the realization that over meant over. There were real tears, lots of them, from both of us. The call went on almost as long as the *Jerry Lewis Labor Day Telethon.*

"On a personal note, I was born in Brooklyn. My folks moved out to Long Island when I was quite young, but once a Brooklynite, always a Brooklynite."

– Mitch Kapor
Communication Entrepreneur,
Inventor of the
Lotus System for
Computers

George C. Parker was known as the greatest con-man in American history, managing to sell landmark items like Madison Square Gardens, the Statue of Liberty and, you guessed it, the Brooklyn Bridge.

In fact, it is reported (whether it's true is another matter) that he sold the Brooklyn Bridge at least twice a week, one time for as much as $50,000. Sometimes the police would have to stop the "new owners" from setting up toll booths in the middle of the bridge.

No Good Deed Goes Unpunished

"He was strong. He lifted up the front of a small car by himself just because he could."

Camp was more than girls and hoof and mouth disease. Here is an "only in camp" ultimate "no good deed goes unpunished" story. It is almost a country song because it involves a girl, a car, a lovelorn drunk, and nearly a murder. Sorry, no train tracks.

Billy Barumshack was half Polish and half Tyrannosaurus Rex. He was an angry man, so angry that he hardly ever spoke, and when he did you didn't want him to be speaking to you. He was also one of the very few staff members who brought a car to camp. It was a '50s Chevy. Word spread quickly. Don't get within fifty feet of that car—or else. Yet, we are taught that a spark of humanity burns within us all and one day, his did, quick as a spark from a flint stone.

Camp was located in between the towns of Hawley (country store and not much more) and Honesdale, a small city, both in the Keystone state. One week, a few of us Junior Counselors were looking for a way to escape camp. Even *Brigadoon* can become wearing, especially when it's filled with mostly over-privileged children. We had few options, the likeliest being to hitchhike, but there were five of us. In the middle of this huddling, Barumshack walked by, and said, "Take my car, but if anything happens to it. And, oh yeah, can you drive a shift?"

"Sure!" I lied. Actually, I had been taught to drive shift, but the shift had been on the floor.

He told me, "This is a little different. The shift is on the steering wheel. It's easy. Just imagine an "H". At three of the points are: first, second, and third gears. At the bottom right of the "H" is reverse. Got it?"

"Sure," I lied again. But we had a car.

Came Saturday he gave me the keys, and said, "Be back by curfew."

As I recall, the car was green, the seats exhaled padding from slits probably made in anger by a knife, and the pedals had no rubber pads. They were polished steel, polished from constant foot pressure, which meant they were slippery. Oh yes, and there wasn't a whole lot of gas in it.

In we piled, and off we went. Driving the car was like driving a Mack truck. It had no power anything—windows, brakes, or steering. Trying to park it was like trying to wrestle a buffalo into a space it didn't want to be wrestled into. For a short while, it was fun and freedom. Then I looked at the gas indicator and realized we needed to gas up. In those days, gas was simple. You had two choices: hi-test or regular. Everything was leaded. It took three of us to find where the gas went and all of us to pay for it. Hawley's Country Store provided a venue for Cokes (actually the hard to find in Brooklyn "Orange Smash" was my summer favorite) and snacks, and off again we went.

Camp, you must understand, was in the mountains, as most summer camps are. That's wonderful for outdoor activities, evening breezes in the dead of summer, and beautiful scenery. It also meant that driving was as unlike driving the straight, flat, grid-patterned streets of Brooklyn as I ever could have imagined. Unfortunately, no one warned me about that little fact. More unfortunately, my realization of it came very suddenly, the first time I fought the "H" trying to get the green monster up a hill and broke out in a cold sweat when I realized I couldn't see what the road did once we topped it. I was staring at the sky. Down, and its direction, didn't come into view until I had to reckon with it—and shift accordingly. It turned out to be both steep and wiggly.

Down was really down. It was a long, steep, slide to the bottom. This meant I had to use the brakes. Now I'm sure up until that point I had used the brakes a bunch. After all, were that not the case, I would have driven right through the Hawley Country Store, hit the gas pumps, and blown us all sky high. But braking down a hill? Uh-oh. I knew you could slow a car by downshifting, so I did that. We slowed, but not a whole lot. I began to panic. This was an emergency, so I pulled the brake that said exactly that. Within minutes, the car was filled with an acrid, burning smoke. I peeked in the rearview mirror to see a black cloud of disintegrating brake adding to the world's growing pollution. Besides bailing out, I had one option, slam on the brakes. I did that. And along with my stomach, the brake pedal went straight down to the floor.

Open windows and mountain breezes couldn't have evaporated the sweat pouring off me. I was literally standing up on the brake watching the speedometer inexorably go up instead of down. By this time everyone in the car knew there was a problem. Someone asked, "What's wrong?"

I croaked, "No brakes." The result was pandemonium brought about by terror.

What's the old saying, "God watches over children and drunks?" Fortunately, that day He had expanded God's definition of children. Eventually the brakes took hold. The toboggan run we were on ended in a long flat runway, and the car stopped acting like it was out to kill us. Fortunately, Stephen King hadn't yet written *Christine*.

We pulled into town knowing we had to have a new set of brakes put on because we had to return to camp on the same highway we had just survived. At the first gas station (in those days they were all full service, with mechanics, and people who actually pumped the gas for you), we asked. The good news, aside from the fact that we had the money to pay for it was that the mechanic wasn't busy and could fix the car that day, but it would take a few hours. We walked into the heart of town, had lunch, and spent the next hour or two watching clocks on church steeples. It gets dark early in the mountains. If there was to be trouble going back, I didn't want it to be in the dark. So back we went for the car, leaving much of the plans for our day off in our heads.

The car was fixed; our day off was over. This time when I stepped on the brakes . . . they worked. As soon as I hit the pedal, the car slowed. All was normal and remained that way as we pulled into camp. I sought out Barumshack to return the keys and give thanks.

"How'd she run?"

"Great," I lied. "We even filled it up for you."

Night fell. The campers slept and so did I. I was drained. I slept the sleep of the dead until that almost became reality.

Most of the bunks were laid out, so they were as secluded as possible, usually surrounded by a stand of trees. My bunk was the most secluded, surrounded by the most trees. It was also furthest from the center of camp. I was awakened by sounds like an angry bull moose might make looking for the interloper in his love affair. Most of what I could understand got clearer because the voice was coming closer to my bunk. By then, I was sorry my hearing was so good. If I cut out the expletives there isn't much else to write. All I can tell you is that words like "Gralnick," "murder the SOB," "where is the so and so?" were what was recognizable. I heard branches snapping and tree limbs falling as if a Tyrannosaurus Rex was approaching. The roar was a bellow. Had it been written yet, I would have thought I was in Jurassic Park. It was obvious Billy had gone drinking and was drunk. In order for him to have gone drinking, he had to use his car. He didn't like the brake job.

But there was more.

Before the more, however, I had to think quickly or die, or if not die, suffer the kind of beating one sees in gangster movies. Camp bunks, simple structures though they are, have a unique feature—rafters. When the campers had unpacked their trunks, they were put up on the rafters, so they were out of the way. They also made it impossible to see the ceiling.

That was it. I leapt from bed, made it like I'd never slept in it, stepped on the curved metal back, and pulled myself up to the rafters settling in a space that had me blocked from view by trunks on both sides of me. No sooner was I hidden than the screen door slammed open ricocheting back into the doorframe with a mighty CRACK and waking half the kids.

Barumshack was raging, but there was a new stanza to his anthem. It had to do with rich kids who always got the girls and how this time he was going to . . . well, fill in the blank . . . he'd never see her pretty boy as pretty again.

"Oh my God!" It hit me like a ton of bricks. He had a secret crush on Cat's Eyes and between the booze, the car, and his unrequited love, he was a murderous madman. I failed to mention that he was strong, very strong. One day he lifted up the front of a small car by himself, just because he could. Funny how some things stick in your mind before you think you're gonna die.

Were there not enough problems, I now had to empty my bladder. While it would have been a form of justice served to have peed on his head, it also would have given me away. He also began interviewing each kid. "Where's your counselor? WHERE IS HE?" They, of course, didn't know, saw my made bed, and assumed I too was out drinking. There were ten kids in the bunk. There was no way I was going to hold my bladder for all these prosecutorial attacks. But God apparently wasn't done with me yet. He sent the cavalry.

A group of Barumshack's friends heard what was going on. They were hot on his trail and finally burst into the cabin. In stage whispers, they told him he was going to get fired and possibly jailed to boot if he didn't get back to where he belonged. They dragged him from the bunk. I assume they threw him in a cold shower and raided the kitchen for black coffee. At 7 a.m., the loud-speakers blared their sketchy rendition of reveille, and in a half-hour we were all assembled on the hill for line up and then breakfast.

But for a knowing glance here and there, it was like any other line-up on any other morning.

As Lily Tomlin's Ruth Ann would say, "And that's the truth!"

Brooklyn, 1879

The Zit

*"With the skill of a nurse's hand, she took
hold of my face. I shuddered."*

You've heard the nasty word *shiksa*. You know that mothers have the same warped ideas on "types" for their sons as they do for their daughters. But there is another type of girl. She causes this reaction: "Okay, so you be happy, I'll go stick my head in the oven." I met that girl at camp.

She arrived with a reputation and had an affinity for the guys who worked at the stables. Somewhat a loner, somewhat aware of the Red "S" everyone put on her chest, the isolation of the stable, when no bunks were scheduled for riding and after five p.m., was her favorite haunt. It wasn't too many days into camp that an edict was pronounced about her, her counselors, and the stable hands. Something to do with immediate excommunication from camp and the potential for arrest if seen with . . .

Of course, I wanted to meet her. And I did. From her last name that started with a "Z", I knew she was of Eastern European heritage. She wore jeans most all the time; they looked like she was born with them on and they just grew as her body grew. She was early developed but not overly busty. She wore mostly snap-button cowboy shirts that had darts that showed off her figure. Topping it off was long hair; down at the bottom were cowboy boots. She wasn't stunningly pretty—a hard, sexy look was hers. Think she made an impression on me?

Girls who are labeled, I learned, often have a chip on their shoulders. They look to do the unexpected, so I don't know if what happened was real or part of a plan. Somehow, I became part of it. It started, like most teenage encounters in my life, very oddly. One day, during a free period, she sat down beside me on the front porch of the main hall. My body shuddered. She leaned over, close, and said very sweetly, "You know, you have the biggest blackhead on your cheek I've ever seen. Let me see that." And with the skill of a nurse's hand she took my face and turned it toward the light and got even closer.

More shuddering.

She was right. I had this small divot in my left cheek; it was about twice the size of a pinhead and black as night. "You ought to get that cleaned out before it gets infected and becomes an ugly zit. I'm very good at that. Want me to do it? I know how. I'll get a warm compress, some alcohol . . ." This was turning into quite the first date. I declined.

She took the offer's rejection in stride and for the next few encounters, she sweetly, but with a come hither if you dare look would say, "How's that zit doin', Billy? I'm ready when you are." It was obvious enough her crew noticed. I began to get knocked around a little up at the stables and was cornered a few times with utterances like, "Stay with your own kind, if you know what's good for you." My luck to have a blackhead that caused a really hot girl to have the hots for me. Does it get more ridiculous than that? Love by blackhead.

Time in camp is unlike time outside of camp. It is endless. The twenty-four hours and what can transpire during them can make a day seem like a week and a week surely like a month. After several come hithers and several warnings, it was time for a camp dance. There was an electrical malfunction in the dance hall and the music stopped.

Our fearless leader asked, "Who's got the closest bunk with a boombox?"

"Lil Miss Come Hither" raised her hand. She was dispatched forthwith, but the Assistant Director whispered to the boss loudly enough for me to hear, "Should we let her go through the woods alone?"

I don't know where this came from, but someone inside my body lifted my hand and its voice said, "I'll go with her."

Everyone knew Billy could be trusted—except Billy. No longer shuddering, I was beginning to sweat. She grabbed me by the hand, yanked me out the door (like she didn't want anyone to change their mind), and pulled me off in the direction of her bunk. In minutes, there we were, alone, just the two of us. There is something atomic about the first kiss you get from someone you know you'd be forbidden to kiss. Especially when that person really knows how to kiss. Wasting no time, she reached behind my neck, pulled me towards her with that same soft grip she used on my face, and went to work. At first contact, my kneecaps disappeared, and my legs began to buckle. All I can say is that it was the first time I had experienced a kiss that electrified my entire body.

This is why I never gamble. I'm a loser.

Here I am, hotter than a pistol, in a bunk with ten beds and no occupants, and having about four minutes before a cavalry is sent out to look for me. Wiser than I, she said, "We better get out of here." She grabbed the boom box, which I had totally forgotten about, grabbed my hand with her other hand, and in minutes we were back to the music hall proclaimed saviors of the dance. To me it was the booby prize.

We didn't have much contact, literal or figurative, after that 'til the end of the summer. One afternoon, I found myself in the same chair and appearing like an apparition was she suddenly next to me. "Let me see that blackhead! You know I really want to take care of that for you."

What the hell. Was I really gonna' get killed by a jealous boyfriend for a blackhead? Yup, I let her do it. I still have the scar on my cheek.

"People from Brooklyn grow up with a certain common sense. If it doesn't ring true, it's not true."

– Judy Sheindlin (Judge Judy)

You Have Eyes Like a Cow

"Talking was my strong point; not talking wasn't."

I've told the tale of the wayward piece of hair—in those days called a fall—masquerading as the back end of a pony that I grabbed hold of (see some chapter in Freud as to why) whilst it was flicking seductively from side to side as my date flitted by me to get her pocketbook. This is another one of those stories. Instead however of taking place around the corner at the beginning of a much sought-after date, this incident took place at summer camp.

The young lady in question was one of those girls who seemed to look better the higher the moon got. During the day, she was a large, well-proportioned fifteen-year-old with powderpuff skin, a round but sweet face, and the manners and demeanor of someone from a small farm town, which she was. And she was painfully shy. It was a period when I had broken up with the then love of my life. I was playing the field and I had been flirting with Miss Farm Girl mostly from a distance for days. Understand, and those of you who went to summer camp for eight weeks know this already, days can be like weeks in camp; eight weeks can encompass the experiences of a lifetime and seem to take that long as well.

There came then the night of a dance. It was a no-date dance, just a camp social. A different girl showed up, or so it seemed. She was wearing jeans and a sweater, penny loafers and no socks, and suddenly she looked no longer fifteen, not at least to my not-so-well practiced fifteen-year-old eyes. To those eyes she looked, well, eye-popping, but not happy. I've learned that it is not uncommon for young women who develop over well, over-early are often not happy about it even while their girlfriends, many still the shape of an ironing board, or boards with small bumps on them, would cut off an arm to be so full-figured. The unhappy girls learn early that there's not much they can do with or about themselves that draw male eyes away from their chest. I learned later, from a friend who had this predicament, that you look a lot older, and boys near to being men, and men who should know better, make assumptions about all kinds of things, the least important of which, except for the law, is about age.

I wasn't too much less shy than she. We danced and chatted, chatted and danced. It was a beautiful, moonlight, mountain night, and I suppose it was I who suggested we go for a stroll. How we managed to get out of the barn under the eyes of the counselors, all of whom were watching us like hawks watch mice in a field, I don't know. I do know that we did and now my teenage heart, near exploding from hormones being pumped through it, had a problem. Simply put, it was what to do. In a textbook sense, I knew what to do, literally. In fact, came that time of my life my mother actually gave me a book about what to do. And I'd heard all the stories of the counselors mostly graphic, and most probably mostly lies, so I knew that at some point one of us would have to stop talking as a signal that something else was going to happen. But talking was my strong point; not talking wasn't.

I must digress to make some sense of the senseless thing that happened next. The camp was in farm country. Memory no longer serves why, some days previous to this story, I was nose to nose with a cow, but I was. Everyone talks about doe-eyes and the limpid beauty of a deer's eyes. I had an epiphany when that cow and I were eying each other. It had the deepest, brownest, clearest, most stunning brown eyes I had ever seen in my life. They were so deep, they seemed to be a pool in which one could go swimming. Would that it had ended there.

Back to the stage. Under the moonlight we strolled. I slowed the pace and slowly turned towards her. There was this powder puff face flooded with moonlight like I had never seen it before. She had the deepest, brownest, clearest, most stunning brown eyes I had ever seen in my life. I felt like I could have jumped in (again see that Freud chapter). Sound familiar?

Sometimes it is best not to think. This would have been one of those times. But I did think. I thought that finally I was looking at some part of her anatomy that wasn't her chest and that she would appreciate it if I said something about it. So, I did. I said, "You know, you have eyes like a cow."

The reaction I got . . . well, let's just say the cow reacted better. Her eyes filled up. She said to me in this crushingly hurt voice, "What did you say?"

Then would have been a good time to think, but I didn't. Rather than finish what went with the statement, I repeated it, "You have eyes like a cow."

Tears rolled down her face. Big tears.

"How could you? I thought you were a nice guy!" She turned, leaving me in full moonlight, stunned, and ran back to the barn. Not only did I not get to tell her the why of the statement, it was thereafter like we were at different camps—miles apart—for the rest of the summer.

I don't see many cows any more but when I do . . . I sigh over the beauty of their eyes, what might have been, and how stupid one fifteen-year-old boy can manage to be.

Cab Calloway, Mr. Hi-de-hi, Hi-de-hi.

A Good Story Should End with a Good Chase

"A genius in geometry was needed, not a bellhop."

The summer in between high school and college, I didn't go to camp; I went to work. It had been made clear to me that other than $20 a week spending money, I'd be living off the land. I needed a grubstake with which to begin college. The Atlantic Beach Hotel was to provide it.

I was told by a friend that there was a whole 'nother summer world I knew nothing about. It was the world of the residential hotels along the Atlantic Beach coast of Long Island. The hotels opened on Memorial Day and closed on Labor Day. In between, they provided everything and anything anyone or anybody needed, from entertainment in the nightclub to shall we call it extra-curricular entertainment-between-the-sheets. In a summer that saw me make over $1,200 on the average twenty-five cent tip, there occurred a novel's length of stories. I will tell you a few and end with The Great Chase.

Johnny Nash:
I told my parents my plans, borrowed the car, and headed out to the man to see, Sam. I learned that Sam was not only the staff manager, but manager of everything that brought in any money, a cut of which went into his pocket. He worked this gig twice. Once in the summer on Long Island, and once again in the winter on Miami

Beach. He was Italian. I had—then—thick hair and a good tan; I too looked Italian. I was hired pretty much on the spot.

I was told to report the week before Memorial Day for orientation. We were sleep-in employees who received room and board, so minimum wage and other such laws didn't apply to us. I believe I got paid $28 a week. Generally, I worked two shifts a day meaning I started at dawn and was done around eleven p.m. In between, the idea was to be wherever someone needed something at the time they needed it. Ice bucket to the room? Drinks out to the cabanas? Set up umbrellas in the burning hot sand? Parking a car, getting a car, giving rides to the men who went to Manhattan every morning—mostly the garment center by train and meeting their trains when they returned? Did it all. That, and some really goofy shit, which is what happens when during the day the hotel is full of women with too much time on their hands. But I was good at it and the quarters rolled in.

During orientation we were told it was a no-no to date any of the guest's daughter's whether they lived on property or not. It would get you fired. Why? The hotel, owned by a Jew, was expected to hire all non-Jews to cut down on the potential attractions because 99% of the clientele was Jewish. In a word, the upper-class Jewish residents didn't want their daughters to be mucking around with the help. The geniuses thought that employing Gentile employees would solve the problem. Not only was that illegal, it was stupid though not the point of this story. Obviously, Dirty Dancing hadn't been made yet . . .

The point of this story is that, in our quarters, I had been hearing a lot of anti-Semitic comments, so I approached my boss about it. He said, "Well, I guess it's because we don't hire Jews, so the guys feel free to say what they want. What do you care?"

"Care?" I said. "I'm Jewish!"

He said, "Holy Shit! How did that happen? Wait 'til Johnny Nash hears this one. I better tell him before he finds out from someone else."

My heart began to race.

Johnny Nash, from Nashville, Tennessee, was everything you'd expect a redneck from Tennessee to be, so I won't bore you with the details. I shortly heard this: "HE'S A JEW? Bill's a . . . GODDAMNED JEW?" The slamming of a door, and footfalls could only mean he was headed my way. Our quarters, probably in violation of the fire code, had but one door and no windows. I was going nowhere.

Johnny and I had had a good time red-necking together that week. That didn't seem to deter his not bursting through the door, blood in his eye. But he stopped after saying, "You're a Jew?" I could hear the gears turning in his head, the smoke building as he struggled to think. He didn't know how to deal with the fact that he actually liked a Jew. Finally, this is what exploded from him, "I like you—it's all those other cheap, Jew bastards I hate!"

Go figure.

Mr. Stein:

Tipping is always an issue. Always was, always will be. Doesn't matter what you're doing, if tips are involved there always will be disagreements. Through the whole summer I never got more than a dollar, except for Memorial Day and Labor Day. Those were the days that involved schlepping suitcases, therefore the tips were bigger. I may have even gotten a few fivers. Some people tipped high, some low, some never. They seemed to have memorized a routine: look in the pants pockets or if a woman in the purse, look on the table and anywhere else except at the bell hop, and then say in muffled tones, "I'm so embarrassed, I just don't seem to have any change on me. I promise I'll catch you next time." Sure.

Then there was Mr. Stein. Mr. Stein's line was, "I'll see you at the end of the summer. It'll be worth your while." Mr. and Mrs. Stein were, of course, very needy. I was always running up to their room with something, or to the drug store to buy something, or to their cabana to bring something, or when they were upstairs and their friends were already out on the Sahara-like sand, taking a message from the Stein's to the friends to tell them they were "on the way." All of these activities always ended up with a promise instead of a quarter.

Mr. Stein was not exactly a fashion plate. He had a closet full of Hawaiian shirts that were cut for someone about six inches taller, so they approached his shins, and multi-pairs of Bermuda shorts, none of which matched the shirts but kept the tops of his socks clean. They too were cut for that same tall person. One day, a little fed up with his promises, I wised off and remarked upon seeing him in the most bizarrely paired outfit yet, "Hey, Mr. Stein. Sharp outfit!" He took me seriously, gave me its purchase history, thanked me—no tip.

Come Labor Day, I had told all the bellhops, "I don't care who's up when Stein calls, he's mine. He owes me." Promises made were about to be fulfilled. About as close to checkout time as could be, the call came. I got the Stein's room. They had enough suitcases to have gone on a safari with camels. Getting them into the car before dropping dead from the heat and humidity was a feat. A genius in geometry was really what was needed, not a bellhop.

Then came the moment. He said, "You know Bill, I promised I'd take care of you. You treated us exceptionally well and I want to give you an exceptional gift." With that, he handed me a large box with a big ribbon and bow. I had no clue what it was, but I knew it certainly wasn't gonna help me much in college because for sure it wasn't filled with money.

What was it? You know that hideous outfit I mentioned? No lie. It was now mine. Good grief.

Cab Calloway:

A number of the hotels on the strip had nightclubs. They competed tooth and nail for the top stars. The pool was deep because it was less than an hour's drive from New York City, so it was easy for a performer to pick up a paycheck at one of these nightclubs on a dark night on Broadway or if you were passing through New York to other venues.

Show night made for a very busy night for us. We were pre-warned, "If you scratch someone's car, bring it around the circle so the scratched side is not facing the driver." Once the car was on the street it wasn't our responsibility. One night, one bellhop got overly excited and drove someone's Porsche into the gravel parking lot, floored it, and misjudged the traction. It went up and over a chain link fence, him in it. In this case, it didn't matter which way he brought it back around the circle . . . .

Another night, someone came screaming through the lobby doors shouting, "Get me my car now—my wife's in labor." He had misplaced the ticket.

"What kind of car is it?" I asked. "BLUE!" he shouted.

"Sir," I explained we've parked nearly five hundred cars and a lot of them are blue." We got it worked out, and the next day I got a thank you and a buck.

But it was the stars who made those nights special. Alan King in his Rolls, Martin and Rossi in their limo. Steve and Edie came in their own car. They were all nice folks. And then came Cab Calloway.

Cab Calloway, in his prime, was one of the great jazz improvisors of his day. He was often mentioned in the same breath as Ella Fitzgerald and Louie Armstrong. His world-famous anthem was "Hi-de-hi, Hi-de-hi." It was a form of scatting. Entire audiences, crowds of thousands at open-air concerts, would pick it up and sing with him.

He was also known as an insufferable ego. The Cab Calloway we got that fateful day was the Cab Calloway past his prime, but not past his ego. Let me set the stage.

He arrives two hours early for his set, probably to have dinner on the house and belt down a few also on the house. We were all given strict orders at the beginning of the season, "No one, and I mean no one, parks in the circle unless Sam okays it."

Circle parking meant money in Sam's pocket. Cab Calloway shows up and parks in the circle and he did it in an aircraft carrier length white, Cadillac Eldorado convertible. Regrettably, I was on duty, and Sam was nowhere to be found.

I approached the car and, in my best-taught manners, I said, "Excuse me sir, but you can't park there."

He snapped at me: "Sonny, do you know who you are talking to?" I said, "Yes, Sir, Cab Calloway."

He said, "So I can park here." (Note, no question mark.) I said, "No, Sir, you can't."

He said, "If I can't park here, I can't perform here," and he starts the motor.

By this time, someone had streaked inside to the Activities Director's office to tell her what was going on and out she raced, mules with cotton balls on the front, flappin' on her feet like loose shutters during a hurricane, badly buttoned blouse holding volleyballs that were bouncing around searching for a net to go over.

By this time, Calloway was around the circle, so she exited the front door behind the car and the scene is her waving her arms in hot pursuit of the white-suited, sun-glassed star yelling like the kid in Shane, "Cab, come back. Cab, come back!" Different ending. He did. And he parked in the circle as well.

But that wasn't the chase I promised you.

Labor Day:

Labor Day was: A) Checkout day. B) Big tip day. C) Payday. All went well until we got to the payday part. "Not so well," doesn't come close. At the end of the day, exhausted, we were all called into the ballroom. We were told by Sam that there had been a screw-up at the bank and the money hadn't come in. We could stay an extra night at the hotel gratis (in, of course, the staff quarters) and we'd be paid at noon the next day. Something was rotten in Denmark. We all smelled it.

I knew the owners were pretty loose with money. About two weeks into the season, I was called into the owner's office, Mr. R. He said, "Look kid, my Eldorado is outside. Here's the keys," which he flipped to me.

On his desk were four or five bags of money, just like you see in the movies in the backs of armored cars.

"Grab these and take 'em to the bank." "WHOA!" Mind you, I'm seventeen.

I scoop them up, wrestled them outside to the car, to find that the top is down, car is locked. I went back in, moneybags causing me to sweat like a pig, to report that I didn't know how to operate the top and he hadn't given me the right keys. I also said, "Mr. R is this stuff insured?"

He said, "Donworryaboudit, kid. Everyone knows my car; nobody's gonna knock you off."

I also informed him I had no idea what bank he used and where it was. That settled, he sent me packing—literally.

I must confess. At seventeen, driving through a beach town in a top down, brand new, red Cadillac Eldorado was beyond cool. I even had my arm resting on the door while I navigated this beast one-handed through traffic. Cooler than that was this line-up of bank bags holding who knew how many thousands of dollars in cash. One or two were piled high with rolled coins; they were heavy as lead, or whatever metal coins were made out of.

I completed my mission unharmed and this became part of my weekly routine, sans tip, I might mention. I thought, however, that being the trusted adjutant of the hotel's owner ought to be worth something over the course of the summer. It wasn't.

We all slept restlessly. Actually, some slept in the lobby, onto which the office opened, and through which you had to go to leave the hotel. Trust was a word that had left the staff's vocabulary. Some slept in their cars in the back parking lot. Distrust and anxiety ran rampant.

By morning, the mood was pitchforks and hangman's ropes. Again, came the call to the ballroom. During what certainly seemed like a very long story with which we were being regaled whose end point was bankruptcy or the like, one of the workers, who was sitting on a windowsill, let out the "Holy S" words and then a string more that would have made an infantryman proud. Everyone raced to the window; there was such a crowd I thought the building was going to tilt.

What was the commotion about?

In our sights were the taillights of the Eldorado hightailing it out of the parking lot and peeling down the boulevard. Unfortunately, our sights weren't attached to guns because we were being robbed.

Now comes the promised chase.

Two things happened at once. While someone was calling the local constabulary, a phalanx of guys headed for the parking lot. Mr. R. had a posse on his tail. He was headed for LaGuardia Airport. Within minutes, we heard sirens and saw police cars emptying onto the Boulevard and falling into line oddly enough behind the employees.

Later, it was reported by the posse, and by the news that the local cops were joined by the state cops and met by the FBI. Short, roly-poly Mr. R. wasn't "stopping fer nothin." Over the bridge he went like a madman, his wife's red hair flying in the wind of the open-air car. Did someone put up a roadblock? No. Did someone try to squeeze the car off the road and then the highway? No. Somehow this Keystone Cops-like chase didn't end until the airport where the culprits were surrounded. They, and the bags, and bags, and bags of money were taken into custody. Obviously not great planners, they had given no thought to what the hell they were going to do with all those bags of money once they got to the airport. Hire a skycap and a hand truck? Even before the days of terrorism and TSA, likely someone would have noticed two frantic looking people at the ticket counter holding bags of money instead of luggage.

Now, I'd like to tell you that later that night someone brought some of the money back to the hotel and paid us.

I can't.

The hotel was put into bankruptcy and Mr. and Mrs. R into jail. The slaves? We got bupkis as the saying goes, but I did have a sweat sock bursting with quarters, a $1200 head start on college beer money and a wicked story to tell.

"I was a Yankee fan in Brooklyn because my father was a Yankee fan. And my father was required to live in Brooklyn with my mother's family, who were all Dodger fans. So he was surrounded by Dodger fans. He was a Yankee fan. So his revenge was to make me a Yankee fan."

– Rudy Giuliani
Prosecutor and
former Mayor of NYC

The Keystone Cops
"They went this way! No! They went that way!"

Conclusion

" . . . they're a lot funnier than when they occurred."

It's a little tricky saying, 'The End' when one is writing about life . . . While this book will be followed by a similar collection that will take us through my bunglings at The George Washington University, titled for the while *I slept with George Washington* not even that will be, hopefully, the end.

After that life gets serious, more important, and less funny. Writing about that is no fun so the memoir writing will stop. I do have two more books I want to write, but the memoir aspect of my third career, writing, except for an occasional piece on my blog (**www.williamgralnickauthor.com**), or stories foisted off on partygoers that no one wants to hear, will be over.

It seems a good place to end this book of tales. *My Fair Lady* is a story of an ordinary girl and her mishaps as she tries to become extraordinary. Much of what happens to her is thrust upon her by others. It is lots of little stories surrounded by the much bigger theme. And it is—mostly—funny. Maybe a metaphor for what you've just finished reading? That was going to be my ending.

But an image popped into my mind. It was of the old movies I love to watch—old as in really old. They all seemed to end with a chase before they went black. I decided, it's my book, I like chases, I'm gonna end with one. Luckily, I had one to use and it actually is, chronologically, the end of the stories for this book.

I'm stopping here for other reasons than just chronology. I've probably enjoyed writing this more than you've enjoyed reading it. One might think that it is a form of self-inflicted torture to re-create all the minor mishaps and embarrassments of one's life. Actually, they weren't so bad and believe me, this isn't all of them. To tell you the truth, they were a lot more amusing, and some downright funnier now than they were when they occurred. Looking into the muzzle of a gun (something that happened to me about ten years later) takes on a whole different perspective when you're sixty some odd years removed from the barrel. Churchill said, "There is nothing so exhilarating in life than being shot at—and realizing they missed . . ." Buying a prophylactic and having it rot in your wallet, leaving a permanent indentation that could be mistaken for nothing else to another who sees it for what it was, leaves a different look on one's face at seventy-four than it did at say fourteen. The frown turns upside down.

I recognize though that here the fun ceases and the challenges begin for me as a writer. Is it a challenge to write seventy or eighty thousand words (believe it or not, that's what you've just read)? Yes. The misery is finding a publisher or an agent. That person surely will not see this as lining up in stature right behind a Shakespearean comedy, or even one by Neil Simon. Hopefully he/she will muse, "Hey this is cute and has potential." Then the work gets harder, the battle over words and wording, what's in and what's out, the ethics of my wife's mantra, "He never lets the facts get in the way of a good story" and, to use one of my mother's favorite non-sequiturs, "All that jazz."

If there is a moral to these stories, it is this: Look in the mirror, figuratively. Instead of concentrating on what you see in there, look through the looking glass, so to speak, into the background (foreground?). You're here and all those memories are deep in the glass. Most of them can't hurt you anymore—though there will always be those few . . . So, pull some out, lay them on a table and smooth them out like you'd do with a cotton sweater just out of the wash. You'll see more sweater than wrinkles. That should give you a smile, and if it does, I'm glad.

Drop me a note on my website **www.williamgralnickauthor.com**. net. Share your stories and good comments. If you didn't like the book—keep it to yourself . . . I've had enough of life's criticism and I'm too old for any more. Thank you for rummaging through the attic of my mind with me, See you in the next book. For now . . .

The End

POST SCRIPT

I wanted to add a P.S. that would tie the book's conclusion to the prelude. Having, as you now know, written, hundreds of letters in my life, many with P.S.'s, I never gave much thought to those two letters and two periods. I thought this time, since this is ending a book and not a letter, I ought to give it some thought if I were tacking it on. Dictionary.com was my helper.

When people wrote letters with actual sentences and complete paragraphs, they often added a Post Script. It is a thought appended to the letter after the signature. We'll overlook the fact that books unlike letters don't end with signatures. Picky, picky, picky. The Post Script is not usually just a random thought left out of the preceding text but a thought or thoughts that add something not just content-wise but thought-wise to the whole shebang. Unnervingly enough, P.S. also has a different meaning in computer language. 'not going there.

A wise and wizened editor told me that readers like to know something about those authors they are reading. Here we come to Yogi Berra's advice: "When you come to the fork in the road, take it . . . ." What more could you possibly want or need to know about me that isn't already in the book you just read? Survey says? The back story I chose not to tell. I have however, given it a re-think, so to speak.

I teased you at the beginning saying that just because I didn't write about psychiatrists didn't mean I didn't need one. As you also know from the book we had one handy, right there in the family. When everyone in the family began to think I was an unhappy kid, which I was but no one bothered to ask me about it, discussions were had, family councils not involving me convened in out of the way corners of whose ever house we were in at the time, and finally referrals were made. Since we had a schizophrenic boy living on the block, in comparison, I seemed to me perfectly fine and thought the idea was nuts. I, however, was just a kid. Couldn't vote in elections. Couldn't vote in family matters, even ones concerning me. And not aware that a little help not from my friends but from a professional might be good for me.

It would not surprise you over the course of a life spotted with therapy sessions, I had some strange encounters. One you've read about. There were others. I saw a doctor who decided I needed a pill. As my son once said, "Daddy, in the old days, when you were young . . ." medicines were like caveman tools. They were clumsy and heavy. I was prescribed something called Stelyzine. It clubbed me into a stupor; after the pill I could have been an extra in a movie about Zombies.

Then there was the strict Freudian trained guy. His office was dark, had a chair for him, a couch for me. After "Hello" he said nothing. The work was mine to do. Often times I told him stories like I've told you. One day he said, "You know, you're a very funny fellow, but it's costing you a lot of money to make me laugh." So, I took the fork in the road and quit.

Finally, there was this rotund, Jewish fellow who had been a classmate of my uncle's. In the first interview, he probed me about what I thought were the issues that pained me. By now I was seventeen. I said, "My mother's an alcoholic and she hits me." He said something that should have been grounds for the cancellation of his license. He said, "You're Jewish, no?" I replied in the affirmative thinking he should have known that since he knew my uncle. "Well then," he continued, "you must be mistaken. Jews don't drink (to excess he meant) and they certainly don't beat their children." I was gone from him faster than I was gone from Dr. Dark and Silent.

Truth be told, while idiots, these doctors were right about something. I was unhappy. I was playing the clown and mostly enjoying it but there was a "but." The "but" was that being a clown is hard work. You have to store up material. You have to think of what material to use and when to use it. You're ever thinking about timing, when to say what to whom. And at the end of the "show" the clown often goes home alone. Even without the makeup being a clown is hard work, and often not fun. It can be rewarding if you need affirmation of self-worth. It also turns life into constant auditions. It is neither an easy way to live nor frankly normal—even for clowns.

The personality of the clown is one of great empathy. He or she senses sadness in others because they know sadness in themselves. Clowns are the super-sleuths of sadness, especially in kids. (Maybe I should have been sent to a clown instead of a psychiatrist . . . or just moved in with my sister-in-law . . .) They are great listeners. They turn their sadness right-side up using it to draw the sadness out of others with their ability to listen and then draw from their own lives, advice given freely to those to whom they listen. This of course is called by my wife "approach-avoidance." You'll notice that in this scenario the clown has willingly faced another's issues but not his or her own.

Now don't get me wrong, you don't have to be pre-suicidal to be funny although as a general group, comedians, especially of the ethnic sort, draw their humor from their own screwed up lives. And some are pre-suicidal and some do end up killing themselves. Those that don't are quick to tell you that.

No better example of walking neurosis is Woody Allen, whose whole life was one of malaprops, and actually still is. Or what was Rita Rudner's life as a kid, day in and day out, that brings forth a line like this: "My mother had it tough. She buried three husbands—the last while he was sleeping on the couch!" Ba da boom.

"So we come to end of it," as my favorite bear, Winnie the Pooh, would say. I leave you with these extra thoughts. There are two pictures to this puzzle, called me. One is of the stories themselves. The second is that the richness, be there any, is not in the writing, or even in the stories. The richness in the picture is in what is not written.

To complete the puzzle, the work is now yours. Some of the pieces are obvious. My mother was an alcoholic and hit me. In some others, not so easy.

What aftermath is left when a young lad watches an apartment building go up in smoke and flames and sees people trapped inside?

What lessons are taught when one comes face to face with anti-Semitism? How long does it take for the fear to wash away from being left in an ocean of child strangers on one's first day of school?

How hard is it on a kid to have to remember that in the presence of grandma he can't ever mention grandpa? And "visa-versa," as we said in Brooklyn.

Is there a lesson in living an upper middle-class lifestyle but living it while one's parents are always worried that the next depression (and I don't mean mental) could be just around the corner throwing the family back into the subbasement, three-room apartment that was my father's childhood?

Can "absentee father" be re-defined as someone you see less of than you want and know less about than you wished as opposed to one who just ups and disappears?

Think about it. And if you have questions, ask. The website is **www.williamgralnickauthor.com**.

An apology before closing. The Post Script is supposed to be short. This isn't. I apologize.

Now I'm done. From here it's up to you. Have it your way. Put the book down and say, "This was fun but who needed all that crap at the end?" Or put the book down and have a good think, think yourself either into my shoes or back to the days of yesteryear into your own. What was funny, what was not and why do you still remember it—and should you write a book about it?

William A. Gralnick, Brooklyn Native

That's All Folks!

CPSIA information can be obtained
at www.ICGtesting.com
Printed in the USA
BVHW070559151220
595603BV00002B/49